VINGTON
NVILLE
MANDEVILLE
LA
MISS.
BILOXI
LACOMBE
SLIDELL
Pearl River
Bay St. Louis
Ship Island Pass
SHIP ISLAND
The Rigolets
Lake St. Catherine
FORT PIKE
CHEF MENTEUR
Lake Borgne
ORLEANS
Chandeleur Islands
Breton Sound
Barataria Bay
Grand Terre Island
Grande Isle
f Mexico
South Pass
Southwest Pass

THE AMERICAN LAKES SERIES

Published:

LAKE HURON by *Fred Landon*
LAKE SUPERIOR by *Grace Lee Nute*
LAKE MICHIGAN by *Milo M. Quaife*
LAKE ONTARIO by *Arthur Pound*
LAKE ERIE by *Harlan Hatcher*
LAKE PONTCHARTRAIN by *W. Adolphe Roberts*

In Preparation.

LAKE CHAMPLAIN and LAKE GEORGE by *Frederic F. Van de Water*
THE GREAT SALT LAKE by *Dale L. Morgan*
LAKE OKEECHOBEE by *A. J. Hanna* and *Kathryn Abbey Hanna*

LAKE PONTCHARTRAIN

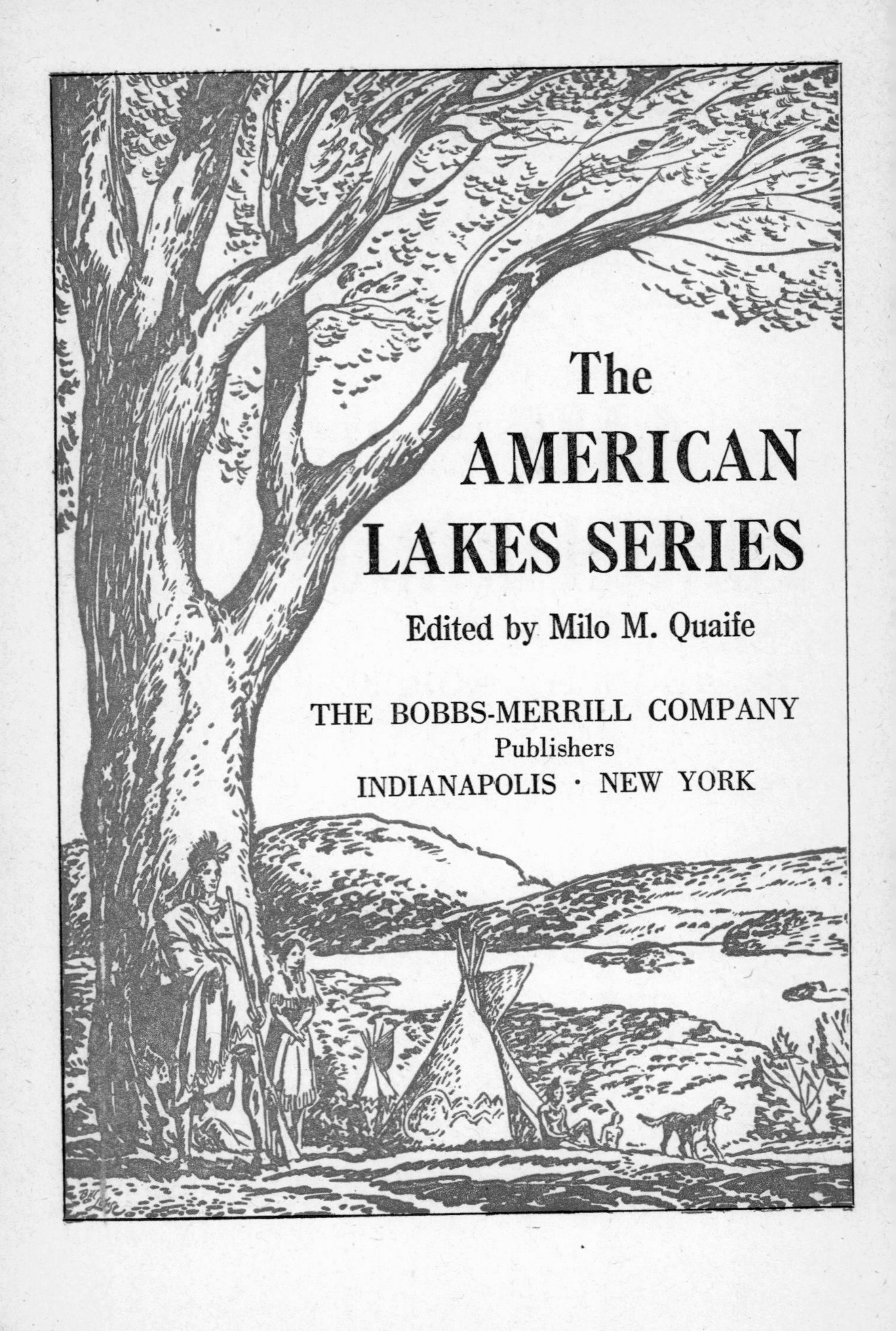
The
AMERICAN
LAKES SERIES
Edited by Milo M. Quaife
THE BOBBS-MERRILL COMPANY
Publishers
INDIANAPOLIS · NEW YORK

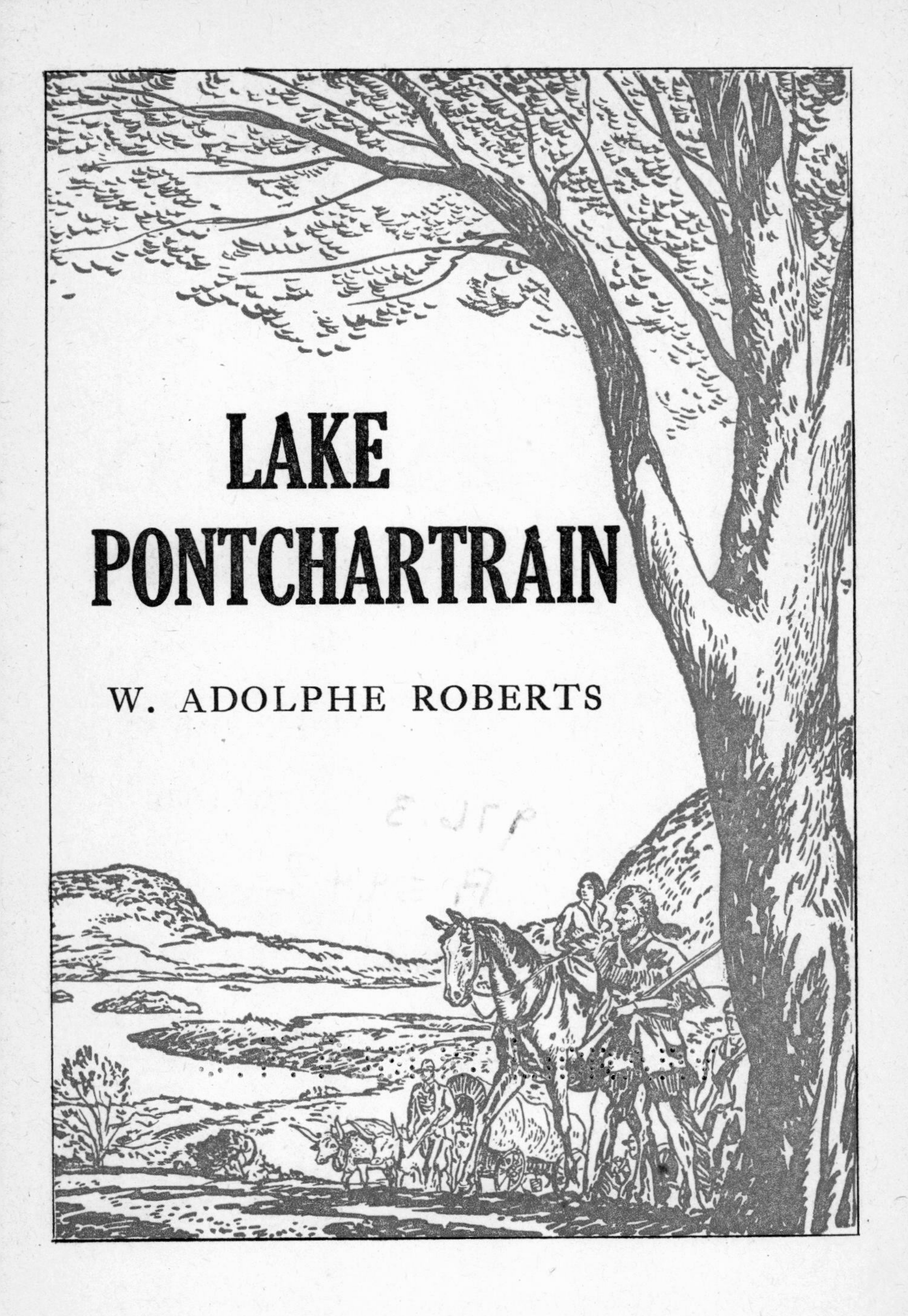
LAKE
PONTCHARTRAIN
W. ADOLPHE ROBERTS

PRINTED IN THE UNITED STATES OF AMERICA

First Edition

DEDICATED TO

NELL

EDITORIAL INTRODUCTION

ALTHOUGH Christopher Columbus was a native of Genoa his voyages of New World discovery were made under the banner of Ferdinand and Isabella of Spain. So it came to pass that the Spanish gained a foothold in the West Indies, from which they quickly extended their activities to the continental mainland of Mexico and the southern United States. Florida was discovered in 1513 and before many years, notwithstanding the desultory nature of the expeditions, the entire Gulf Coast was traced and the Gulf itself became a Spanish Sea.

More than a century passed before the Spanish dominance of the Gulf Coast was successfully challenged. In 1608 Champlain founded Quebec and took up the search for a water highway to the Indies which had first lured Columbus westward. Two generations later, still pursuing the same will-o'-the-wisp, Intendant Talon of New France assigned to Louis Jolliet the task of finding and exploring the Great River of the West, whose existence had been reported by the Indians to the traders and missionaries around Lake Superior.

There ensued the momentous voyage of discovery of the Upper Mississippi in 1673. In two bark canoes manned by five voyageurs and provisioned with a little smoked meat and Indian corn, in May 1673, Jolliet and Father Marquette embarked at St. Ignace upon a voyage "whose duration they could not foresee." Four months later they were back at the Green Bay mission house, having completed without accident or loss a journey of 3,000 miles. They had found and descended the Mississippi as far as the mouth of the Arkansas; they had determined that its outlet was the Mexican Gulf rather than the Sea of California; and they had driven the first stake of France's claim to the greatest river and the richest valley in the world.

A new governor now guided the destinies of New France, and Jolliet, who before the age of thirty had added the Detroit, Wisconsin, Illinois and Mississippi rivers to the map, was never again permitted to visit the West. Nine years after his return to Canada the new favorite, Robert Cavelier, Sieur de La Salle, completed the task which Jolliet and Marquette had left unfinished by descending the Mississippi to the Gulf. There on April 9, 1682, he formally annexed the entire valley to France and named it Louisiana in honor of the reigning sovereign.

Thus was Louisiana born and thus was the Spanish hold upon the Gulf Coast rudely shattered at its very center. La Salle's own colonizing effort ended in failure and tragedy but other hands took over the task of establishing an outpost of France at the mouth of the Mississippi. Although Spanish rule was to return for a time in the latter half of the eighteenth century, and American rule to become permanent at the opening of the nineteenth, the French culture and race still remain firmly entrenched along the lower reaches of the Great River. Alone among the forty-eight commonwealths of the Union, Louisiana adheres to the Code Napoléon as the basic law of the state, and chiefly to her French element New Orleans owes her fame as the most glamorous city of America.

Central to all this Gulf Coast development is Lake Pontchartrain. Some miles to the eastward lies Biloxi Bay, site of the first French settlement on the Gulf, made by Iberville in 1699. This same winter the leader rediscovered the Lower Mississippi and discovered and named Lake Pontchartrain. The capital, after being several times removed, was finally permanently established at New Orleans, which had been founded in 1718, its site determined by its location on the Great River in close proximity to Lake Pontchartrain.

Mr. Roberts, who has assumed the task of adding Pontchartrain's story to The American Lakes Series, has conceived a lifelong interest in the history of all the lands around the Caribbean Sea and the Gulf of Mexico. He is a native of Jamaica and in boyhood lived at Port Royal, ancient capital of the buccaneers who infested the Caribbean area. He has written biographies of Sir Henry Morgan, pirate and governor, and of Raphael Semmes, Confederate sea rover. His *The Caribbean* surveys the history of the entire region from its first discovery by Columbus down to the present day. He has also published a study of *The French in the West Indies* and two historical novels portraying the French society of nineteenth-century New Orleans. During World War I he served for two and one-half years as an American newspaper correspondent in France. In him Lake Pontchartrain finds not merely a sympathetic chronicler but one whom the studies and activities of a lifetime have admirably equipped to narrate its story.

—M. M. Quaife,

Detroit Public Library

PRELUDE

A GLANCE at any relief map will show that the land about the mouth of the Mississippi River is a true delta, which may be defined as a triangular-shaped deposit of alluvial soil bisected downward from its apex by the main stream, and veined by lesser exits of that stream. Obviously such a formation is created by the river itself. The soil has been brought from the interior, and its emergence above sea level is comparatively recent. Study the map more closely and it will become apparent that the entire plain as far north as Cairo, Illinois, partakes of the nature of a delta. This indeed is what it once was. At the beginning of the Tertiary period, the Mississippi emptied into the Gulf of Mexico near the mouth of the Ohio River and gradually filled up the space to the present coast line. Each hundred miles south may have taken thousands of years. Approximate dates would only be confusing. But it is safe to say that when Babylon flourished the site of the city of New Orleans was still covered by water.

Topography is not architecture. By that is meant that the earth never shapes itself evenly and with the balanced accuracy of a blueprint. Numerous irregularities occur, some of them vast. Lake Pontchartrain falls into the latter category, in the region we are considering. The lake has an area of 600 square miles and is about 40 miles long by 24 miles wide, connected by a narrow channel with a sound and the Gulf beyond. The logical course for the Mississippi would seem to be through the basin of which Pontchartrain is the main feature. Instead the river curves to the south. Separated at the narrowest point by a mere 5 miles from the lake, it twists and loops with a general southeasterly drift for another 110 miles. Its great delta has become a peninsula which promises to be indefinitely extended.

There is ample reason for believing that the existing channel of the Mississippi below Cairo is not the only one that has been utilized. The river was located farther to the west in Louisiana at some remote prehistoric time. There have been other major changes, and it is barely possible that the Mississippi did follow the Pontchartrain route for an eon or so. In that event the lake was a product of the river, which then deserted it and left it linked tenuously with the ocean. If they were never united their close juxtaposition is a singular phenomenon. One way or the other, the effect upon man's projects in the immediate region has been considerable.

Outsiders think of New Orleans as being strictly a Mississippi town. It lies on the strip of land between lake and river, but although it was built facing the river, early communication was very largely through a back door in the form of a bayou running from the lake. Today the city fills the intervening space. It has a lake front as well as a river front. It owes much to Pontchartrain. Contrariwise, if it were not for New Orleans, Pontchartrain would be unimportant in the modern economy of the country. There are no other big cities on its shores, nor is it likely that there ever would have been one save at the spot where New Orleans stands. The waters of this inland sea are too shallow to float vessels of deep draught. A partnership with the river was necessary.

The best scientific opinion regards Pontchartrain as part of a former arm of the sea, isolated in the long process by which southern Louisiana was molded. The basin as a whole certainly gives that impression. Approaching along the coast westward we pass Ship Island and Cat Island and Pearl River Island, then come to Grand Island in the mouth of a broad inlet enclosed on three sides, called Lake Borgne. A short distance farther on we find a strait, the Rigolets, 400 yards wide and 10 miles long, through which we enter Lake Pontchartrain. At the far end is the Manchac Pass, another strait, 300 yards wide and 7 miles long, which leads into Lake Maurepas. The last-named is roughly of the same oval shape as Pontchartrain, but is less than one-sixth the size.

In the opinion of William Duffy, writing in 1817, "the mind could not resist the conviction that the lakes Maurepas, Pontchartrain, and the Rigolets at the mouth of Pearl River, were once a prolongation of Lake Borgne."*

The school which maintains that the Mississippi once passed that way has never lacked for proponents. *Louisiana—A Study of the State,* by Mabel Brasher and others, which was published first in 1929 and is used as a textbook in Louisiana, contains the following flat assertion: "Lake Pontchartrain [and this would include Maurepas] was formed as deposits of sediment were made on either side of the river channel to the

---

* *Geographical Description of the State of Louisiana.*

Gulf." But a more tenable theory is that it was formed by the drowning out of the deltas of lesser southward-flowing rivers.

The chain is not one of true lakes, whatever else it may be. Borgne is a salt-water branch of the ocean; its very name is satirical, the word in French meaning "a one-eyed man" and carrying the implication that this is an incomplete or defective lake. Pontchartrain is a lagoon, the saline content of which is scarcely noticeable during the season of heavy rains and floods from the upcountry. The water becomes brackish when the level is low, or when storms drive exceptional amounts of sea water through the Rigolets. Maurepas is a subsidiary lagoon, and is virtually fresh because of its remoteness from the ocean.

Nevertheless, Pontchartrain lives up to all practical definitions of a lake. Its landlocked area with which we are familiar has been stable for centuries. It is fed by its own system of streams. The vegetation surrounding it is not that of the seacoast. Aquatic creatures which cannot live in salt water are encountered. Traffic by human beings on its surface has benefited by the protected location. From the lightest Indian canoe to modern skiffs, types of craft that could not face the open sea have ever traversed Pontchartrain in good weather. Its storms—and devastating ones occur—are those characteristic of a shallow lake.

Pontchartrain has an extreme central depth of 16 feet, while that of Maurepas is 12 feet. Around the edges the bottom shelves gradually, though not evenly at all points. A hundred yards from shore in many places a plumb line will show but 4 or 5 feet. The waves are consequently short and choppy. A vicious ground swell can be whipped up in a few minutes.

When it is perfectly calm, the beauty of the water is unforgettable. The first thing noticed by early travelers was its opalescence. They described a film which seemed to overlie the surface like a varicolored paint, flashing in the sunshine. Possibly they referred to patches of mineral oil that had seeped in from adjoining marshes, known today to be sources of petroleum. However, the vivid hues everywhere may be ascribed to the refraction of light in water resting thinly on a bed composed of decaying vegetable matter, sands from the glacial age and countless billions of sea shells.

There are many surprises in connection with Pontchartrain. Historically it once formed part of the boundary between Louisiana and Florida. Yes, Florida. Dr. Nelson Gowanloch, of the Louisiana Conservation Commission, agrees with the late David Starr Jordan, president of Stanford University, in calling it "on several grounds, the most interesting, barring none, of the American lakes." Assertions of the kind cannot be dealt with in a prelude, where they serve merely to titillate the imagination. Their significance will emerge in the main body of the story.

TABLE OF CONTENTS

Part I

THE EARLY LAKE

Part II

A CENTURY OF ROMANCE

TABLE OF CONTENTS—*Continued*

Part III

THE WAR PERIOD

Part IV

THE LAKE IN OUR TIMES

LIST OF ILLUSTRATIONS

List of Illustrations — Continued

Part I

THE EARLY LAKE

Chapter 1

The Discoverers

SPANIARDS starting from Jamaica under Alonzo Alvárez de Pineda in 1519, thirteen years after the death of Columbus, skirted the northern shore of the Gulf of Mexico for the first time. They noted but did not enter the mouth of a great river, which the leader named for the Holy Ghost. In 1527 Pánfilo de Narváez, an unlucky captain who had fought in Jamaica, Cuba and Mexico, obtained the Gulf Coast as a grant from the king and took a large expeditionary force there. He and all his men were lost, save Cabeza de Vaca and three companions whose epic journey across the continent ended almost ten years later at the Gulf of California. Then came Hernando de Soto. His course in 1539 was from Florida, inland and westward to the Mississippi, of which he was the titular discoverer. He was buried in its waters, and his party hastily abandoned the march of conquest.

Thereafter the great river was virtually forgotten by the Spaniards, though it appeared vaguely on some of their maps as the Escondido, a word which means "hidden" and which refers to the difficulty of identifying the stream's main outlet through the delta to the sea. They continued to lay claim to the entire region. The French working down from Canada came to know the upper reaches of the Mississippi. One hundred and forty-three years passed. Then in 1682 René Robert Cavelier, Sieur de la Salle, one of the ablest of the French pioneers, struck out from the Great Lakes to verify the discoveries of Jolliet and Marquette, retraced their voyage to the mouth of the Arkansas and continued on down the Mississippi in birchbark canoes to its mouth. His lieutenant, Henry de Tonty, who had lost a hand in battle and replaced it with one of iron, came shortly in his tracks. The upshot was the annexation by France, in defiance of Spain, of the territory called Louisiana.

Strangely, none of the above explorers happened upon Lake Pontchartrain, or if they did so they failed to mention it in their chronicles. Cabeza de Vaca missed it by taking to boats in the Gulf far east of that longitude, and De Soto passed well north of it. The men who navigated the river were often close to the lake and at one point within five miles of it, but they appear not to have made any of the practicable overland forays which would have revealed it to them. The honor fell to a brilliant young Canadian whose mission was to develop the newly acquired colony.

Louis XIV had backed La Salle in a project to establish a province and found a port. This had ended disastrously with the death of the explorer, astray in Texas, on his second voyage.* Members of the king's entourage had remained interested, and after the Peace of Ryswick they brought to his attention the brothers Pierre le Moyne, Sieur d'Iberville, and Jean Baptiste le Moyne, Sieur de Bienville, as promising talent. The first was in his thirties, the second only eighteen. They were sons of a Quebec family that had greatly distinguished itself and had been raised to the rank of the petty nobility. That was why Pierre and Jean Baptiste were termed *sieurs,* or lords, of separate landed estates held by their father. The two had already seen action against the English in Hudson Bay, Iberville as the commander of a vessel that had whipped three opponents. It was decided by the Court that they had a better chance of succeeding on the Mississippi than anyone else in sight. Iberville was given charge of the expedition, with Bienville and the Sieur de Sauvole as his chief lieutenants.

A frigate, the *Badine,* was fitted out at Brest and sailed on October 28, 1698. The ship carried the main body of adventurers, but along with her went a second small frigate, the *Marin,* under the Chevalier de Surgères, while a royal warcraft, the *François,* joined

* There is the strongest presumption that Tonty of the iron hand must have heard of Lake Pontchartrain, or seen it, during his fruitless search for La Salle at this time. But we know only that Tonty descended the Mississippi and made several forays from both banks into the interior, in pursuit of rumors about his chief.

them on the way to assist in case they were attacked. Iberville went first to the West Indian colony of Saint Domingue, where he remained for a month loading supplies and enlisting recruits. He accepted the services of Laurens de Graff, a reformed buccaneer who had been notorious in his day, and who had some knowledge of the Gulf Coast. Thither Iberville repaired in January 1699. He had a bloodless argument with the Spaniards at Pensacola Bay, their sole outpost, and proceeded westward, keeping close contact with the land. He was searching for the mouth of the Mississippi, but had only a vague idea where it might be. Some authorities assert that he was relying mainly on a description of the appearance of the delta which he had had from La Salle's own lips. This seems improbable, for La Salle's last contact with civilization had been in 1684, and at that time Iberville was a boy.

Inspecting Mobile Bay en route, he now pushed on to Ship Island, where he dismissed the *François* and anchored his two frigates. The shallow waters of the sound, the Chandeleur islets, the low-lying mudbanks and bayous of the mainland below: all these confused him. He felt it had become an affair for smaller boats. So he equipped two barges, each carrying twenty-five men. Accompanied by Bienville and Sauvole, he edged his way south, finally entered the river on March 2 and mounted against the current to a point well beyond the site of Baton Rouge. There had been numerous friendly contacts with Indians.

On his way back in the last week of the month, Iberville was told by natives that there was a short cut to the "great water." He concluded to try it, while sending Bienville and Sauvole out in the barges by the route they had come. Indians showed him a bayou connecting with the Mississippi on its east bank a few miles below Baton Rouge, which they called the Ascantia, according to the French rendering. Subsequently it was known by the straight Choctaw name of Bayou Manchac, the meaning of "manchac" being a back entrance. It was ten feet wide, by three or four feet deep. Iberville's party consisted of four men in two canoes. One Indian accompanied him as a guide.

The first day it was necessary to make fifty portages over fallen trees and vegetable debris matted into rafts that blocked the waterway. Despite the annoyances of this crawling progress, Iberville was fascinated by the country, its rich earth, fine timber and plentiful game. He noted great flocks of wild turkeys. The second day, the guide deserted. But the Frenchmen had solved the nature of the difficulties and had no intention of retreating. Twenty miles from the Mississippi, the bayou merged with what is now the Amite River. Conditions at once became better. The channel was deeper, with a gravelly bottom, and the water of the Amite ran clear. The canoes speeded ahead for another nineteen miles and debouched suddenly into a broad lake.

Most of the oval surface lay to the south. A far shore was soon visible, and directly opposite the point of ingress there appeared a new strait, wider than the Bayou Manchac, easier to navigate. As Iberville was in a hurry he did no exploring, but paddled through the gap called the Manchac Pass. At the end of seven miles he found himself, to his astonishment, in a much larger lake than the first one. Its extent could not be readily divined. He would have taken it for a gulf of the sea, had it not been that its water was brackish rather than salt.

The canoes skirted the shore, though whether to the right or left is uncertain. Camps were made several times on low, grassy points. Iberville reported that on these occasions he was tortured by clouds of mosquitoes, which he described as "terrible little animals, to men in need of rest." Nothing more formidable than the insects was encountered, however, and presently the passage later known as the Rigolets was discovered. The leader calculated shrewdly that he had come a sufficient distance to bring him close to his ships, so to attract their attention he lighted a bonfire on the east coast of the lake. At dawn the next day he traversed the Rigolets without trouble, and was met by barges that had been sent to look into the matter of the fire. He was aboard his flagship, the *Badine,* by midday. Only eight hours later he was joined there by Bienville and Sauvole, at the end of their longer but easier journey down the Mississippi and up the coast. The date was March 31.

Iberville was enormously impressed by the two lakes through which he had passed, superficial though his observation had been. He had lacked the leisure even to make soundings. That such fine bodies of water must play an important part in the opening up of the country to European commerce appeared certain to him. He decided to name them both for the powerful Phélypeaux family that had taken a special interest in this voyage to exploit the discoveries of La Salle. Louis de Phélypeaux, Comte de Pontchartrain, was the royal Minister of Marine, and with the king's consent had organized the expedition. Iberville, therefore, called the larger lake Pontchartrain, and the smaller one Maurepas after Jérôme de Phélypeaux, Comte de Maurepas, the minister's eldest son.

The immediate job was to build a fort before the supplies on the ships gave out. Instructions had been to do this on the Mississippi, but Iberville had seen for himself that the lower reaches of the river were scarcely distinguishable from the surrounding morass. Any spot chosen within seventy-five miles of the sea would be in constant danger of floods at high water.* Without giving up the idea of a river port, he felt that the first settlement must be easily accessible. He seriously thought of placing it just inside Lake Pontchartrain, but finally settled on Biloxi far to the east. There a building was hastily erected and garrisoned with a discontented handful of soldiers and artisans. They were supposed to start the colony by planting crops. Sauvole was placed in charge, and Bienville made second in command. Iberville sailed to get reinforcements. He reached France at the end of June.

His report dazzled his patrons, notably Jérôme de Phélypeaux, who a few weeks after Iberville's arrival succeeded by the resignation of his father to the office of Minister of Marine. Later he became Comte de Pontchartrain. The younger man, a protégé of the

---

* The French had christened the river the St. Louis, but the Indian name persisted. An interesting translation of Mississippi, other than the common "Father of Waters" is "River Everywhere," from the Outouba words *missi,* everywhere, and *sipy,* river. The impressive fact to the natives was that at floodtime the river took possession of the land.

illustrious military engineer Vauban, proved to be a less fortunate statesman than his father had been. He had a visionary streak in connection with the New World, a fault which was shared by so many ministers of the colonizing powers that it would be unfair to single him out for ridicule.

Along with the wherewithal for a new expedition, the second Pontchartrain issued a set of written orders. He had heard of a hill of greenish earth from which emeralds were dug, and of pearls fished from the Gulf with the greatest of ease. So he urged attention to these sources of ready wealth. Yet gold and silver would be more important in the long run, he said. Naturally they existed in a Golconda like Louisiana. "The grand affair is the discovery of mines," he wrote. Stock raising and farming should not be neglected. The wild cattle (bison) had shaggy coats of wool; they must be domesticated as a future source of cloth goods, and abundant hints how to accomplish this were furnished. In that mild climate silkworms would probably flourish; the care of them would constitute a logical activity for the Indian women and children, while harder labor was assigned to the males.

Iberville understood the true nature of his problem, but he was too clever to disillusion a patron. He concentrated on recruiting Canadians, men who had wrestled with the wilderness since boyhood. In the port of La Rochelle he found a number of sturdy fellows remembered from the Hudson Bay fighting, who gladly reenlisted. His seventeen-year-old brother, the Sieur de Chateauguay, joined him, and so did the Sieurs de Boisbriant and Juchereau de Saint-Denis. Instead of miners or would-be miners, a few Breton peasants were taken aboard.

On regaining Biloxi early in January 1700, Iberville received a pessimistic account from the sluggish Sauvole, a far more stimulating one from Bienville. The latter had spent his time in roaming widely through the country, visiting as many of the Indian tribes as possible, and learning their dialects and customs. He had had with him a literate man-at-arms, a carpenter by trade, named André Pénicaut, who served history by keeping a journal. An instructive side trip had been made into Lake Pontchartrain by way of the Rigolets. Pénicaut describes the beginning of the journey, after the sound had been reached, as follows:

"We left the sea on the larboard side, and at three leagues we came to an island which we called Pea Island because a sack of peas was left there through forgetfulness. We hurried off an hour before daylight, to get rid of the annoyance of swarms of small flies, or *cousins,* which the Indians call *maragouins,* and which puncture even to drawing of blood. The stream we had met with [the Rigolets] communicated with this place. Four leagues further on we detected a large lake, which M. de Bienville styled Pontchartrain. This is about twenty-eight leagues in circumference and seven wide. Its embouchure, at the entrance, is a quarter of a league from one side to the other.

"Both sides of the pass, or entrance, are covered with shells, and in such quantity that they form an elevation, which was the reason it was called Pointe-aux-Coquilles. When one has passed through this channel, you perceive on looking ahead at a distance of a league and a half to the left a projection of land called Pointe-aux-Herbes, where the boats were placed under shelter; because, in this place [the lake] the water is shallow, and in heavy gales canoes are sometimes lost there. Six leagues further on is a small river called by the Indians Choupicatcha, which the French afterward called Orleans, or Bayou St. Jean."

Pénicaut also tells of camping not far from the site of the future city, under great cypresses which served at night as perches "for innumerable Indian fowls [wild turkeys] weighing nearly thirty pounds and all ready for the spit." These birds, he notes in astonishment, were not frightened by gunshots.

Bearing steadily to the left, Bienville circled the lake and arrived at the point on the northern shore where the town of Mandeville now stands. There he landed to establish relations with the Acolapissa Indians, relatives of the Choctaw. He had with him a chief of the Bayagoula as a guide. The French were given a reserved welcome by the Acolapissa, who numbered 300 warriors. A long powwow followed. That it ended with a mutual pledge of amity was due to the tact and the strong, courteous personality of Bienville, for he always could get along with Indians. His hosts told him a startling story. They were accustomed, they said, to go on distant hunting excursions, and often had had clashes with English colonists in the backwoods of South Carolina. Only two days before Bienville's coming, their village had been unsuccessfully attacked by 200 Chickasaw led by two Englishmen. The English had been the first seen so far south. Nothing more about them has been recorded. We may assume that their eyes rested on the lake, and if so they missed being its white discoverers by only a few months. This and other curious matters were reported by Bienville to his brother. The pair agreed that Englishmen and warlike Chickasaw made a threatening combination.

Every student of the period knows that the young Bienville was the man of destiny in the founding of Louisiana, the genius whose unique gifts were precisely those required by the semitropical location, whereas the older brother was by nature a trail breaker of the north. The chronology we are tracing is that of Lake Pontchartrain, Iberville's find, and for the moment Iberville remains the dominant figure.

His first project on his return to Biloxi was to go to the Mississippi through his short cut. He believed that it could be done without traversing the entire length of the two lakes and the Bayou Manchac. The little bayou not far beyond the Rigolets seemed promising. He equipped two barges manned by sixty men, which he took to the spot on the southern shore of Pontchartrain described by Bienville. Sure enough, the inlet proved navigable, and at its end a short portage brought him to the river. He emerged at the exact spot where New Orleans was eventually to be built, but he failed to appreciate the excellence of the site. He contented himself with planting cuttings of sugar cane on a ridge near the portage, then dropped down the stream and built an ill-fated blockhouse eighteen leagues from the Gulf, at a point which the Indians had assured him was above the flood mark.

Turning rightabout face, he mounted the Mississippi with the intention of charting it to its confluence with the Red River, and exploring the latter. But Iberville's health was not standing up well against the rigors of the climate. He had had a fever the previous year. Now he suffered from a badly infected foot, as well as a general debility that probably was malarious. Somewhere in the land of the Big Tensas, he ordered Bienville to proceed up the Red with twenty Canadians, retired to his miserable little fort in the lower delta and lay ill there for weeks. He made his way by sea at last to Biloxi, and sailed for France at the end of May. During his long absence Sauvole died. Bienville became acting governor of the colony, greatly to its advantage from the standpoint of morale and practical measures taken to develop the planting and trapping that would make it self-sufficent.

Iberville's third and last arrival on the Gulf Coast was in December 1701. He came with elaborate plans. Bienville was placed in charge of the construction of a new fort on Mobile Bay, which Iberville had come to regard as a better site than either Biloxi or the mouth of the Mississippi. A warehouse and station for handling immigrants were located on Massacre Island, later called Dauphin Island, off Mobile Bay. A request was filed in Paris for serious settlers rather than adventurers, and particularly for women. The Ministry of Marine intended to co-operate. But in 1702 the War of the Spanish Succession broke out, and the entire business of colonizing Louisiana was necessarily slowed up. Iberville himself was made commander of a warship and sent to the Caribbean. He distinguished himself there, up till his untimely death of yellow fever in Havana, in 1706.

Bienville had inherited the governorship. He was allowed to keep it, at first by default, and afterward because the Court realized dimly that this extraordinary youth was superior to anyone who could have been sent to supplant him. The story of the next decade is that of Bienville's struggle against natural obstacles, with little support from the homeland. He continued to familiarize himself with the immense territory from Pensacola to Texas and south of Natchez. He made allies of as many Indian tribes as possible and organized them to beat back those, such as the Chickasaw, whose hostility could not be overcome.

At the start Bienville had favored the move to Mobile, and that it was a good place to build a city is evidenced by the fact that one has stood on the bay ever since. But his realistic mind would not allow him long to ignore the Mississippi. The river which drained the heart of the continent fairly cried out for a port. With the connecting inland waterways by means of which the Great Lakes could be reached, the French had a chance to make themselves the masters of North America if they exploited the mouth of the Mississippi. They could thus squeeze the English possessions from the north, west and south. Furthermore, the immediate business of a colony in Louisiana would be best served by developing trade on the giant "Father of Waters."

He returned to the scene over and over again. The fort at the eighteen-league point had been drowned out and abandoned. After weighing all the possibilities, he concluded that the ideal spot was the fairly high ground where he and Iberville had crossed from Lake Pontchartrain to the river in 1700. The existing Indian camp on the site was called Chinchuba, the Choctaw word for "alligator." There he would establish his chief city, on a crescent bend of the Mississippi with the Bayou St. Jean at its rear. It would be a port with two water fronts, each of them handling a different kind of traffic. Craft from upcountry and the larger ships from Europe must necessarily use the river. But small coastwise boats and barges to which cargo had been transferred would find it easier to come through the lake and bayou, instead of struggling against the powerful current of the Mississippi.

Bienville never wavered in his advocacy of this idea. He urged it in a detailed memorandum sent to Paris in 1708, and he repeated the plea at intervals for years. Pontchartrain found various reasons for withholding his consent. He and the king were disgusted by the heavy financial cost of the attempt to launch the colony, no mines or pearl fisheries having materialized. They were unwilling to invest in the building of a new port. In 1712, Louisiana was farmed outright to a promoter named Antoine Crozat, and Bienville was replaced the following year as governor by La Mothe Cadillac. The latter had been active in the settlement of Detroit, and had commanded for a short while at Michilimackinac, the vital way station between Lake Huron and Lake Michigan.

A rehearsal of Crozat's almost total failure would contribute little to this narrative, for the entrepreneur did not touch the region of Lake Pontchartrain. His visionless scheme was merely to set up a monopoly of imported goods, for which he charged exorbitantly, and to buy furs from the colonists and Indians for a song. The customers being indigent, there was no basis for an even break, much less a profit. However, immigration from Europe, including women, rose slightly. In September 1715, Louis XIV died. Shortly afterward Crozat asked to be released from his contract. The Duc d'Orléans, regent for the infant Louis XV, agreed gladly, because a new plan was in the offing, one of the wildest fantasies that ever possessed the minds of men. This was John Law's so-called Mississippi Bubble.

Law, a Scotsman, a fugitive in Paris from the consequences of a London duel that had ended fatally, remarked the difficulties of the French Government over its *billets d'état,* a species of bonds issued as promissory notes to postpone payments due on the national debt. The circulation of these *billets* at ever-increasing discounts had turned them, in effect, into a debased paper currency. Soon they would be valueless, and the people might tear down the throne in vengeance. Law got Orléans to allow him to form a bank, shares in which could be bought for twenty-five percent cash and seventy-five percent *billets d'êtat.* By means of adroit juggling, this institution became a financial success. Orléans, delighted, gave it official backing.

Then Law proposed to found the Company of the West, popularly known as the Mississippi Company, the shares in which would be purchasable only in *billets d'état.* Its purpose would be to develop Louisiana, and the enormous profits anticipated for this venture would soon make possible the redemption of the entire national debt. The ready money needed for initial expenses would be furnished by Law's bank, a going proposition as everyone knew. The Scotch gambler's intent was to rake in a personal fortune from the commissions on his huge stockjobbery, but he appears to have believed that an empire in Louisiana might produce a bonanza and make everything come out all right.

The public was happy enough to get rid of its *billets d'état* by exchanging them for shares. Then Law, with the regent's consent, issued three billion livres' worth of unguaranteed paper money, and some of these "funds" were used to finance the promotion: an advertising campaign of unexampled flamboyance in France, a disorderly effort on the Gulf Coast to create prosperity from the void. Law launched forth in September 1717 under a franchise which gave him Louisiana for twenty-five years, with the right to assign lands to colonists free of feudal obligation and exempt from taxation for the period of his trusteeship. He undertook to place 6,000 white settlers and obtain for them from Africa 3,000 Negro slaves.

As the ships loaded with immigrants and all-too-scanty supplies began to sail for America, the Mississippi Company took its most intelligent step. It appointed the Sieur de Bienville to the governor generalship, and when he promptly asked permission to establish a port near the mouth of the river it told him to go ahead. However, his proposal that the new town should be the capital of the province was vetoed for the time being. In February 1718 he started to clear the site he had chosen so long before. The name he gave it was La Nouvelle Orléans, in honor of the regent.*

Bienville had been in the country nineteen years. The phase of

* On slim evidence, which he admits is but "tradition," André Cajun (the nom de plume of Andrew J. Navard) says in his *Stories of New Orleans* that the Sieur de Chateauguay, Bienville's younger brother, conducted a trading post on the site of New Orleans years before the founding and should be regarded as the city's father.

Bureau of New Orleans News

THE CABILDO IN NEW ORLEANS

Built in 1795, the Cabildo is one of the most famous buildings in the old French Quarter. It was first used as the seat of the Spanish Government in Louisiana. Today it houses the Louisiana State Museum.

Louisiana State Museum

JOHN BAPTISTE LE MOYNE,
SIEUR DE BIENVILLE

Louisiana State Museum

PIERRE LE MOYNE,
SIEUR D'IBERVILLE

Louisiana State Museum

JACQUES PHILIPPE VILLERÉ

Louisiana State Museum

GOVERNOR W. C. C. CLAIBORNE

pioneering was over for him, and he stood at the threshold of great achievement. This is the juncture at which he may best be appraised. He was short but stocky, his face somewhat square in shape, with a deceptively gentle and reserved expression. As a stripling he had shown his ability to lead men much older than himself and to command respect from his foes. He shared with La Salle a remarkable gift for penetrating the intricacies of the Indian mind, and dealing with the savages according to their accepted traditions and in their own languages. He could learn a new dialect in a few weeks. Thus he dispensed with interpreters, who almost invariably were cheats. Bienville's Canadian followers gave him unswerving loyalty. Those Indians who took the French side, as against the Spanish or English, called him "Father." He had considerable military aptitude, but he shone more brilliantly as explorer, diplomat and administrator. Without question he was the outstanding architect of French power on the Gulf Coast of North America.

While he pushed the work of laying out New Orleans, Bienville made arrangements for the reception and distribution of the colonists from Europe. He designated Dauphin Island off Mobile Bay, already an immigrant station, as the place where all the newcomers must be landed. It was not his fault if the Company showed little judgment, or downright indifference, about the suitability of those it sent, and failed to inform them that they should carry food and the means of shelter for the first few days ashore. The financial aspects of the "Bubble" were all that mattered to the speculators in Paris. To hold public confidence there must be a tide of settlers moving westward, but anybody would do. Certain seigneurs who had been granted great estates in Louisiana came well provided, and with a gang of field hands. The rest formed as bizarre a throng as ever faced the wilderness.

There were recruits who thought they knew what they were about, robust French peasants eager to make their fortunes in the new land. However, not enough of these had volunteered. Law filled his quotas by means of government edicts which authorized him to empty the prisons of murderers, robbers, debtors, prostitutes and other types of convicts; to impress vagrants and beggars in the streets, and even to collar persons with bad reputations as libertines and infidels. The Louisiana boats proved to be a handy way of getting rid of undesirable relatives under one of the above categories. Some men went to the length of denouncing their personal enemies and having them seized as colonists. Unoffending young men and women were at times kidnaped by the Company's street agents who were known as "the Mississippi bandits."

The hundreds dumped on Dauphin Island at the end of each voyage struggled for survival under horrifying conditions. Diseases they had brought with them and fevers peculiar to the climate killed many. Others perished of famine. Bienville employed the few boats at his command to get the survivors as quickly as possible to the lands they had been promised, or to destinations chosen by himself. He displayed his usual energy and had greater success than could have been expected in the circumstances.

There were several main channels of dispersion for the immigrants, and one of these flowed through Lake Pontchartrain.

Chapter 2

The Island of Orleans

As ITS founders and many subsequent generations know it, New Orleans was located on an island. Iberville's historic voyage of discovery in canoes accounted for this. Since you could mount the Mississippi from the Gulf to the entrance of the Bayou Manchac, then pass through the Bayou and the Amite River to the lakes and the Gulf once more, the land wedged between those boundaries was actually an island. It was so described in treaties signed by France and Spain. But in a more limited sense the site on the narrow strip with the river on the right hand and the lake on the left appeared insular. You could come down the Bayou St. Jean from Pontchartrain, and at other points to north and south you could turn into bayous from the Mississippi and reach Pontchartrain after an easy portage. So the land in the immediate vicinity of the town was commonly referred to as the Island of Orleans.

Bienville began his work of building with some fifty men, of whom twenty-five were ex-convicts, and soon complained in his diary that he was "grieved to see so few persons engaged in a task which requires at least a hundred times the number." He had scarcely cleared a few arpents of cypress forest and canebrake, and erected barracks on ground which he calculated to be ten feet above sea level and safe from floods, when the Mississippi rose and inundated his settlement to a depth of from six to twelve inches. He promptly postponed everything else to throw up the first levee along the water front and dig a drainage ditch at the rear of his site. Thus New Orleans' eternal problem—the struggle against the encroachments of water—was faced from the start. How serious the matter of drainage was may be judged from the fact that, as the town took form, each square block was ditched all round, with lesser ditches separating the building lots. In consequence, the settlers called a square block an *îlet,* or "islet," and that is the term used in Creole French to this day.

Aided by the engineers Le Blond de la Tour and Adrien de Pauger, Bienville planned the city after the checkerboard pattern typical of Spanish rather than French colonial construction. The length of the whole was 4,000 feet and the width 1,800 feet. At the center, fronting the river, space was reserved for a parade ground to be called the Place d'Armes, and along the far inner side of this was to stand the administration building, the church and a house for the clergy. Otherwise, the squares were to be divided by five streets running parallel with the levee and twelve shorter ones running in the opposite direction. The pathways outside the ramparts on what became Canal Street, Rampart Street and Esplanade Avenue were not to count as municipal thoroughfares. Five forts were designed, two on the river corners, two on the rear corners, and one at the middle of the landward border of the parallelogram.

The early homes naturally tended to cluster about the Place d'Armes, with the south quarter where Bienville had fixed his own residence preferred to the north. The rudest log cabins were erected, and in those days a citizen used the greater part of his lot as a vegetable garden. The excellence of the soil was one of the governor's favorite themes. "Everything will grow there," he noted in his diary and frequently reported to Paris. Others did not share his enthusiasm, for it was only rice, or vegetables suited to very marshy soil, that flourished. It was better on the banks of the Bayou St. Jean, where some of the immigrants preferred to halt as they followed the short coastal route in from Lake Pontchartrain. Let us hear from one of the most interesting of these, the historian Le Page du Pratz.

He was an urbane eighteenth-century gentleman, lettered above the average of his class, and fairly well-to-do. Two influences attracted him to Louisiana: the fact that he had met and admired Bienville in France, and the hypnotic effect which he credits whimsically to certain pages of John Law's propaganda in the *Mercure* of Paris. After reading those glittering words, he says, it was impossible for him to doubt that New Orleans—then only a few weeks old—was already a rich port, embowered in gardens, and its hinterland an earthly paradise where a man of energy was assured of making his fortune. Antoine le Page du Pratz's *Histoire de la Louisiane* is, in part, a personal record set down simply and with a regard for truth.

"They sent, in 1718, a colony of eight hundred men, some of whom found homes at New Orleans, while others formed the settlement of the Natchez," he begins. "It was with this embarkation that I passed over to Louisiana." The three vessels composing the flotilla sailed from La Rochelle in April, lost their direction and fetched up at Puerto Rico. Steering westward, they paused at Cape François in the colony of Saint Domingue after a voyage of two months. They took another month, by way of the coasts of Jamaica, the Cayman Islands and Cape San Antonio, Cuba, to reach Dauphin Island on August 25. No one had died or been seriously ill aboard during the trip, an unusual circumstance in those days. So passengers and crews joined in singing a *Te Deum*.

Such rosy conditions could not last. Put ashore with all their effects, the colonists found that no provision had been made for their comfort except a few thatched huts. Those who had been too poor to bring their own food starved, for there was little to be bought and that little at the highest prices. A hummock of human bones, the result of a mass slaughter of Indians by another tribe, was pointed out to Le Page du Pratz as the origin of the old name of the place, Massacre Island. It was a nice irony, in his opinion, because the evidences of a newer and more avoidable havoc lay up and down that coast. He saw on one beach the scattered bones of immigrants from Europe who had died of want or of exotic maladies, and for whom not even graves had been furnished.

Nevertheless, the personal experiences of the historian were not so harsh as some translations of his work into English make out. These renderings, particularly the contemporary ones, omit whatever fails to suit the translator's purpose and even twist the text so as to create an impression that all French attempts at colonizing were bungled. Later writers, unfortunately, have trusted the old English versions and perpetuated their falsehoods. It is necessary to go back to the original. This shows that the favored Le Page du Pratz lodged comfortably on Dauphin Island with M. de la Pointe, a retired Canadian sea captain, whose table was loaded down with fish from the Gulf.

Before long Bienville arrived from New Orleans and had a friendly talk with the distinguished newcomer. The governor asked right away whether Du Pratz had brought a compass. There was none in the colony, and the administration urgently needed one. The answer was yes. A little reluctantly, we gather, Du Pratz sold his compass "at a fair price." He then explained that he had picked his concession in advance from the map. It was to be somewhere between Lake Pontchartrain and the city. Bienville replied that he was pleased to learn he intended to settle so close to the capital, "because a good farm near a town is often more valuable than a seignorial manor in the woods, the second being suitable to the chase rather than to commerce."

The stay at the Dauphin Island landing station was supposed to be for no longer than four days, but a regular schedule was out of the question. Weeks often passed without a boat to the mainland. Despite Bienville's promise of help, Du Pratz had to wait almost four months. He took it philosophically. At no time did he or his half-dozen servants lack for food. At last he was able to charter a small craft, which was loaded with his abundant baggage, including seeds and bulbs for planting, and he set forth.

"After passing the bay of St. Louis," he writes, "we entered the channel which leads to Lake Pontchartrain. We lay to and camped on the Ile-aux-Coquilles at the mouth of the Rigolets. . . . On the south shore of the lake is a great creek (or bayou, a stream of dead water with little or no observable current) called Bayou St. Jean; it comes close to New Orleans and falls into this lake at the Pointe-aux-Herbes which projects a considerable way into the lake. We passed near that point, which is nothing but a quagmire. From thence we proceeded to the Bayou Tchoupic, so designated from a fish of that name. The many rivulets which discharge themselves into this lake make its waters almost fresh, though it communicates with the sea, and on this account it abounds not only with sea fish but with freshwater fish, some of which, especially carp, would appear to be of monstrous size in France."

Bayou St. Jean and Bayou Tchoupic were the same, though the above does not make that clear. Tchoupic, or Choupic, was the Indian name and has also been translated as "muddy." It was later confined to an inland branch of the bayou. Turning into the natural canal, the party went up it for a league, a measure of distance which is vague, as the old chroniclers used it. The French league is generally estimated as being equal to three English miles, and this was about what Du Pratz meant, since he says that he landed at the site of a deserted Acolapissa village halfway to New Orleans. The Acolapissa, as has been said, were one of the branches of the large Choctaw nation, like the Tchoupitoula and others encountered on the journey. The Tchouchouma, also found near the bayou, were a remnant of the Houma people.

"On my arrival," continues Du Pratz, "the Sieur Lavigne, a Canadian, lodged me in a cabin of the Acolapissa, from whom he had bought the village. He gave other cabins to my workmen, and we were pleased to get ourselves under shelter so promptly in a wild country. A few days afterward I purchased from a neighbor a native female slave, so as to have a woman to cook for us. My slave and I could not speak each other's language; but I made myself understood by means of signs, which these natives comprehend easily. My slave was of the Tchitimacha, with whom the French had been at war for a long time."

Pressing on still farther toward the Mississippi, he "chose a spot at a short half-league from the place where the capital was being founded. At that moment all that there was of New Orleans was a shed covered with dry branches, where the commandant lodged. I selected my site with a view to disposing easily of my crops, which would not have to be transported any distance. I notified the commandant of my choice, and he came and put me in possession in the name of the Company of the West. I built for immediate use a barracks on my land, a stone's throw from the Bayou St. Jean, while awaiting the completion of my house and quarters for my men." As he looked about him, he found the location good. If not the pioneer, he was the first eminent settler in a tract that was soon to become the infant city's finest suburb.

It is a pity that recorders like Le Page du Pratz rarely draw a portrait, and care to describe only what they regard as imposing: a native civilization, a completed outpost in the wilderness. Mainly they tell of deeds performed. Our man is as disappointing in this respect as any. He dismisses Lake Pontchartrain in a few words, and does not evoke a picture of Bienville's historic clearing on the shore of the great river. The opportunity to make character come alive is muffed. That female slave of his, for instance. She was evidently a vigorous personality and not devoid of charm. If he had devoted a few paragraphs to her real self, he might well have created a Pocahontas in the lore of the region. But he does not even given us her name. During their first days together, she astounded him by waving him aside when he was about to shoot an alligator that had come ashore near their dwelling, and destroying the beast herself with a stick as her sole weapon. Otherwise she figures briefly, though always interestingly.

"I was settled on my plantation," he writes, "yet I had reason to believe that the air was not of the best. The country was extremely aquatic, and this caused an unwholesome atmosphere which no longer exists since the land has been drained and a levee built in front of the city. The soil is of very good quality, and everything I sowed came out well. In the spring I found some peach stones which had commenced to germinate and I planted them. The following autumn the shrubs were four feet high with branches in proportion. [One questions seriously whether they could have been what we know as peaches.] Despite these advantages, I decided to quit this plantation and take another a hundred leagues further up country."

Friends of Du Pratz, including M. Hubert, a director of the Company, were heading for the Natchez bluffs. The slave was eager that he should join them and take her with him. She said that she had relatives among the Natchez people, who would help out in many matters. "That is a fine country, where one lives well and men last to a great age," she added. Her old father, hearing of the plan, came with an offer to buy her back from servitude. She would have none of it, and the father then performed a ceremony of the placing of hands which transferred her to the white man as a ward.

Le Page du Pratz lingered in New Orleans itself for two months. He acquired a Negro man and woman, each twenty years of age, who had come in a consignment from Africa. The price paid was 1,320 livres, the equivalent of $764, for the pair; he thought it a bargain. Again packing everything he owned—growing plants now, as well as furniture and tools—and with his Indian girl at his side, he mounted the river in several canoes. His stay on the Bayou St. Jean appears to have been for about two years.

In 1720 the Mississippi Bubble burst. John Law's bank failed, and the shares based on the supposed treasures of Louisiana became almost worthless in the general crash of the financial system in Paris. The Company, however, continued to function for some years, and it must be admitted that the gamble launched by the Scots adventurer had at least resulted in building up the white population of the colony. This had advanced from 400 permanent inhabitants in 1717 to about 5,000 in 1720. Bienville was authorized to remove the seat of government to New Orleans in May 1722.

The first complete census is dated November 24, 1721, and signed by the Sieur Diron d'Artaguette, inspector general of troops in Louisiana. These are the figures for New Orleans and adjacent villages, or concessions, such as Bayou St. Jean and Gentilly:

Men (meaning accredited settlers and officials) . .	293
Women	140
Children	96
French servants	155
	684
Negro slaves	514
Indian slaves	51
	565

Also listed were 231 horned beasts and 28 horses.

"It is absolutely necessary to send many Negroes to the colony, for they are better suited than whites to work on the land," a postscript to the census report advises in familiar terms. "Just as the islands of America [the West Indies] became prosperous only when they got Negro slaves, Louisiana will never be successful until a sufficient quantity of them are sent here. They are marvelously suited to the climate, and the only suggestion is that they be properly clothed in winter, which does not cost very much."

An occupational breakdown of the colonists shows that there were eighteen government employees, headed by Bienville, and forty-eight in the service of the Company. Among the forty-eight independent persons of property we find three carpenters, one baker, one pastrycook, one armorer, one locksmith, one harness maker, one turner, one house furnisher, one tobacco maker, one engraver, one gardener and one tailor.

The other side of the picture is to be had from the passenger lists of ships arriving from France. Here large groups of immigrants are baldly designated as exiles, vagabonds, deserters from the king's army, persons ordered to be deported for crimes, and in the case of many women the euphemism "seized for frauds." Throughout history members of the underworld have adopted spicy nicknames, which the authorities note as a means of identification. A few, taken at random from the earliest New Orleans rosters, are both amusing and suggestive:

Claude Duval, alias Sans Souci (Without a Care)
Pascal de Guisse, alias Sans Souci (Without a Care)
Nicolas Joussain, alias La Bonté (Good Fellow)
Jean Duval, alias St. Jean (St. John)
Joachim Claude, alias Sans Façons (Without Pretensions)
Antoine Medieu, alias Belles Fleurs (Pretty Flowers)
Jacques Jeune, alias Baguette (The Wand)
Claude Fortier, alias Sans Regrets (Without Regrets)
Joseph Deschamps, alias La Rose (The Rose)
Vincent Roger, alias Pied de Chat (Cat Foot)

We have seen that there were officials with their reports, diarists and at least one historian to tell the tale of pioneering in Louisiana. No artist capable of producing a work of the imagination emerged among the early colonists. It would have been indeed a long shot that one should do so. Yet a great romantic story that two centuries have not blunted was partly inspired by the gaudy madness of the Bubble, the dreams and hardships of those who went out voluntarily or otherwise. Written contemporaneously, the Abbé Prévost's *Histoire du Chevalier des Grieux et de Manon Lescaut* gives many a glimpse of the human side of the migration. The fact that the Abbé was never anywhere near the Gulf Coast and made some geographical blunders is of little consequence. He had observed what happened on the French end and he had listened profitably to the talk of returned voyagers. Manon, heroine of his novel and of the opera founded on it, is more than literature to New Orleans; she is folklore derived from truth, and that there was an original of her pathetic lover is pretty generally believed.

Antoine François Prévost joined the Benedictine Order at the age of twenty-two, following "the unhappy end of a too tender attachment." He made a bizarre churchman after a pattern that the eighteenth century regarded indulgently, was often in trouble with the authorities, and spent a few years in exile in England and Holland. His real *métier* was that of popular writer. He turned out more than one hundred volumes, of which the best known were a series entitled *Mémoires et Aventures d'un Homme de Qualité qui s'est Retiré du Monde.* These shoddy chronicles, all action and intrigue, were suddenly interrupted in 1731 by the Manon story presented as Volume VII of the series. The contrast was startling.

An honest, beautifully written study of character, the first novel of its kind in French, a work that was to create a school and seriously influence such authors as J. J. Rousseau, Mme. de Stäel and George Sand, had come as if by magic from a hack's pen. Paris was delighted with it. But it offended the police in that age of license under the young profligate, Louis XV. Copies were seized in the bookstores. The *Journal du Court* spoke of "decent folk melting for pity over a sharper and a whore." Nothing could halt its success, and before long we find the Abbé serving as almoner to the Prince de Conti, of the noble family after which one of the streets of New Orleans had been named. Restored to favor by the Church, Prévost rose to be prior of Saint-Georges de Gennes. He never wrote another masterpiece.

Briefly, this is the plot of *Manon Lescaut:* The narrator, the fictional *"homme de qualité,"* traveling in Normandy, comes upon a band of twelve girls being escorted by archers to a port where they are to be shipped to Louisiana. Along with the group is a young man who has been bribing the guards at so much an hour to let him keep one of the girls company. He has just run out of money and is in despair. The narrator gives him some gold coins. Years later he meets the same young man, who is the Chevalier des Grieux, and learns his story.

The chevalier had met Manon when she was sixteen and had induced her with remarkable ease to go and live with him without benefit of clergy. This involved hiding from his family. The atmosphere of true love is evoked from the start, despite the fact that the chevalier is a weakling throughout, and Manon one of the most incorrigible little wantons in literature. The pair have various scabrous adventures. Des Grieux takes to cheating at cards as a means to fortune, and Manon deceives him with any rich man who will pay her price. He is devoured by jealousy, but eternally forgiving. Always in the man's case and sometimes in the woman's, the sins are committed for the other's sake, to provide luxuries or to avert bankruptcy. Des Grieux moralizes, but Manon never does. The two characters are sharply etched, different, plausible. One believes that they are utterly devoted to each other—and with a singular inner purity—no matter what the appearance of things may be.

Finally Manon is thrown into the Hôpital, the foul women's prison of the day, and is ordered deported to Louisiana, to be disposed of by the governor there as the wife of some settler. Des Grieux accompanies her the whole way. Aboard ship he pretends that she is his wife, and the governor agrees that they shall not be separated. They go to live in a hovel, "built of planks and clay," in New Orleans, and they are happy. Unluckily, Des Grieux gets the belated idea that they should really be married. He has to ask permission of the governor. The governor's attitude immediately changes, for his nephew had wanted Manon, and if she is not a legal wife it is his nephew that shall have her and not Des Grieux.

The couple flees into the wilderness. Manon cannot stand the exposure. She dies in her lover's arms, and is buried by him in the sand dunes on the shore of Lake Pontchartrain. He makes his way back to France. There are variations in the librettos of Massenet's and Puccini's operas, not the least absurd of which is the placing of mountains near the death scene. One would have to travel north to the Great Smokies between the Carolinas and Tennessee to find such a range.

From our point of view, one of the most interesting features of *Manon Lescaut* is the treatment of the heroine as a deported convict of the type known in old Louisiana as a "correction girl." On the third page of the novel, the narrator observes "among the twelve girls chained by the waist, six by six," one whose "face and carriage were so little in accord with her condition that in any other circumstances I should have taken her for a woman of the highest rank. Her sadness, the dirtiness of her linen and of her clothes did so little to disfigure her that the sight of her inspired me with respect and pity." Later, when Des Grieux is telling his story, he says that "to imagine Manon confined in the Hôpital was torture indescribable. Apart from the infamy attached to the place, I did not know how she was being treated there; the memory of some details which I had heard of that house of horror renewed my agony each moment." Women in eighteenth-century prisons—and particularly the Hôpital—were shamefully misused by their jailers unless friends or relatives paid to have them protected.

On the road to Le Havre, Manon is again described as being chained by the waist and seated in soiled linen on some handfuls of straw. The chief of the archers guarding her concedes bawdily that he will charge Des Grieux a sum equal to "the regular price in Paris" for time spent with Manon, for he can imagine only one motive on the young man's part. When he realizes that he is dealing with a sincere lover, he boosts the tariff sky-high.

"After a voyage of two months," writes Prévost, "we reached the desired shore at last. The country had nothing agreeable to offer us at first sight. There were barren and uninhabited fields, where one saw only some reeds and a few trees stripped by the wind. No trace of men or animals. However, the captain having ordered some of our guns to be fired, we soon perceived a band of citizens of New Orleans approaching us with the liveliest signs of joy. We had had no view of the town: it is hidden on that side by a little hill. [Needless to say, there are no hills near New Orleans, though the levee may have been meant.] We were received like people who had come down from heaven. These poor folk tumbled over themselves to ask us a thousand questions about the state of France and the various provinces of their birth. They embraced us like brothers, like beloved companions who had come to share their poverty and their solitude.

"We joined them on the road to the town; but we were surprised to discover, as we advanced, that what had been vaunted to us up till then as a fine city was only a collection of a few poor cabins. The latter were inhabited by five or six thousand persons. The Governor's house seemed to us a little distinguished from the rest by its height and its location. It was defended by some earthworks, around which ran a large ditch.

"We were at once presented to him. He had a long talk in private with the captain, and then, returning to us, he appraised, one after the other, all the girls who had come by that ship. There were thirty of them, for we had found another company at Havre which was attached to ours. The Governor, after he had inspected them closely, summoned various young men of the town who were languishing in expectation of a bride. He gave the prettiest to the more important, and lots were cast for the rest. He had not yet spoken to Manon, but after he had ordered the others to withdraw he bade us both stay behind."

The governor, having decided to befriend them, keeps the two lovers to supper and finds a lodging for them. Prévost evades any description of the life of the pioneers in New Orleans. When Manon and Des Grieux are compelled to flee, he speaks vaguely of their crossing barren plains with "not a single tree" to give them shelter, of wild Indians near by, and ravening beasts. There is no realization of the swampy environs, crisscrossed by bayous. Des Grieux has little difficulty at the last in opening a grave in the sandy soil, with a sword as his only implement.

Now what foundation of truth is there in all this? The brutalizing of correction girls before they reached the colony is, of course, authentic. The historian Michelet writes: "The mere transportation from Paris was so severe that it drove many to despair. A body of girls arose in revolt from maltreatment at La Rochelle. Armed only with their nails and teeth, they attacked their guards. They wanted to be killed. The barbarians fired on them, wounded a great many and killed six."

That Prévost's characters should be regarded as actual persons is something else again. Grace King, the New Orleans woman of letters, declared in 1895 that Manon's grave had until recently been shown to the curious, she did not say just where, and that "relics of her" were still being sold in the local antique shops; that a Chevalier des Grieux was on the register of those arriving in the colony, served as a royal officer, and was buried in an early cemetery not far from the river. A house on Bayou Road, near Roman Street, was long pointed out as Manon's residence, though no building of that type could possibly have existed at the time she was supposed to have been living in New Orleans.

Subsequent research has revealed some more provocative leads. *The Louisiana Historical Quarterly* published, in Vol. 2, No. 3, 1919, a monograph by Victorin Dejan entitled *Manon Lescaut, the Real versus the Ideal.* Dejan first dismisses the hypothesis of Arsène Houssaye, Henry Harisse and other authors, that the Abbé Prévost had merely narrated a love affair of his own youth. It is then established that Des Grieux was the name of the captain of the *Comte de Toulouse,* a ship that came several times to Louisiana and notably in 1718, when she transported a great many convicts to Biloxi. If this genuine Des Grieux did not know Manon, "he certainly heard of her adventures." For there was a girl who comes close to being identifiable with the abbé's heroine.

One Manon Porcher was exiled from Angers, France, at about the same time that the Chevalier Avril de la Varenne left that city for the New World. In January 1716, La Mothe Cadillac, governor of Louisiana, reported to Paris:

"I have the honor, my Lord, to inform you that a young man of rank called Avril de la Varenne, from Angers, has come here in the storeship *La Dauphine.* He brought with him a woman said to have been married, and who actually may have been, for she left three children in France. She first took the name of Froget [this could have been a corruption of Porcher] and at present bears that of Quantin, declaring herself married to the said Sieur de la Varenne, which was confirmed by M. Raujon, M. Crozat's director."

The conclusion is, therefore, that the Abbé Prévost fictionized a true story, setting the date forward from 1715-1716, and gave his hero the name of the sea captain from whom he may well have learned the circumstances. What became of Avril de la Varenne and his sweetheart is not known. But the myth surrounding them is immortal.

Chapter 3

Pioneer Days of a Capital

THOUGH begun in 1718 and made the capital in 1722, New Orleans did not actually function as the seat of government until 1723. It then had a population of about 1,400 souls, slightly more than half of whom were white. An increasing amount of shipping arrived directly, instead of unloading at Mobile and Biloxi. The engineer Pauger had demonstrated that the passes at the mouth of the Mississippi were navigable for the largest craft, a question which had been in doubt. Barges and little boats of all kinds continued to prefer the lake route. It is impossible to tell how many ships cleared the port up to 1724, because the records of several months for the whole colony frequently are lumped together with nothing given but the number and names of passengers. Cargoes are ignored, or referred to vaguely as "stores." But there are numerous references in reports and private memoirs which indicate the things most needed from abroad: comestibles, including wines and brandies, for the colony was still far from being self-sustaining in the matter of food; clothing, building materials, tools and weapons, gewgaws for trade with the Indians.

Next to the pioneer task of learning how to live in a new and utterly strange environment, the Indians constituted the chief problem for the settlers. The lower part of what is now the state of Mississippi and the part of Louisiana which lies north of Lake Pontchartrain was the country of the Choctaw. Tribes affiliated with them, such as the Tangipahoa, the Tchoupitoula and Acolapissa, had settlements south of the lake, where a few true Choctaw also had penetrated. Around the shores of Lake Maurepas lived the subtribe called Quinipissa. Bienville had never lost the influence he had established over the natives of the coast and the vicinity of New Orleans. He was on particularly good terms with the Choctaw, who considered themselves allies of the French and who so remained with but few lapses. North and east of their territory, however, lay the land of the warlike Chickasaw, who favored the English and with whom the French never succeeded in coming to terms through the long years ahead.

Between Choctaw and Chickasaw, on the east bank of the Mississippi, was the small but fiercely independent Natchez tribe. Their holdings were among the most desirable in the region, and shortly after the coming of Iberville and Bienville the French had planted a settlement there. The fort built to protect it was named Fort Rosalie in honor of the Comtesse de Pontchartrain. As early as 1716 Bienville had had to suppress a revolt of the Natchez. He marched against them again in 1723, restoring order with some severity.

The near-by Indians west of the great river and among the lower bayous were the dispirited Houma, who gave little trouble. Much farther west, the savage Attacapa, eaters of human flesh, loomed as a half-legendary, ominous bogey to the colonists of Louisiana.

The friendly Choctaw figured for two centuries in the annals of New Orleans. Some students hold that the superior qualities and traditions of the Choctaw indicate that they were of Aztec origin and had wandered north from Mexico. Their manners and customs differed from those of other Red Indians of the Southwest. For instance, they did not live in tepees, but built fairly solid dwellings, some circular, some square. The great round hut seen in many of their villages was probably the ancient council house. Later, in imitation of the French, they adopted the log cabin. Their food consisted of fish, wild fowl, fruits and vegetables, principally corn. Alligator and turtle bones have been unearthed in their old kitchen middens. The men wore their hair long in two braids on either side of the head and cut straight in a bang above the eyebrows. The women tied back their thick tresses, occasionally plaiting them in a single loose rope. Both sexes painted, the preferred decorations being yellow crescents outlined with blue on both checks. Tattooing was used, but less than painting.

They hunted with blowguns. Their dugouts were hollowed from a single log of black gum. In these craft they traversed Lake Pontchartrain and all its adjacent waterways, fishing and going to special localities where sport was good, according to the season. Thus it was Choctaw from Chinchuba Creek on the north shore of the big lake whom the first French had discovered camped on the future site of New Orleans. Asked about themselves and the place, the Indians had replied "Chinchuba," meaning "alligator." Probably the saurians were no longer running lively on the creek, and the chase had been carried to the Mississippi. Choctaw liked alligator meat. But the French naturally enough were confused and thought it the designation of a separate tribe.

Being the original finders of the spot and having a good opinion of it as a resort, the Choctaw continued to come after the city got started. For generations they were seen about the French Market on the levee, which was a site their people had once used for bartering. They brought ornaments, baskets, seasonings and herbs to sell. Or they solemnly paraded the streets until these became distasteful to them because of the growth of wheeled traffic. But they could not be happy long away from the pine woods of Okwá-ta, or Ok-Hata—the Wide Water—as they called Pontchartrain.

Pauger, the practical architect of New Orleans, tore down in 1721 all the squatters' houses that displeased him because they were irregularly located, and forced the owners to build anew. For this one irate woman attempted to slap his face, and he retaliated only by calling her a sow. He fixed the levee side of the Place d'Armes (now Jackson Square) at forty paces from the riverbank. The rue de la Levée (now Decatur Street) then ran its entire length parallel to the shore. The current of the Mississippi has since shifted, and a triangle of new land lies from southwest to northeast in front of the Vieux Carré, its narrow end beyond the Place d'Armes.

Bienville built his house at the corner of the Quai, or rue de la Levée, and the street thereafter called by his name. Its dimensions were twenty-one by thirty-two feet, two stories high, and it had a shingled roof. It contained eight rooms, and in the yard behind stood a kitchen built of stakes driven into the ground, and roofed with bark. No glass was available, so the window frames were filled with transparent cloth. It is an odd circumstance that the space in front of the governor's residence was not cleared of forest growth for several years. Pauger's specificiations had called for an initial measure of cutting down the trees for four squares in from the river, and three squares on either side of the Place d'Armes. If Bienville chose to establish himself outside that zone, he would have to wait for services. The governor appears not to have minded having to reach his front door by a narrow pathway from the Quai.

Another elaborate dwelling, relatively speaking, was the house of Captain de la Marque on the rue de Chartres. It was forty feet in length, and surrounded by a gallery. On the ground floor was a great hall with a fireplace, an adjoining room with two closets. Above there was a garret, and the roof was of bark. Two wings flanked the courtyard, the first being employed as a kitchen with rooms for the servants, and the second as a storehouse. It sounds more pretentious than Bienville's home, but all accounts agree that the latter was the handsomest and best furnished of early New Orleans houses.

The first church on the site of the Cathedral was a poor wooden structure, which in 1724 was followed by a brick building, also far from imposing. The next, and for a long while the only other brick edifice, was the jail, behind the municipal hall and adjoining the church.

Complaints having been filed against the administration of Bienville, he sailed for France in 1725 to submit himself to an inquiry, and left his cousin Boisbriant in command. The political uncertainty lasted for two years, during which the colony grew steadily and traffic with France increased. In 1726 Louisiana exports were silk, tobacco, rice, indigo, pitch, tar, lumber, masts, sassafras and some rather inferior drugs. These were the products of the newly settled coastal region. Furs from the Illinois, as the limitless upcountry was called, were rafted down the Mississippi and constituted the most important item shipped from New Orleans. Much of the fur traffic, however, passed directly from the river into the "manchac" leading to Lake Maurepas and Pontchartrain, and the Gulf ports beyond.

The Company of the Indies, as the old Company of the West had become, was interested in making tobacco the chief crop for export. It therefore offered to pay a small bonus, and quick results followed from growers close to New Orleans and in the Natchez settlement. The business of producing pitch and tar commenced at Mobile and was developed later on the shores of Lake Pontchartrain. An average of some 12,000 barrels per year at each locality was obtained, a large commercial activity for the times. Indigo showed a gain, but silk languished because the European mulberry on which the worms fed was not at its best in that warm, damp climate. A start was made in the cultivation of cotton, destined to be one of the region's great staples.

More exports naturally led to a boom in imports, some of which began to arrive from the French West Indian islands. It is necessary to jump ahead several years to find a detailed manifest of cargo, but we may rest assured that the difference between the needs of the 1720's and those of 1747, when the following list is dated, was one of quantity rather than kind.

352 barriques of wine, four to the ton,
5 ancres [10 gallons each] of brandy,
200 barrels of flour,
60 cases of soap,
110 cases of molded candles,
12 cases of brandied fruit,
25 cases of capers, olives and anchovies,
50 ancres of salt pork, 28 to the ton,
50 firkins of butter,
39 cases of olive oil,
22 barrels of goose thighs,
10 large packs of linen paper,

5 large packs of woolen cloth,
2 hogsheads of hams,
10 barrels of salt beef,
2 hogsheads of trumpery, glass beads, etc.,
20 sacks of salt.*

Such was a typical shipment from Europe. We find cattle and other domestic animals being landed in Louisiana from Saint Domingue in 1720, indigo seed and rum in 1722; again a fair number of beasts, rum and Spanish silver to be used as currency in 1726. Rice, timber, pitch and tar were the products most needed by the islands. There was a shortage of lumber for building in Martinique, and the demand there for Louisiana cypress and pine grew brisk.

An even curve of progression might have been maintained if the wise Bienville had returned, as expected. The Company was unluckily inspired to replace him, and instead it sent Etienne de Périer, a man who knew nothing about Indian psychology and was incapable of learning. He arrived in 1727, and immediately he dropped all those officials who had been closely connected with his predecessor. To be commander at Natchez with its 300 prosperous colonists he appointed a certain Sieur de Chépart, an avaricious, cruel, drunken officer who was soon hated by all the inhabitants, white as well as red. The French settlers brought charges against him. He was tried before the supreme council in New Orleans and was about to be dismissed when Périer stupidly insisted that he be pardoned and gave him back his post.

Chépart was puffed up with conceit when he resumed his duties. He had long had it in mind to mark out an estate for himself in the region. His eye now fell on a village of the Natchez, called the White Apple village, where a perpetual fire was kept burning in a sacred place on a hill. The head chief, whose title was the Great Sun, was ordered to vacate the site within two moons and turn it over to Chépart. The Indians could not believe at first that the decision was serious. They pleaded for a reversal,

* *Archives Nationales, Colonies;* Paris: Sér. C13, Vol. XXXI, fol. 252.

but were insultingly rebuffed. It is evident that they then calmly plotted the massacre of every Frenchman they could lay their hands on.

The Great Sun's crafty subterfuge was politely to invite Chépart to a feast on November 27, 1729. The commander accepted and took most of his officers along, including the storekeeper Ricard. They were served vast quantities of food and intoxicating drinks. At about three o'clock in the morning, Chépart staggered back to Fort Rosalie and went to bed. He was awakened shortly afterward by Lieutenant Macé and the interpreter Papin, who told him that the Indian mistresses of some soldiers had just warned them that the French were all about to be butchered that same day. The commander threw his nightcap at them, called them weaklings and had them clapped in irons. A couple of hours later, a very prominent settler named Kolly arrived with his son and their overseer Longuay. They had heard the same rumor as they came out from early Mass and they wanted some action taken, but Chépart had them also locked up for disturbing his peace with calamity howling.

Shortly after daylight on the twenty-eighth, scores of Indians drifted into the fort and posted themselves in twos and threes at the door of each house. They used the pretext that they were organizing a hunt and needed to borrow gunpowder. They asked to see the head of the family and prolonged the powwow with friendly gossip. Meanwhile the Great Sun appeared, displaying the calumet and attended by several braves carrying furs, fowls and pots of oil, as gifts for Chépart. He was awakened for the last time. He was so pleased with the tribute offered that he sent for the five men he had jailed. "Look, look! I am master of the savages!" he shouted as they entered the room. The disgusted Kolly and the rest left as quickly as they could.

The first blow was delivered at the river landing, where Ricard the storekeeper was superintending an unloading. An Indian leaped onto the boat, caught its owner from behind and decapitated him. Simultaneously the members of the crew were shot down with guns. Ricard had the luck to drop into the river unscathed; he swam to the shelter of some woods, and was one of the few survivors. The sound of the guns had been the signal for the massacre at the fort. Promptly every Indian fell upon the man with whom he had been talking. In less than half an hour nearly all the male colonists had perished. The party headed by Kolly was struck down on its way home. The vicar, Bailly, was slain in his bed. Chépart fled in craven panic to his garden, where the Natchez chief ordered him clubbed to death by an Indian slave since he was too low for a warrior to bother about.

Two white men were spared, a carpenter and a tailor whom the Indians felt they could use. One chronicler has it that Great Sun and his brothers, Little Sun and the Serpent, wanted the tailor to make over the more showy French uniforms to fit them. It does not sound much like the austere Natchez spirit, but the intent may have been derisive. The Negroes, the women who were not obviously *enceinte,* and the French children were preserved as slaves. Diabolically, the pregnant women were slashed open, their unborn infants torn out and flung to the dogs. Every building was burned to the ground.

One soldier who had crawled through the chimney of a bake oven and two men who had chanced to be out hunting game succeeded in joining Ricard in the forest. These started for New Orleans to raise the cry of vengeance. The historian Le Page du Pratz is among the best critics of the affair. He had seen through Chépart from the beginning, had felt it so certain that the bully's methods would lead to an explosion that he had left his plantation and moved to within a few miles of the capital. On the morning of December 2 he was told by a black boatman that terrible news was circulating in the city. He hurried there and was among the first to learn official details. Everyone congratulated him on his foresight in quitting the danger spot.

Governor Périer mustered all the soldiers within reach and sent them against the Natchez. But a Canadian irregular named Le Sueur got there first, at the head of some 700 Choctaw. The Choctaw detested the Natchez, and eagerly falling upon them, they rescued 51 of the white women and children. It developed into a regular war, with the Natchez retiring west of the Mississippi to secret fastnesses, and both sides committing the atrocities usual in Indian fighting.

The difficulties did not justify the treacherous policy adopted by Périer the next year. Late in the summer he had assembled a large number of troops in the Ouachita district. He then proposed that the Natchez chiefs come in under a flag of truce to discuss a peace settlement. Great Sun agreed because he realized that his tribe was hopelessly outnumbered. But while the conference was in progress, Périer's men closed in on it, seized the chiefs and held them as hostages. All their followers must surrender on a guarantee that their lives would be spared, Périer announced, or the chiefs would be put to death. Forty warriors and some 400 women and children did capitulate; they were double-crossed, since several were set aside for execution. The others, including the chiefs, were sold into slavery in Cuba and Saint Domingue. There remained fewer than a hundred warriors who had decided that no faith could be placed in the word of a man who had violated a truce; these fled back with members of their families in a rainstorm to wilder country, east of the river.

The massacre by the Natchez and the way Périer handled the incident had a profound effect on the history of Louisiana. That the lives of so many seasoned colonists should have been lost and their ten years' work destroyed was bad enough, but the resulting atmosphere of mutual terror proved even more expensive. French planters regarded all Indians as suspect and tended to huddle closer to Mobile and New Orleans for protection. The Indians, on the other hand, concluded that friendship with whites was an illusion; even the Choctaw were not unaffected by this feeling. As a tribe the Natchez had been destroyed, yet the tale their survivors carried to the bloodthirsty Chickasaw and other rovers of the middle border stimulated new wars. Without question, progress was retarded for at least a decade because Chépart had reached for the White Apple sacred village.

Périer's administration was marked otherwise by the arrival of a group of Ursuline nuns. They came through the efforts of the Jesuit Order which was all-powerful in the Illinois country, but found itself supplanted in New Orleans by the Capuchins. The latter had a contract with the Company of the West, later the Company of the Indies, to found churches and furnish religious consolation in the coastal settlements. Determined to uphold their prestige, the Jesuits sent fathers to preach in New Orleans, and that was the start of a feud which raged for many years. But in the matter of the nuns the Jesuits had had a happy inspiration which all Catholics praised then and afterward.

Different versions of the special mission of the Ursulines have come down to us, and all are based on truth. The nuns were to superintend virtuous young girls sent from France until husbands could be found for them; they were to seek the reformation of the many loose women already in the city; they were to be nurses and teachers. The last-mentioned activity is the one that caused them to be longest and most gratefully remembered. For a hundred years they furnished the best type of female education to be had in New Orleans.

The original band of Ursulines sailed from France in the ship *Gironde,* early in 1727. Delayed for months by bad weather, they were given up for lost, finally went ashore at the Balize, a disembarkation point inside one of the Mississippi passes, and came up the river in small boats, beating the *Gironde* to the city. They were temporarily quartered in Bienville's house, and two years later in a plantation house west of the ramparts, the property of Mme. de Kolly, whose husband and son had been killed in the Natchez massacre. One of their early duties was to take care of the orphans resulting from that disaster. The building of their great convent (which still stands), about midway between the Place d'Armes and the Esplanade, was not completed for seven years.

A sister named Madeleine Hachard, whose nature was optimistic and powers of observation keen, has left an account of the pioneering adventures of the Ursulines. The following will serve as an example of her sprightly style:

"The roofs of the houses are covered with shingles which are cut in the shape of slates, and one must know this to believe it, for they have the appearance and beauty of slates. The colonists are very proud of their capital. Suffice it to say, they sing a song in the streets here to the effect that this town is as fine a sight as Paris. . . . The women here are extremely ignorant as to the means of securing their salvation, but they are very expert in the art of displaying their beauty. There is so much luxury in this town that there is no distinction among the classes so far as dress goes. The magnificence of display is equal to all. Most of them reduce themselves and their family to the hard lot of having nothing to eat at home but *sagamite* [corn mush], and flaunt abroad in robes of velvet and damask, ornamented with the most costly ribbons. They paint and rouge to hide the ravages of time, and wear small black patches on their checks as embelishment."

The part played by the Ursulines in arranging marriages for worthy immigrant girls should not be overlooked. It is tied up with one of Louisiana's favorite traditions, and none too accurately, as modern research has shown. The story goes that, to offset the scandal of the "correction girls," who were transported to the colony at the start of the Bubble, the king ordered that maidens of decent families, properly trained in domestic duties and of irreproachable character, should be chosen by a bishop and sent out. These were called *filles à la cassette,* or casket girls, because each one was provided by the Company with a small chest containing articles of clothing, such as blouses, undershirts and headdresses. A kind of trousseau, in short. It is generally stated that they began to arrive in 1728, were placed under the guardianship of the Ursulines and were easily disposed of, "so great was the want of the country," the supply continuing at fairly regular intervals until 1751.

But Laville Bremer and others have demonstrated that no less an authority than Pénicaut recorded the landing of the first and only casket girls—eighty-odd of them—at Biloxi in March 1721. This would have been a normal outcome of the king's ruling, which had been signed the previous year. Contrariwise, it is unlikely that his wishes should have been ignored for eight years, as the 1728 date implies.

The truth seems to be that, having sent a single consignment according to specifications, the Company quietly dropped the troublesome business. Other eligibles doubtless came from time to time under Church and Court auspices, but they were not authentic *filles à la cassette*. When the Ursulines reached New Orleans they naturally were asked to take charge of such cases.

In Louisiana, descent from a casket girl is claimed with the pride that a New Englander attaches to *Mayflower* ancestry. Cynics have pointed out that the fertility of the charming creatures must have been prodigious, whereas there is no evidence of offspring left by a single correction girl.

The complications springing from the Natchez calamity ended by breaking the Company of the Indies. It had been put to heavy expense to wage the punitive military campaign and to repair the material losses. Furthermore, it was threatened with endless damage suits by the families of the murdered colonists. In 1731 it surrendered its charter to the Crown. Louisiana again was a royal province, and the monarch could find no one better fitted to be governor than the Sieur de Bienville. He had never been tried on the flimsy charges brought against him, but had been living quietly in Paris. His reappointment was the most complete vindication possible. His authority was to be on a plane of dignity denied him when he had been the servant of a coterie of gamblers and financial sharks. Yet even he could not master the menacing new conditions which had arisen during his absence. It was too late in his career for him to begin all over again.

On his way out, Bienville stopped over in Saint Domingue, where he talked with the enslaved Natchez Suns. These fierce braves honored him; they were among the many Indian chiefs who had accorded him the title of "Father." Now they explained that they would not have dreamed of striking at the French if it had not been for the cumulative injustices practiced under Périer. Bienville frankly sympathized with their viewpoint. But he must have felt that it would be bad for discipline on the mainland to seem to condone their deeds as individuals. So he left them where they were, failing to recommend a pardon.

He was back in New Orleans in March 1733, found that Périer had moved into his house after the Ursulines vacated it, and brusquely threw him out, dispensing with the courtesies generally shown a retiring governor. Delighted to see their natural leader again, the citizens gave him an ovation. At once he began to correct abuses in the administration, while doing his best to revivify planting and extend trade.

Then, moving cautiously, he tried to patch up relations with the Indians. In this he met little but discouragement. The only important tribe he could seriously hope to hold, he learned, was the Choctaw and there was a division of loyalties among them. One of their chiefs, Red Shoe, admittedly favored an alliance with the Chickasaw and English. When Bienville dispatched an expedition of thirty Frenchmen and nearly a thousand Choctaw, the native force was bought off by the Chickasaw and returned to New Orleans after a mere pretense of a battle with its ancient enemies. Two years later, the governor led a campaign in person, and for the first time in his life was defeated by Indians. The trouble was with his Choctaw levies, which in action attacked at the wrong time and in the wrong place, and generally speaking proved unruly. Still a third foray was repulsed by the Chickasaw, and in the end Bienville was forced to conclude a peace he regarded as humiliating to him.

The struggles of nearly a decade are here condensed into a paragraph. Fighting more serious than that against the Natchez occurred, but it was waged far east of the Mississippi, and the effect upon the Island of Orleans was indirect. The details do not concern this narrative; only the fact that the standoff in the wilderness saved the double port on river and lake from being temporarily overwhelmed by red foes is important.

One perceives clearly enough today that Bienville's policy of friendship and co-operation with the Indians, excluding the Chickasaw, would not have worked out as a permanent thing. It was motivated by French as opposed to Anglo-Saxon imperialism. Bienville, the Canadian, wanted to use the aborigines whom he influenced to crush the English and their native allies. He saw Louisiana as a southern extension of Canada and hoped that the two jaws of the pincers would finally meet in the rich territory on the eastern seaboard. Had this taken place the French would not have long remained on good terms with the Indians. They would have turned upon and despoiled them, as Europeans of all races did everywhere in North America, because Indians were fanatic individualists who declined to be regimented. Indians would not have accepted French culture, as Negroes gladly did.

But even the notion of Louisiana as a legitimate child of Quebec was false. What had been established on the Gulf Coast was a colony similar to France's island possessions in the Caribbean. Lawless men of the buccaneer type who had conquered Saint Domingue formed the bulk of the early settlers, as against the solid Normans and Picards who had gone to Canada. Hot-country crops were the staples: tobacco, indigo, rice, cotton and subsequently sugar. These required an ever-increasing number of black slaves, as the census taker of 1721 had stressed. The loss of Indian friendship was less significant in the long run to the destiny of Louisiana than the fact that two large shiploads of blacks from Africa had arrived in each of the years 1727, 1728 and 1729. Briefly, whites were outnumbered in New Orleans. The Negroes continued to come, and with the restoration of order on the plantations after the Natchez massacre they were distributed more widely.

In 1743 Bienville was relieved as governor at his own request. He informed the court with some bitterness that he had outlived his usefulness. His departure for France was the clear-cut ending of a period in the history of the colony he had helped his brother discover, had virtually created and had more than once preserved from mortal peril.

Louisiana State Museum

NEW ORLEANS IN 1803

This view of the city is from Fort Saint Charles. The original, an engraving by J. L. Boqueta de Woiseri, was found in the Cabildo.

Association of Commerce

PONTCHARTRAIN RAILROAD

The lake terminal of the Pontchartrain Railroad with piers and bathhouse in the distance.

Louisiana State Museum

DON ANDRES ALMONESTER Y ROXAS

Louisiana State Museum

GOVERNOR ALEXANDER O'REILLY

Chapter 4

Ancien Régime

THE appointment of Pierre Cavagnal de Rigaud, Marquis de Vaudreuil, as governor in succession to Bienville, both pleased and flattered the people of Louisiana. Vaudreuil's father had been governor general of Canada, and the family was influential in France. Charles Gayarré, the Louisiana historian, expresses it as follows: "His nomination was received as a token that the government intended to make serious efforts to put the colony on a more respectable footing, and it was presumed that the marquis would not have accepted the post of a petty governor in so insignificant a colony if he had not received promises that the province over which he had been called to rule would soon be destined, under the powerful patronage of the mother country, to acquire more importance than it had so far possessed." These hopes were dashed. But an immediate and remarkable change in the social life of New Orleans manifested itself. One may say that the rude pioneers then took on that gloss of the *ancien régime,* that elegant hauteur masking a touchy pride, which thereafter was typical of Creole culture.

Vaudreuil inherited two problems: the recurring wars with the Indians, and a rivalry within the administration caused by the soaring pretensions of the king's intendant. The trend of native affairs was sketched in the previous chapter. It need only be added that the difficulties became progressively worse, with the English of the Carolinas egging on the Chickasaw, and the Choctaw dividing into pro-French and anti-French parties. Vaudreuil asked no better than to hold the fighting at a distance, and this he was fairly successful in doing. The gadfly of an intendant was something else again.

Every French colony had an official of this title, a royal delegate set to watch and check the governor, audit accounts and see that the public services were properly conducted. He regulated the collection of revenue, notably customs duties and taxes, and he supervised its expenditure. He could interpose an absolute veto on the governor in financial matters, and challenge any of his acts if he regarded them as despotic. In other words, he was resident inspector general for the Crown, with certain arbitrary powers of his own and the annoying privilege of making secret reports on everything. The system nearly always led to venom between the two high officials—and a decline of that efficiency which it was thought to promote.

Bienville had known how to dominate intendants, though even he had his troubles with them. Vaudreuil, less forceful and aware that some of his acts were open to censure, shrugged them aside. But in the administration that followed his, an intendant was the cause of the utmost discord.

When the marquis really cared about was the little court that he set up in New Orleans and over which his sharp-tongued, avaricious, but socially brilliant marquise delighted to preside. The military officers were, of course, the first ornaments of this imitation Versailles. "Who says officer, says everything," is reported to have been the criticism of an intendant and then of the disgruntled planters and merchants. The latter, however, soon learned to value an invitation to the governor's mansion, especially as their women had joyfully hailed a regime that promised them a taste of the amenities of European life.

Gayarré tells many stories to illustrate Vaudreuil's generosity, marked as it was by a slightly sardonic note. Having been informed by the marquise that one of his favorite servants had behaved insolently toward an officer, Vaudreuil agreed to dismiss him. He sent for the man, paid him his back wages and then handed him 300 livres from his private purse as a bonus. Annoyed, his wife objected that he was putting a premium on misbehavior. He did not answer in words, but negligently tossed another 300 livres to the servant. Then, as the marquise flushed with rage, he drawled: "I do not reward him for his offense, Madame, but for his former fidelity, and if you show too much distaste in the poor devil's presence I shall give him the whole purse as a salve for the humiliation you now inflict upon him." One may suppose that Vaudreuil was glad of the chance thus slyly to rebuke his wife for her well-known greed in money matters.

On another occasion a servant accused of mislaying, perhaps stealing, a valuable piece of plate was brought before him. He fixed the trembling man with a look and questioned him sternly. Then he smiled and turned to his butler. "Fetch a bottle of my best wine and give it to this poor fellow to cure him of his fright," he said. The lost silver utensil was found soon afterward. He did not trouble to ask whether it had been restored through gratitude for his leniency.

An officer had written a letter against Vaudreuil to the ministry in Paris, and it had been sent back to the governor. He ignored it until a day when the officer in question offered him gross flattery to his face. "What, sir!" exclaimed the marquis. "Do you dare give the lie to your own written assertions?" The other swore that he did not know what was meant. Vaudreuil referred more positively to the letter, at the same time strongly advising that he be not forced to produce it from his files in proof. Receiving no further answer, he bowed ironically. Never again did he open his lips on the subject, according to Gayarré, or show by any act that he remembered the circumstance.

Vaudreuil gave great encouragement to Leblanc de Villeneuve, a member of his staff, who aspired to be a poet and dramatist. This young officer was allowed to share his company at any hour of the day or evening, while those who came on business errands were often kept waiting for hours. There followed a play in verse, by Villeneuve, which was the first to be written and produced in Louisiana. It was called *The Indian Father,* and it dealt with an incident that had occurred the year before. An Acolapissa had killed a Choctaw for sneering at his tribe as "mean-spirited dogs of the French." Vaudreuil had tried to persuade the relatives to accept presents as damages, and failing in that had ordered the arrest of the murderer. The criminal was said to have hidden in New Orleans, but could not be found. Then his old father went to the Choctaw and let himself be tomahawked in the guilty son's place, a solution that Indian ethics regarded as most honorable. Villeneuve's drama was acted in the governor's house, to the delight of Vaudreuil and his friends.

This graceful executive differed widely indeed from those who had preceded him, and notably from Bienville. But Louisiana remembered him with a nostalgic affection. It did no real harm that Michel de la Rouvillière, the intendant, could write to the French Government in 1751:

"The soldiers are allowed to do what they please, provided they drink at the liquor shop designated to them; and they carry out of it wine and spirits, which they sell over again to the Negroes and Indians. This has been proved ten times for one; everybody knows it, and yet the abuse is not stopped. I have frequently spoken to the Marquis de Vaudreuil on the subject. But this nefarious practice, instead of being checked, has grown more active. It is M. de Belleisle, assistant to the major, who has the lease and administration of the liquor shop, and who pays a certain sum for it to the major—others say to the Governor's lady. . . . Moreover, the Marquise de Vaudreuil is capable of carrying on a still baser kind of trade. She deals here with everybody, and she forces merchants and other individuals to take charge of her merchandise, and to sell it at the price which she fixes. She keeps in her own house every sort of drugs, which are sold by her steward, and in his absence she does not scruple to descend, herself, to the occupation of measurement and to betake herself to the ell. The husband is not ignorant of this."

In 1752 Vaudreuil was promoted to his father's old post, the governor generalship of Canada. Strange to say, the selection was made because trouble on a grand scale was brewing between

France and England, and a strong man was needed on the St. Lawrence. Stranger still, he lived up to what had been expected of him, defending his province bravely and well when it was invaded four years later. From dilettante in the wilderness to proconsul, at a bound. One wonders about him.

The new governor of Louisiana was Louis Billouard de Kerlerec, an aging Breton captain in the king's navy. He had had twenty-five years of active service and had been wounded several times. Kerlerec reached New Orleans in February 1753, and at once launched forth on a policy of conciliating all Indians with the exception of the Chickasaw. It did not work out. He had come with a preconceived idea that the natives were more reasonable than they had been given credit for, and that to win their friendship it was necessary only to entertain them at banquets and to distribute gifts lavishly. The method worked at first, because he had brought large quantities of stuff the Indians wanted, and they flocked to collect. He discovered that he had placed himself in the position of paying tribute, and at a figure which it was hard to maintain. We soon find him imploring the government to send him the wherewithal for further largesse, to stave off attacks. One year he writes of the Choctaw: "I am satisfied with them. It seems to me that they are true to their plighted faith." The very next year he states that he has become sufficiently acquainted with these ancient allies "to know that they are covetous, lying and treacherous, so that I keep on my guard without showing it."

Kerlerec's entire term was marked by perils from without and unrest within the colony. He did not have Vaudreuil's talent for charming the people, and the times were unpropitious, anyway, for social gaiety. Heavy fighting with the English along the Ohio Valley frontier started in the early 1750's. These were the operations called in American history the French and Indian Wars. It was feared that they would extend to Louisiana, and although this did not occur they proved to be the overture to the terrific Seven Years' War, the first conflict among European nations which spread to all parts of the known world. The destiny of France in the Western Hemisphere was at stake.

Troops were sent from New Orleans to the Ohio country. Reports of the action seen by these men kept New Orleans at a high pitch of excitement. One such incident was that involving Jumonville and Washington. Lieutenant Jumonville de Villiers was dispatched from Fort Duquesne to carry a message warning the young Virginian George Washington against further encroachment on territory claimed by the French. Washington, learning from a scout, of the approach of the French, surprised them, and in the action that followed Jumonville was killed. When Coulon de Villiers, brother of Jumonville, received the news at Fort Duquesne, he decided to avenge his brother's "assassination." With a company of several hundred men, many of whom were volunteers from the Illinois country, he was successful in catching Washington immobilized in the unhappily situated Fort Necessity, and forced him to surrender and sign incriminating articles of capitulation. Such happenings lost nothing in the telling in distant New Orleans.

The English established a naval blockade in the Gulf of Mexico. They cruised continuously between Cape San Antonio, Cuba, and the coast of Yucatan, this being the route always taken by merchantmen coming from France via Saint Domingue. Another flotilla watched the Florida Strait, while privateers under English letters of marque pounced on even the smallest craft trying to enter the Mississippi, Lake Borgne or Mobile Bay. Louisiana was cut off from the mother country, and before long there was a serious shortage of foodstuffs, wine and manufactured articles. Kerlerec believed that there would be an attempt to force the mouth of the river. He showed energy in fortifying the approaches, but no assault from that quarter materialized.

"The governors of Virginia and Carolina have offered rewards for our heads," wrote Kerlerec in 1756, as the Seven Years' War got under way. "I believe that the English government is not aware of it; otherwise it would be an abomination. Our Indians have frequently proposed to bring to me English scalps, and I have always rejected their offer with indignation."

He had a plan to unite all the Indians of the coast and lower Mississippi Valley and lead them against the English, striking at the Carolinas. The hope was to cause a diversion in favor of Vaudreuil's defense of Canada. But nothing came of this, and the marooned sea dog was left to struggle with the domestic problems of an administration that was shot through with treachery.

His first intendant had been quarrelsome, yet not impossible to work with. This man died, and a new one ran the English blockade in 1758. His name was De Rochemore; between him and Kerlerec there sprang up a vendetta which reached grotesque proportions. The intendant had scarcely had time to examine the records of his office when he accused the governor of failure to maintain discipline, of extravagance and profiting from an illicit traffic with the Indians. He made a vitriolic report, to which Kerlerec retorted by informing Paris that Rochemore had annulled certain concessions of lands and transferred them to members of his own family, had given contracts for public works to men with whom he had formed secret partnerships, and had played fast and loose with the king's merchandise. The charges and countercharges were endless. It would be absurd to resurrect them all. Sufficient to say that the colony divided into two parties, and that some military officers saw fit to support the intendant against their commander in chief.

Kerlerec won the first round. The ministry ruled that Rochemore had placed himself under grave suspicion and dismissed him from his office. It did not send out a successor, however, and according to custom he continued to function until one should arrive. Kerlerec, meanwhile, seized and forcibly embarked a number of the subordinate figures who had been most offensive to him. It turned out to be an error. Among those deported was Antoine Philippe de Marigny de Mandeville, an officer of marine troops, son of one of the oldest colonists and a powerful personality on his own account. Marigny, backed by his companions, insisted so clamorously that Rochemore was right and Kerlerec wrong that the ministry reversed itself. It was not until 1761, and as the result of fresh complaints, that Rochemore was definitely recalled. The new intendant was named Foucault, a crafty man who feigned such sympathy for the governor that the latter praised him in dispatches, but who vilified him on paper no less savagely than Rochemore had done.

In June 1763, partly on these cumulative charges and partly through the influence of Marigny de Mandeville and his friends, the bluff Kerlerec was deprived of his post. When he arrived in Paris he was thrown into the Bastille. It took him years to clear his name. His successor was Philippe d'Abbadie, who did not come to New Orleans as governor but merely as director of the colony or what seemed to be left of it. Abbadie knew that his was to be a sad task. But the darker part of the secret that lay behind his dubious title had been withheld from him.

France had lost the Seven Years' War, lost it so disastrously that the previous February she and her ally Spain had signed a treaty which gave England every foot of soil east of the Mississippi on the continent of North America, except only the Island of Orleans, and all the rich lands of the Ohio and the prairies south of the Great Lakes. Louisiana was to be cut in two. Spain had ceded Florida to England as a consideration for the return of Cuba, which England had captured toward the end of the war.

In the Caribbean, France got off more lightly. Saint Domingue had never been invaded by the English, though they had once had a plan to that effect, and cession of the great sugar colony was not demanded. All the smaller islands belonging to the French had been seized, but Martinique and Guadeloupe were now restored and the "neutral" Carib island of St. Lucia thrown in as a gift. England annexed Grenada, Dominica, St. Vincent and Tobago. The tiny fishing stations of St. Pierre and Miquelon, off the coast of Newfoundland, were left in the hands of the French.

Article Seven of the treaty read as follows:

"In order to re-establish peace on solid and durable foundations, and to remove forever all causes of dispute in relation to the limits between the French and English territories on the continent of America, it is agreed that, for the future, the limits between the possessions of his Most Christian Majesty and those of his Britannic Majesty in that part of the world shall be irrevocably fixed by a line drawn along the middle of the River Mississippi, from its source to the River Iberville [the Manchac and the Amite], and from thence by a line in the middle of that stream and of the Lakes Maurepas and Pontchartrain to the sea; and to that effect, the Most Christian King cedes, in full property and with full guaranty, to his Britannic Majesty the river and the port of Mobile, and all that he possesses, or has a right to possess, on the left side of the Mississippi, with the exception of the town of New Orleans and the island on which it stands, and which shall be retained by France, with the understanding that the navigation of the Mississippi shall be free and open to the subjects of his Britannic Majesty as well as those of his Most Christian Majesty, in all its length from its source to the sea, and particularly that part of it which is between said island and New Orleans and the right bank of the river, including egress and ingress at its mouth. It is further stipulated that the ships of both nations shall not be stopped on the river, visited, or subjected to any duty."

Abbadie went ahead with the physical surrender, hauling down the flag at Natchez, at Mobile, at Biloxi, and making arrangements to take care of French citizens, including some Indians, who refused to live under the English. Simultaneously he had to enforce the order of expulsion against the Jesuits decided upon by the governments of France, Spain and Naples throughout their possessions. All Jesuit property in Louisiana was confiscated and sold for the equivalent of $180,000, a large sum for the times. Arrears of bonuses to the Indians were paid—to avert a massacre, in the director's opinion—though with the loss of the northern shore of Lake Pontchartrain most of the Choctaw were outside the French domain.

What Abbadie did not then know was that the mutilated colony in his charge was itself no longer the property of France. The War of the Spanish Succession at the beginning of the century had confirmed a French prince as monarch in Madrid. The two countries had thereafter framed an agreement known as the treaties of the Family Compact, under which they were pledged to aid each other in singular and devious ways. This had brought Spain into the Seven Years' War. And in November 1762, three months before the capitulation to England, Louis XV decided to indemnify his royal cousin for losses about to be sustained. By an act which was not made public, the whole of Louisiana had been ceded to Spain, the *Bien-aimé* averring that he had been moved only by "the pure impulse of his generous heart." The real object of the Duc de Choiseul, chief minister, who had engineered the matter, was dual. He wanted to rid France of a colony that had always shown a deficit and that would become more of a problem now that it was geographically isolated. Also, he desired to extend Spain's sovereignty from Mexico to the Mississippi, in the hope that the westward march of the Anglo-Saxon would be permanently halted at that line.

The Spanish Government appeared to have been taken by surprise. It hesitated, but accepted with the proviso that the deal remain in abeyance for a while. Then, in February, came the peace treaty with England. Spain acquiesced silently in letting that country have the section of Louisiana east of the river. France continued to administer the rest of the province. The situation could not well have been more equivocal. In the next decade Spain was to argue that while she had yielded old Florida to England, the cession of West Florida (the new name for the region between the Perdido River and the Pontchartrain-Mississippi line) was illegal, because enacted by France who had ceased to own it.

Nobody consulted the wishes of the colonists. That the latter might seriously object to choosing between the loss of their nationality or their holdings was an idea that did not occur to officials who believed in the divine right of kings. But when Abbadie, in 1764, at last received a letter from Louis XV informing him of the transfer to Spain and sorrowfully published it, there was an immediate explosion in New Orleans. A group of the leading men, headed by the attorney general, Nicolas Chauvin de Lafrénière, protested that they were unalterably French at heart. They appointed one of their number, a young merchant named Jean Milhet, to go to Paris and plead with the throne to reverse its decision.

The climax of that *démarche* had the quality of tragic drama. Milhet, despairing of reaching the king and in doubt whether he would even be able to see Choiseul, asked the Sieur de Bienville himself to intercede. The founder of Louisiana was then in his eighty-sixth year, a proud old man, feeble but with mental faculties almost unimpaired, who had long since ceased to concern himself with affairs of state. He took Milhet past the lackeys and clerks, straight into the minister's office, and asked permission for the delegate to present his case. Milhet did so. Then, without waiting for an answer, Bienville cut in. The historian Gayarré says that he spoke like a father suing for the life of his child. Choiseul muttered, courteously enough, that it was too late to reopen the question. Tears came to Bienville's eyes. He took the duke by both hands, actually bent his knee and implored that at least the Island of Orleans be saved. Choiseul was known as a cold-hearted realist. He replied firmly that he had been the one to propose the transaction with Spain, and that he neither could nor would change his advice to the king. Bienville tottered out, leaning on Milhet's arm, his last public act a disillusionment which no heart but his own could fully appreciate. He died in seclusion less than three years afterward.

It took months for Milhet's report to get to New Orleans. The loyalists did not accept it as final, perhaps because their delegate had remained in Paris and they thought that he still hoped to accomplish something. Three other important events marked the year 1765. Abbadie succumbed suddenly, and the administration was taken over by the ranking military officer, Commandant

Philippe Aubry. There arrived some 650 refugees, chased from Nova Scotia by the English; these were the first of the Acadians, who were to prove such sturdy settlers west of the Mississippi. The Superior Council of New Orleans received a letter from Havana announcing that Don Antonio de Ulloa had been appointed governor. But the months slipped by, and the Spaniard did not come.

One of the strangest interregnums in the annals of any American community was only at its halfway point. If we count from November 1762, when Louisiana was secretly ceded, to the date of the definite solution in 1769, the period lasted for about six and a half years. Most accounts concentrate upon the political maneuvering between the French and Spanish, and neglect what the English were doing in the neighborhood of New Orleans. The present story, however, is primarily that of Lake Pontchartrain, in and about which the English were being extremely active and fairly indifferent as to what flag was to fly opposite theirs. Let us catch up with them.

The treaty had made a frontier of the lake and its connecting waters, which thereby had become an international route to the Gulf. It had also provided that the navigation of the Mississippi was to be absolutely free. But the English knew that ways of hampering them on the river could be found. So they planned from the start to use the Mississippi below the Iberville Passage tentatively, while developing the lake route to its utmost capacity. They even dreamed of strangling New Orleans by founding an upriver port to intercept the trade from the interior.

The moment they were in possession of the east bank they garrisoned Natchez and Baton Rouge, encouraged merchants to settle at both places, and designed strong forts. A Lieutenant Philip Pittman was sent to survey the Bayou Manchac, particularly with a view to building a town and fort at its juncture with the Mississippi. He reported:

"The inhabitants and traders who reside at Pointe Coupée, at

Natchitoches, Attakapas, Arkansas [all still French], the Illinois and the Post of St. Vincent's on the Wabash, would rather trade at this place than at New Orleans if they could have as good returns for their peltries and the produce of their country; for it makes a difference of ten days in their voyage, which is no inconsiderable saving of labor, money and time. The goods which these people take, in return for their peltry, furs, tobacco, tallow and bear's oil are spirituous liquors, grocery, dry goods of all kinds, and all the articles necessary for their commerce with the savages."

Pittman recommended that the Manchac should be dredged, and that on the north bank, the one the English owned, "the trees should be cut down forty feet back from the riverside, so that a road might be made for carriages when the waters are low, at which time the bed of the river [the Manchac] is dry from the Mississippi; when the waters are high it will still be necessary for the navigation, as vessels may be tracked up by horses or men to the Mississippi, in the same manner as lighters in England."

A few months later, in 1764, George Johnstone, the governor of West Florida, then stationed at Mobile, wrote enthusiastically to England:

"The passage by the Iberville* to the Mississippi is now so opened and cleared by Captain Campbell that it may be depended on as a fact that vessels of six feet water may pass from Lake Pontchartrain through this channel as soon as the Mississippi rises. . . . The opening of the Iberville is regarded by all as one of the luckiest events which could have happened to this colony; but to render the effect entirely certain, it is judged necessary to take post at Point Iberville [he means the site of the projected town of Manchac] with six cannon, two officers and forty men. The advantages which will attend the occupying of this post, besides keeping so material a passage open and protecting the navigation in this

---

* Iberville River, or Iberville Passage, always means the Bayou Manchac *and* that part of the Amite which completed the connection with Lake Maurepas. Manchac Pass means the link between Maurepas and Pontchartrain.

passage, will be the securing of our possessions on the north of that channel and rendering New Orleans dependent on us for all things instead of our being dependent on New Orleans."

Johnstone was anticipating and substituting the hope for the deed. The Manchac was never cleared to a depth that would float vessels of any size. But Pittman's proposed road was eventually built part of the way to the Amite, and this link served as a successful portage to and from the lakes. A mushroom port sprang up, as expected, and flourished from the beginning. The fort was completed in 1765; it was called Fort Bute in honor of the British prime minister, while the commercial part of the settlement went by the name of Manchac.

Governor Johnstone was not far wrong, after all. An odd personality, this Johnstone. Aubry characterizes him as follows in a letter to the ministry, in 1765:

"The correspondence which I am obliged to have with the English, who write us from all parts, and particularly with the governor of Mobile, gives me serious occupation. This governor is an extraordinary man. As he knows that I speak English, he occasionally writes to me in verse. He speaks to me of Francis I and Charles V. He compares Pontiak, an Indian chief, to Mithridates; he says that he goes to bed with Montesquieu. When there occurs some petty difficulties between the inhabitants of New Orleans and Mobile, he quotes to me from the Great Charter (Magna Charta) and the laws of Great Britain. It is said that the English ministry sent him to Mobile to get rid of him, because he was one of the hottest in the opposition. He pays me handsome compliments, which I duly return to him, and upon the whole he is a man of parts, but a dangerous neighbor against whom it is well to be on one's guard. The ordinary communication from Mobile to New Orleans is through the Lakes and Bayou St. Jean. So far, we have always permitted the English to pass in that direction. I have lately, however, refused this privilege to Mr. Farmer, who is going to the Illinois with three hundred men. He has the river; let him use it."

An Englishman named Captain Henry Gordon kept a *Journal of an Expedition along the Ohio and Mississippi* which has been preserved among the Shelburne Papers. He has nothing of consequence to say about New Orleans, but the account of his departure from that city in the spring of 1766 casts a light upon the lake route:

"Our Boat & Baggage being carried to the Bayou de St. Jean, for which we Paid 20 Dollars for the Boat alone, & is only 2 miles distance, we left New Orleans the 15th in the Evening, & lay that night at the Bayou. To this place the trade from Mobile comes, & all manner of Smuggling. There are three Schooners, constantly ply between the East side of Lake Pontchartrain & here employed in bringing Tar. There is a good Harbour for Craft here. The 16th in the Afternoon we went along the Bayou which is 2 Leagues long, & only Twenty-five feet wide in many places. It is deep Enough, but the Windings are so short sometimes that a Schooner has Difficulty to turn; The grounds on each side were under water except in three or four Places where Rice had been cut off, & in general the Country is overflowed, between Lake Pontchartrain and the Mississippi, to within 2 Miles of the last; this particularly in high Easterly Winds, which was now the cause of the Waters Height.

"At Dusk we passed the Blockhouse at the opening into Lake Pontchartrain, in which was a Serjeant & 12 Men, French and Spaniards, and some small Cannon mounted. We continued Rowing till 11 o'clock & rested. Next day by noon we were across the Lake, the wind in our Teeth. That Afternoon we went down the Regolets which is the Communication between the Lake & the sea; It is 2½ Leagues long, deep from 4 to 5 fathom."

One of the first imports brought by the English, and in quantities far beyond their own needs, was black ivory from Africa, transshipped at Jamaica. It was against the customs laws for them to sell Negroes directly to the French planters, but they engaged in the business openly at every settlement, not excluding New Orleans itself. Other contraband was also smuggled by them on a large scale. The commerce of Louisiana was said to have doubled in a year. Most of it was illicit, but Aubry looked the other way, apparently on the theory that as France was about to lose the colony he might as well allow its residents to stock up before the Spaniards arrived. In that age of mercantile autarchy, nation by nation, the practice of free trade took such a firm grip on the region that the incoming rulers were never able to break it.

Slaves formed the easiest cargo to ship by the lake route, for they could traverse the final portage on their own feet. They may be said to have inaugurated the new era of Pontchartrain's value as a medium of traffic. This was to last for almost exactly a century, divided into three periods: fifteen years of English frontier rivalry, thirty-five of Spanish and then American control during which the Iberville Passage remained open, and fifty years during which the big lake alone was important. After that, railroads would be built and the picture change once more.

Chapter 5

Lafrénière's "Cry of Liberty"

Nicolas Chauvin de Lafrénière, chief of the party that wanted to keep Louisiana French, was an exceptional man for any colony to have produced. He has been undeservedly neglected in American history. Ulloa and Gayarré say that he came of an obscure family, but that is scarcely true according to New Orleans standards of importance in the middle of the eighteenth century. His father was a Canadian named Chauvin, one of four brothers who had been among the earliest followers of Bienville. All of them had raised large families. The clan had staked out plantations south of the Vieux Carré, in what is now the American section of the city, and as they flourished they had tacked on various names to distinguish them one from the other. There was a Chauvin de Lafrénière, a Chauvin de Beaulieu, a Chauvin de Léry, a Chauvin de Boisclair. They cultivated rice and indigo, raised cattle, and owned many slaves. One of their houses was the first recorded country residence of brick in the Mississippi Valley.

The young Lafrénière, as it will be simplest to call him, was sent to France for his education, which must have been most unusual in pioneer days. He took law and quickly displayed striking gifts of analysis and eloquence. He had an individuality which can be described only as flaming, both as to appearance and manner. This son of a backwoodsman looked so kingly that he was nicknamed "Louis Quatorze." He was passionate, domineering, a lover of costly pleasures, and at the same time a sincere libertarian: the combination of aristocrat and democrat which has so often made a successful tribune of the people. That he had absorbed the ideas of the Encyclopedists is manifest, but along with his fervor for them went great personal ambition.

Why such a man failed to test his talents in Paris is not clear. He could probably have had a career during the last days of the monarchy, and should have figured in the company of Mirabeau. He chose to return to New Orleans, where he was active in politics and law, and neglected his plantation. Curiously, he received direct from the Throne the appointment as attorney general on January 1, 1763, after the secret cession to Spain and a few weeks before the Treaty of Paris with the English. In this capacity he had had to be the actual confiscator of the property of the Jesuits, an unpopular role, which, however, had not destroyed his popularity.

The principal supporters of Lafrénière in his protest against the treaties were the intendant and comptroller Foucault, who was cautious about it; Pierre Marquis, a captain of Swiss mercenaries; Joseph Villeré, planter and commander of militia at the German Coast up the river, whose half-sister was Lafrénière's wife; Jean Baptiste de Noyan, a retired captain of cavalry married to Lafrénière's daughter, and Bienville, a lieutenant in the navy, both men nephews of Louisiana's founder; Balthasar de Masan, a rich planter who had been decorated for military services; Hardy de Boisblanc, a former member of the Superior Council; Julien Jérôme Doucet, a lawyer; Joseph and Jean Milhet, Pierre Caresse, Pierre Poupet and Joseph Petit, merchants.

After the receipt in 1765 of the letter from the new Spanish governor, Don Antonio de Ulloa, Lafrénière continued to mark time, hoping for better news from Jean Milhet in Paris. But when Ulloa finally reached New Orleans in March 1766, accompanied by three officials and only ninety soldiers, a policy of resolute obstructionism was put into effect. The Spaniard was a naval officer best known for his fine attainments in science, as an astronomer and naturalist. He had never been a colonial administrator, and he fumbled the business of being one now. He was not prepared, he said, to take over the colony until more of his troops arrived. Aubry must continue to govern, though he would indicate what he wanted done. Thus he played straight into the hands of Lafrénière, who was able to arouse a widespread spirit of resentment.

Aubry considered it his duty to co-operate with Ulloa, to whom he denounced the colonists as "a set of reprobates, infected with the rebellious spirit of republicanism." That is a very early use in America of the term "republican," perhaps the earliest at a moment of crisis. Aubry could only have been interpreting the views of Lafrénière, and probably of Marquis, the Swiss. The mass of loyalists were devoted to the king. Even Lafrénière was careful never to speak against Louis or say that he would defy an absolute veto from Versailles, but he may well have dreamed that the success of his movement would inspire the French people to demand a voice in their government.

The most effective authority in New Orleans during the next two years was the Superior Council, which was dominated by Lafrénière. This body rendered it difficult for Aubry to carry out any order that it did not approve. Its debates were a continuous flouting of Spanish sovereignty. Astoundingly lethargic, the Court of Madrid made no move, did not send Ulloa his reinforcements. And Ulloa behaved in still more singular fashion. He absented himself for months at the Balize, at the mouth of the river, where he was joined by his fiancée, the Marquesa de Abrado, a comely Peruvian heiress. They were married in a shack by Ulloa's private chaplain. When they at last opened an official salon in the capital they were ignored by the majority. About the only practical accomplishment of this governor was the taking of a census of Spanish Louisiana; it showed a total white population of 5,562, and roughly an equal number of Negro slaves. He also exhibited an interest in the remote settlement of Natchitoches, where he paid a long visit and looked carefully into the means of communication with Mexico.

Late in 1767 Jean Milhet returned from Paris. His detailed oral report plainly convinced Lafrénière that Choiseul and the king would pay attention to nothing short of a *fait accompli,* for the members of the movement now became active conspirators. They met secretly at Masan's house in the city, and at the country home of Madame Alexandrine Pradel. This interesting woman is generally dismissed carelessly as the mistress of Foucault. She was the widow of the Chevalier de Pradel, deceased only in 1764, who had helped in the founding of New Orleans and whose estate, Mon Plaisir, across the river from the Place d'Armes, was one of the colony's show places. The intendant, a comparative newcomer, had sought to marry their daughter, but the girl had given her heart elsewhere and had had her own way about it. That Foucault then had paid suit to the mother appears likely. She gave supper parties for the loyalist group, and the plotting took place in her garden—some accounts say the garden of her town house.

A revolt against Ulloa was decided upon, with the forms of allegiance to France carefully preserved. A rank and file of volunteers was enrolled. Villeré's militia agreed to follow him in the enterprise. Acadians who had been ashore scarcely a year rallied under Noyan. Marquis organized a troop composed in part of regular soldiers, and the Swiss was appointed military commander in chief of the insurgents. It is hard to see how Aubry and Ulloa could have overlooked a plot of the kind, but they professed to have known nothing about it until October 25, when it was too late for them to act effectively. Foucault convened a meeting of the Superior Council, announcing evasively that its deliberations would be free and that he personally was not taking sides. During the night of the twenty-seventh, the guns at the Tchoupitoulas gate in the south wall of the city were spiked, and in the morning the volunteers from the country poured through that gate.

Lafrénière then adroitly called a mass meeting, which he and the two Milhets addressed fervidly. Little of what they said has been preserved. The upshot was a petition to the Superior Council to expel Ulloa and restore French rule. It was signed by about 500 citizens. The way had been cleared for the Council to maintain that it had no choice but to carry out the will of the people.

Aubry mustered the 110 soldiers still willing to obey him and swore that he would die in Ulloa's defense, yet ended by advising the governor to go aboard his frigate in the river. Ulloa weakly did so.

The Superior Council met on October 29. It took up the petition of the day before, upon which Lafrénière spoke. This was his great moment. After assailing the legality of the Spaniard's exercise of authority, seeing that he had never presented his commission, and complaining that there had been tyranny and the flouting of local customs, Lafrénière generalized in formidable terms. It was a foretaste of the oratory of the American and French Revolutions. How any historian dealing with this period could resist citing his phrases it is difficult to see:*

"Without population there can be no commerce, and without commerce no population. In proportion to the extent of both is the solidity of thrones; both are fed by liberty and competition, which are the nursing mothers of the State, of which the spirit of monopoly is the tyrant and stepmother. Without liberty there are but few virtues. Despotism breeds pusillanimity and deepens the abyss of vices. Man is considered as sinning before God only because he retains his free will. Where is the liberty of our planters, our merchants and our other inhabitants? Protection and benevolence have given way to despotism; a single authority would absorb and annihilate everything. All ranks, without distinction, can no longer, without running the risk of being taxed with guilt, do anything else but tremble, bow their necks to the yoke, and lick the dust.

"The Superior Council, bulwark of the tranquility of virtuous citizens, has supported itself only by the combined force of the probity and disinterestedness of its members, and the confidence of the people in that tribunal. . . . Often did discontents and disgusts seem to force you to resign your places, but you have always considered it as a duty of your station of counsellors to

---

* Some of these passages are also quoted in my book *The French in the West Indies* (Indianapolis: The Bobbs-Merrill Co., 1942).

the Most Christian King to alleviate and calm the murmurs of the oppressed citizens. The love of your country and the sense of the justice due to every citizen who applies for it have nourished your zeal. It has always, this justice, been rendered with the same exactness, although you never thought proper to make representations on the infractions of the act of cession. You have always feared to give encouragement to a mass of discontented people threatened with the most dreadful calamities; you have preferred public tranquility. But now the whole body of the planters, merchants and other inhabitants of Louisiana apply to you for justice."

In attacking monopoly, Lafrénière was subtly attacking the French system along with the Spanish, though he extolled the "benevolence" of the former. France had always insisted on what she called *"l'Exclusif"* in trade with her colonies. He was also asking the Superior Council to overrule the king at the last in the matter of the cession to Spain and then to plead for royal sanction of that stroke.

Lafrénière swept everything before him. The resolution adopted was practically the text of his speech with the citizens' petition tacked on to it. Three delegates were appointed to take it to France for approval. Meanwhile, Ulloa was ordered expelled, with Aubry officially dissociating himself from all of this. The Spaniard departed quietly, but from Havana he wrote a cool, devastating report which was sure to rouse the Court of Madrid to vengeance. He called Lafrénière a "turbulent spirit," and said of the popular petition: "It bears the stamp of Lafrénière's style, which is easily detected. In that document are to be found those arrogant expressions, that superciliousness and that insolent freedom with which he is in the habit of declaiming against our nation."

Ulloa had not had a chance to see the final memorial, as the planters and merchants called it, which was issued after he sailed. This document, obviously written by Lafrénière, was printed by Braud, the colony's official printer, on the orders of Foucault. It said in part: "What harm have we done in shaking off a foreign yoke? What offense have we committed in claiming back our laws, our country, our sovereign? Are such laudable attempts without an example in our history? Have not more than one city in France . . . and even whole provinces . . . repeatedly broken with patriotic courage the English yoke, or refused to be fettered by foreign chains? Noble resistance to the decree of our natural-born sovereigns, far from kindling their wrath, stirred up the fountains of their attachment and forced them into helping their loving subjects, and thus wrought their deliverance!"

In New Orleans Aubry resumed the governorship willy-nilly. Why did Lafrénière not stand ready to seize the power and proclaim the independence of Louisiana if the French Government repudiated the revolt, as he must have known was quite likely to occur? The thought was in his head, for Marquis advocated publicly while the king's answer was being awaited—and the Swiss certainly would not have done this without his leader's consent—that New Orleans be declared a free port with its own bank and currency, and that a republic be formed in which "the oppressed and the needy among all the nations of the earth would find a refuge and a home." The response was lukewarm. There has never been an example of French colonists wanting to break away from France, no matter how violently they have put special demands. The chiefs concluded, anyway, that a republic would not be tolerated by the three powerful monarchies that ruled America, and the thing was dropped.

Nearly nine months passed without a reply from Versailles, or the least hint of what Spain intended to do. Little is known about conditions in New Orleans during that time of maddening suspense. The English smugglers furnished most of the imported goods. A few ships came legally from Saint Domingue, and from Cuba and Jamaica under flags of truce, but there was practically no traffic with Europe. Among the arrivals was Oliver Pollock, a young Irishman who had spent five years in Havana, learned Spanish and established some solid connections. He was a merchant and shipmaster. His announcement that he would like to stay for a while in the restless port on the Mississippi attracted no attention. It had a hidden significance. We must assume that he had heard from Cuban friends that there would soon be a coup by Spain. The statement in many histories that Pollock first appeared at New Orleans after that event is erroneous.

On July 24, 1769, the city was thunderstruck by the news that a Spanish fleet of twenty-four vessels, carrying 2,056 troops commanded by General Alexander O'Reilly, had cast anchor at the Balize. O'Reilly, an Irish-born adventurer of military talent, inspector general of the forces in Mexico and the Caribbean colonies, bore a commission as emergency governor of Louisiana. He was one of the age's strong men, a complete realist, soft-spoken but ruthless. His permanent limp came from a wound suffered in the War of the Austrian Succession. A graduate of Spain's Hibernia Regiment, he had fought also under the French and Austrian flags, and on his return to Madrid had had the luck to save the life of Carlos III in a riot. Naturally the king favored him and would have sent him on no trivial errand. The army he brought was only a thousand less than the entire population of New Orleans.

O'Reilly's personal representative, Francisco Bouligny, proceeded up the river the same day and was greeted almost obsequiously by Aubry. Marquis had attempted a hostile manifestation, but not many turned out with him, so great was the popular dismay. Aubry said to Bouligny: "Tell General O'Reilly that I am ready to deliver this province at any time to his Excellency, and that should the colonists make the slightest opposition to it I am determined to join my forces to his." A love feast and talks to the populace followed. Aubry declared over and over that he had reason to believe there would be no stern reprisals.

Lafrénière's safest course would have been to escape to the interior. This he scorned to do. None of the loyalist leaders made any such plan except Villeré, and his suspicions were finally lulled by the half promises of clemency. In a day or two Lafrénière announced that he, Marquis and Joseph Milhet would call on O'Reilly and explain their position. They made the trip to the Balize in Bouligny's barge, were formally presented and received with a show of cordiality. Lafrénière spoke without prevarication of "the revolution which took place in the colony." He said that it had been caused by Ulloa's harshness in denying the old French privileges. But since it had not been upheld by Versailles the people would now submit quietly to the new regime. "We beg your Excellency not to consider Louisiana as a conquered country," he added. "The orders of which you are the bearer are sufficient to put you in possession of this province, and they impress our hearts more than the arms which you bring."

O'Reilly made a bland, very Celtic reply. He would study the facts. He was well-disposed and would hate to injure anyone. He had no prejudices and was aware that things which look black at a distance often prove white enough when seen close at hand. He would be guided by the true spirit of justice. Then O'Reilly invited his visitors to dine with him, and showed them every courtesy. He sent them back without placing restrictions on their future movements.

In the leisurely manner of the day, entry into New Orleans was put off until August 18. It was then staged with pomp, the ships lining up along the water front and firing salutes; flags and martial music accompanying the soldiers as they disembarked in close ranks. O'Reilly came ashore preceded by mace-bearers, accepted the keys of the city gates from Aubry, witnessed the hauling down of the French standard and the raising of the Spanish, and entered the cathedral where a *Te Deum* was sung. That same afternoon he vigorously took over the administration.

He demanded from Aubry a confidential report of the recent troubles, urging him to be frank about men as well as events. Aubry obliged with what Gayarré calls "a precise and fatal indictment," ending with an apology for his own inability to put down the revolt. On August 21, O'Reilly summoned to his house, supposedly for a routine conference, the twelve men of whom he had decided to make examples. Nine came, headed by Lafrénière.

They were placed under arrest and imprisoned here and there, so as to foil a possible rescue plot. The other three were seized about town. Villeré's case was notably tragic. He had just been taken aboard a frigate in the river when his wife, who had heard a rumor about it, had herself rowed out by slaves and begged to be allowed to see him. She was brusquely refused. But Villeré had recognized her voice. He struggled to reach her, and was bayonetted to death by his guards.

Foucault was added later to the list of the accused. He argued that whatever he had done was in his official capacity of intendant of the French king, and he refused to answer questions. Let them send him to France, where he was willing to stand trial, he said. O'Reilly concluded that that would be the best solution. Foucault was deported, and on his arrival in Europe he was thrown into the Bastille.

The joint trial of the twelve, including the dead Villeré, was held in October. It was a cut-and-dried affair. The judges interrogated the prisoners privately and separately in their cells. They also examined witnesses in secret and did not permit the accused to know who the witnesses were. In court the royal attorney presented the cases at considerable length, and a verdict of guilty was handed down. O'Reilly, as presiding judge, condemned Lafrénière, Marquis, Noyan, Caresse and Joseph Milhet to be hanged; the memory of Villeré "to be held and reputed forever infamous"; Petit, Masan, Doucet, Poupet, Hardy de Boisblanc and Jean Milhet to varying terms of imprisonment.

Many pleas for mercy were made by the women of the colony, and even by certain Spanish officials who had come with Ulloa. But O'Reilly remained obdurate in his suave way. He agreed to only one modification of the sentence. No white man willing to perform the hanging could be found, and it was thought that race prestige would suffer if a Negro were employed to put such prominent citizens to death. Execution by a firing squad was therefore authorized.

At three o'clock in the afternoon of October 25, the five martyrs were taken to what is now the northeast corner of Jackson Square at St. Ann and Decatur Streets. The site appears to have been a barracks yard on the Place d'Armes in 1769. The prisoners were pinioned, but otherwise received courteous treatment. "They were well dressed," writes the contemporary chronicler Baudry de Lozières, "and perfectly calm and self-possessed; conversed with one another as they went along, looking around them kindly and returning salutes addressed to them." They refused to have their eyes bandaged, or to sit on a bench that had been placed for them. Lafrénière, as ever, struck the keynote. "I am French! The cry of liberty has been heard!" he shouted as the volley was discharged.

The epoch-making fact is that seven years before the American Declaration of Independence, eleven years before Tupac Amaru, a descendant of the Peruvian Incas, revolted against Spain, these Louisiana Frenchmen strove for self-determination and uttered phrases of mordant import. Theirs was the first European colony to challenge the old order.

It must be remembered also that, for a Spanish official, O'Reilly had been merciful. He chose but twelve men for punishment, admitting later that he had intended from the start to execute six and imprison six, and he took no action whatever against the many others who had supported Lafrénière. When one of the first six, Villeré, was killed before he could be tried, O'Reilly did not even substitute another name on the "hanging list." Before long the Crown pardoned Jean Milhet and the others who had been jailed, and allowed them to go to Saint Domingue. O'Reilly is said to have acquired Lafrénière's cook, a slave named Artus, and to have shown no resentment when the Negro threatened to poison him in vengeance. Such feelings were natural, he declared, and sold him to someone else.

A policy we would consider brutal today was moderation itself two centuries ago.

Chapter 6

New Orleans under the Spaniards

O'REILLY's reorganization of the government of Louisiana was an intelligent and thorough job. The province was made a dependency of Cuba, yet local autonomy was permitted to a greater degree than in most Spanish colonies. Part of the French system, including some French laws, was retained. Athanese de Mézières, a veteran who had served Bienville, received the post of lieutenant governor. In New Orleans a *cabildo,* or municipal corporation after the Spanish pattern, replaced the Superior Council, but all the members of the new body were Creoles. Residents were appointed as agents to deal with the Indians. A militia was enrolled and officered by prominent citizens; as soon as it was functioning smoothly O'Reilly sent most of his soldiers back to Havana. These marks of confidence won over the majority of the people, and in a few short weeks the general was being warmly acclaimed.

His essential tolerance and Irish sense of humor helped him. It is said that a sharp bit of repartee by a Creole lady irritated him into snapping, "Madame, do you forget who I am?" "No, sir," replied the lady, bowing. "I have known men higher than you, however, who never found it necessary to remind anyone of what they were." O'Reilly instantly left the house, but was back the next day with a smiling apology.

His chief object was to turn Louisiana into a profitable colony. To this end he dealt severely with the English smugglers, chasing away ships that were nothing but floating stores and had long been anchored brazenly off the New Orleans water front and the Bayou St. Jean, and prohibiting any further contacts with Spanish soil. He could not prevent the Creoles from going to Manchac,

Baton Rouge and Natchez to shop. But during the few months of his rule he did keep the English traders within their own boundaries, and he allowed heavy commerce only with Havana and the ports of Spain. Nevertheless, he was not in full sympathy with the school of state mercantilism whose only use for colonies was to exploit them, and he persuaded the Court that Louisiana should be allowed to buy and sell certain commodities without paying the usual crushing imposts.

What is more, O'Reilly made an exception in favor of one Anglo-American merchant. Oliver Pollock, who was mentioned in the preceding chapter, had found New Orleans suffering from a shortage of foodstuffs. At an undetermined date before O'Reilly came, Pollock had departed for Baltimore where he had cemented old business relations of his, had loaded a large vessel, the *Royal Charlotte,* with flour and sailed back to the Mississippi. The expeditionary force had landed while he was away, and as was commonly the case at that period the commissary arrangements were faulty. The addition of 2,000 soldiers to a population of 3,000 had brought the city close to famine.

Pollock at once offered his cargo to O'Reilly at the latter's price. He said that the relieving of human want was more important to him than profits, but the general insisted on allowing him a small margin of gain. In reporting this transaction to the king, O'Reilly recommended that Pollock be rewarded with a permit to trade freely at New Orleans forever after, and it was granted. The two men of Irish birth became close friends as a result; that, at least, is the story. One earnestly suspects that they had met in Havana, and that the plan had been worked out between them. At all events, Pollock prospered under O'Reilly's successors, and his connection with New Orleans was to prove fateful in the history of North America.

The mission of O'Reilly had been to start Spanish Louisiana as a going concern, no more than that. He was considered too valuable a man for a small colonial post. Indeed, he brought with him Don Luis de Unzaga, the colonel of the Havana Regiment, who had already been commissioned as governor. O'Reilly formally installed Unzaga on December 1, 1769, but as the Crown's special representative he remained his superior until his own departure in March 1770, after a stay of less than eight months. On his return to Spain he was promoted in the army and finally ennobled as the Conde O'Reilly.

Unzaga came close to being the ideal ruler at that juncture. He was not particularly strong, but was a good administrator, just, amiable, slightly cynical, and bent on bringing the various elements of the colony together. He married a Mlle. St. Maxent, daughter of one of the best Creole families, and many of his officers imitated him. With a broad-mindedness that would seem liberal even today, he smoothed over the difficulties when a fanatical Spanish priest attacked the morals and orthodoxy of the easy-going French Capuchins. He winked at the smuggling on the river and lakes, allowing it to revive on the theory that the Spanish system was too strict for Louisiana where manufactured goods were badly needed. But he relaxed none of the military precautions against the English along the Mississippi frontier.

Under Unzaga there commenced the amalgam of two Latin strains that gave New Orleans its lasting character—with surprises that none could have predicted. The Spaniards had been inefficient in many of their colonies. They were efficient here, perhaps because they had French foundations on which to work. Government, the courts, the police, business houses, the near-by plantations—all made long forward strides. Immigration increased. The architecture struck a Hispanic note, the low cottages with steeply pitched roofs yielding to gracious structures built around patio gardens, and restful with broad, shadowy balconies. Oddly, the Spanish tongue never made headway. Military and official affairs were conducted in it, but French remained the language of society. That is why we think of New Orleans and its Creole civilization as being French, whereas at its height it became Ibero-Gallic.

Meanwhile, the Indians had ceased to be a serious menace. Dating from the cession of the east bank of the Mississippi to England, who had poured colonists into her new territory, and the advance of Spanish power from Texas to the west bank, the wild tribes had been more or less cowed. The sporadic outrages they committed fell short of being a threat to the existence of Louisiana.

The English had divided their vast Florida holding at the Apalachicola River, calling one province East Florida and the other West Florida. The capital of the latter was fixed at Pensacola, which had never been French. But prosperity boomed in the opposite direction, at Manchac and at points picked long ago by Bienville, such as Natchez and Mobile. As discontent rose in the thirteen colonies on the Atlantic seaboard, men of Tory sympathies moved to West Florida. The province seemed destined to be a real stronghold of anti-republicanism. Who could have foretold than an Irishman and a Spaniard in Louisiana would see to it that that did not occur!

In 1776 the American Revolution started. It was a great worry to the aging Unzaga, who believed that if England won she would try to extend her empire beyond the Mississippi. He maintained a type of neutrality on the river and lakes that favored the colonists. Charles Lee, then second in command to Washington, sent a messenger to Unzaga asking for arms and other military supplies. Oliver Pollock, who had been made commercial agent in New Orleans for Virginia, immediately approached the governor and successfully urged him to sell 9,000 pounds of gunpowder from the king's stores. Lee's messenger was temporarily placed under arrest to delude the British in West Florida. Another man took the powder north, delivering it to Forts Pitt and Wheeling in time to save those posts from capture. This was the only deal of its kind to which Unzaga would consent. He was anxious, anyway, to relinquish the governorship. Madrid granted his request toward the end of the year, promoting him to be captain general of Caracas and appointing as his successor one of the most brilliant young men who ever served Spain in the New World.

Bernardo de Gálvez belonged to a family that wielded enormous influence at the time. His father, Matías, was Viceroy of New

Spain (Mexico), while his uncle, José, was Minister of the Indies, an office only one step below the Throne. Bernardo had won his spurs as a lieutenant in the army, fighting the Portuguese, and then the Apache on the Pecos River in the wilderness of Mexico's northernmost reaches. On his return to Europe, a captain, he had served under O'Reilly himself in Africa and was advanced to the rank of lieutenant colonel. At the middle of 1776 he came to New Orleans as colonel of the Louisiana Regiment, which constituted the permanent garrison. The official notice sent in advance to Unzaga carried a postscript in O'Reilly's handwriting:

"The aforesaid bears his instructions and will present them shortly. He is an individual whom I esteem highly, and his uncle, the Minister of the Indies, is my particular friend; wherefore I will thank you for any attentions you can show him."

Gálvez was then about thirty years of age, dynamic, handsome, excessively attractive to women, and able to win the loyalty of men. It appeared to take him by surprise when he was made governor of Louisiana. Unzaga turned over the office to him on January 1, 1777, saying, among other things, that if Spain was going to side with Great Britain, "Oliver Pollock should not remain in the country twenty-four hours," but that if it were to be the other way about, the Irishman was the best foreign merchant for him to confide in. Actually, the camp which Spain would favor was scarcely in doubt.

Instructions had just arrived permitting trade with France and the French colonies. Certain restrictions were specified, but Gálvez interpreted these liberally. Nor did he interfere at first with the English contrabandists. The commercial activity on the lower Mississippi surpassed anything that had been seen before. At the end of four months however, Gálvez seized eleven ships engaged in smuggling and issued a proclamation ordering all English subjects to leave Louisiana in a fortnight. The action was not made to apply to colonists in revolution against England. Pollock had got the ear of Gálvez, and from then on the pair worked in the closest harmony.

State Parks Commission

RUINS OF FORT PIKE

State Parks Commission

MOAT AT FORT PIKE
The fort is on the Rigolets

Louisiana State Museum

BATTLE OF LAKE BORGNE, 1814

Space is lacking to trace the intrigues of the next two years. Gálvez showed his friendship for the American cause over and over. In addition to forwarding a secret gift of arms and medicines from the king of Spain, he contributed supplies of every description from the government warehouses. He sheltered Revolutionary privateers in New Orleans and allowed them to sell their prizes there; he did as much for the land raiders, under James Willing, who had plundered Tory Natchez. He backed the credit of Pollock, enabling him to spend $300,000 in behalf of the Thirteen Colonies. We should bear in mind, of course, that whereas the Irishman had thrown in his lot with embattled democracy, Gálvez was motivated by no such sentiment, but was seeking to cripple an ancient foe. A weak new republic would be a more agreeable neighbor, in his opinion, than the British realm.

But unless Spain declared war there was a point beyond which he could not go. He prepared for the eventuality by demanding reinforcements of troops and strengthening the militia. He settled a group of colonists from the Canary Islands midway of the Iberville Passage, pointing out that they would help to safeguard the Island of Orleans from an English surprise attack. Near the same place, American refugees built a small village and called it Gálveztown in his honor. He welcomed them as an additional source of strength on the lake route.

These acts of Gálvez were well received by the French Louisianians. He cemented his popularity by doing as Unzaga had done and marrying a Creole, Felicitée d'Estréhan. He was presently to triumph more signally by making himself their military leader and hero.

France signed the Treaty of Amity and Commerce with the American Colonies in 1778 and struck at England. It should be only a matter of months now before Spain joined. Gálvez rallied his forces and collected armaments, comprising ships and guns. The Creoles rushed to enlist. Small detachments of regulars were sent to him from Havana and Vera Cruz. In 1779 he learned ahead of the British garrisons on the Mississippi that his country had at last entered the war, and he decided to take West Florida by surprise, beginning with Manchac. A terrific hurricane swept over New Orleans on the eve of his departure, leveling many buildings and destroying shipping and crops. The military arrangements were thrown into the utmost confusion. But Gálvez refused to be halted. The day following the hurricane he addressed a mass meeting at which support was pledged to him, and the day after that, August 19, he recognized the independence of the United States "by beat of drum" and public crier.

On August 27 he set forth up the east bank of the river with 667 men, of whom somewhat more than 500 were Spaniards, 60 Creole militiamen from the city, 80 free blacks and mulattoes, and seven American volunteers. Oliver Pollock was along as the general's aide-de-camp. At the German Coast the main body of the French militia joined, 760 strong, including many Acadians, a number of colored men, and more than 100 Indians. The terrain through which the little army now marched was a tangle of woods and swamps. It took ten days to cover 115 miles, and in that time a third of the force dropped out from illness, hardships or plain desertion.

The English had heard that Gálvez was coming, but were in doubt as to his intentions. They still did not know about the declaration of war. Fearing that he would at least facilitate an American coup, they concentrated most of their regulars at Baton Rouge and left only a handful in Fort Bute, Manchac. The fort was surrounded by Gálvez on the night of September 6, and the next morning Creole militia under Gilbert de St. Maxent, Unzaga's brother-in-law, stormed it easily.

Pressing on to Baton Rouge a few days later, the Spanish governor besieged the fort there. It was a strong position, mounting thirteen cannon and surrounded by a moat. Gálvez had only ten guns which he used cleverly. A tongue of woods approached the fort on one side and seemed the natural starting point of an assault. There he posted on the afternoon of September 20 a detachment of troops with orders to chop down trees, throw up earthworks, and keep up a continuous fusillade with muskets as if to safeguard the job. The English were deceived into bombarding the woods all night, shifting some of their heaviest pieces for the purpose. Gálvez spent the time in moving up his guns silently to a garden within small-arms range of the fort on the opposite side. In the morning he opened a concentrated fire that breached the walls. The garrison sent out a flag of truce at 3:30 P.M. Colonel Alexander Dickson, commander of all British forces on the Mississippi south of the Chickasaw Bluffs (the site of Memphis) agreed to surrender not only Baton Rouge but the fort at Natchez as well. This was carried out, with a total capitulation of 550 regulars who were sent to New Orleans as prisoners, and more than 500 armed colonists and Negroes whom Gálvez released.

In the meanwhile there had been colorful activity along the Iberville Passage and on the lakes. Spanish gunboats darted out of Bayou St. Jean, advanced beyond Lake Maurepas, and at Gálveztown captured three galleys and a brig which had delivered supplies at Manchac; they also took two cutters loaded with provisions from Pensacola. Carlos de Grandpré, commanding Creole militia, crossed the Amite River and seized two English posts. He then cut the communications between Baton Rouge and Natchez.

The English had a frigate, the *West Florida,* which for two years had dominated Lakes Pontchartrain and Maurepas, and long before hostilities started had caused ill feeling by confiscating boats laden with tar for New Orleans. She carried five guns, the largest of which was a nine-and-a-half-pounder. Her crew numbered about thirty. The Spaniards had no craft that dared to tackle her. But an American privateer named William Pickles fitted out a sloop, the *Morris,* mounting only two-and-a-half-pounders, and with a necessarily small crew. He was on Pontchartrain looking for trouble within a few days of the declaration of war. Overhauling the *West Florida,* Pickles ordered her to surrender. The English captain, Paine, laughed at him. Shots were exchanged simultaneously. Pickles ran in close, boarded the enemy and subdued her in hand-to-hand combat. Four Britishers were killed, including the captain. On the American side, Pickles reported that he had lost only one: "Brown Traitor to our Cause swimd ashore." Whether he meant a gentleman of color or a sailor named Brown he did not explain.

On September 21, the same day that Gálvez was receiving the surrender of Baton Rouge, Pickles raised an American flag on the northern shore of Lake Pontchartrain. He found white settlers in the pleasant pine country between Bayou Lacombe and the Tangipahoa River, and these gladly took an oath of allegiance to the United States. For some reason, 122 Choctaw, whose ancestral land it was, wanted to be transferred across the lake to Bayou St. Jean, and Pickles obliged them. The Spaniards could hardly believe he had brought in the formidable *West Florida* undamaged. She was later turned over to Pollock, who agreed with Gálvez that she should be kept on the lakes as a cruiser "for the common cause."

An equally sensational exploit, in its way, was that of Vincent Rillieux, a New Orleans Creole who was given command of a Spanish sloop of war. Learning that a heavily laden English barque had entered the Amite (from which direction is uncertain) he landed his entire crew of fourteen and some small guns. He chopped down trees and built a sort of masked battery. When the barque came edging along, her sides virtually parting the vegetation, Rillieux opened point-blank on her. Field pieces and muskets roared, and the hidden men yelled so loudly that the English sailors were convinced that they had been trapped by an overwhelming force. Panic-stricken, they rushed below deck. Rillieux and his companions leaped on board, where by simply closing the hatches they captured the vessel and every soul in her. Even then, they did not dream how big the prize was. It transpired that there were one captain, one first lieutenant, two second lieutenants and fifty-four grenadiers of the Waldeck Regiment in the hold, not to mention the crew of twelve who if they had kept their heads could easily have run the craft to safety. One of the

English army lieutenants was killed resisting arrest—the sole casualty.

The victories on land and water had in less than a month given Gálvez control of West Florida from the Mississippi to where the Pearl River runs into Lake Borgne.

He had definite instructions from Madrid to capture Mobile and Pensacola. As he saw it, this called for sea-borne expeditions and support from Havana. He was energetic enough in preparing the campaign, but the dilatory methods of his superior, the captain general of Cuba, delayed him. In the early days of February 1780, he descended to the Gulf of Mexico with a frigate and half a dozen smaller vessels, carrying 754 soldiers. The flotilla encountered stormy weather and suffered losses. A hazardous landing was made at the entrance to Mobile Bay, and the troops advanced on foot to the environs of the town. Then the promised reinforcements arrived. There was an investment of the feebly-held English position, a concentrated bombardment, and on March 12 Mobile fell to Gálvez.

The capture of Pensacola proved to be far more difficult, because the English there got help from Jamaica. It is outside the scope of this book and can be dismissed in a paragraph. Operating now from Havana, Gálvez assembled large naval and land forces, executed several daring preliminary maneuvers, besieged Pensacola and reduced its forts after desperate fighting. The capitulation took place on May 10, 1781, and by its terms the English surrendered the entire province of West Florida. Gálvez was made governor. He then planned the conquest of Jamaica, but did not receive the necessary backing and sent a lieutenant to overrun the Bahamas instead. He was seen in New Orleans only at long intervals.

The peace treaty of 1783, which established the independence of the United States, gave both the Floridas to Spain. In 1784 Gálvez, ennobled, was appointed captain general of Cuba, while retaining the governorship of Louisiana and the Floridas. He found his old friend Oliver Pollock in jail in Havana for the mountainous debts incurred as agent of the Continental Congress, and secured his release. This was the last direct service rendered by Gálvez to the American cause. The following year he was promoted to the viceroyalty of Mexico, in succession to his father who had just died.

It will be noted that although the Spaniards had encouraged Anglo-Saxon republicans to resist the British east of the Mississippi, and had smiled on such gestures as the "annexation" by Captain Pickles of the north shore of Lake Pontchartrain, there was never any question of waiving claim to a foot of land that had once been part of French Louisiana. Spain seized and held the region she had failed to get after the Seven Years' War, maintaining that Louis XV had ceded it to her at that time and that the English had been in wrongful possession of it. The young United States thought differently. This was to cause trouble in the near future. But for the moment West Florida, restored to its original eastern limits at the Perdido River, was a Spanish domain.

The new governor at New Orleans was Esteban Miró. Like Gálvez he had been colonel of the local regiment of regulars and had often acted as executive during the absence of his chief. He had married Marie Céleste de Macarty, a Creole of French and Irish blood, and this carrying on of the tradition set by Unzaga and Gálvez had helped to make him liked and willingly accepted by the people.

It is not intended to characterize all the Spanish governors, or even to record their principal acts. Suffice it to say that until the end of the century, when Louisiana again changed hands, the post was held by Miró, Baron Hector de Carondelet, Gayoso de Lemos and the Marqués de Casa Calvo. We have leisure only to pause over certain high lights of history, with special reference to the development of New Orleans and the increasing importance of the lakes.

After Spain recovered West Florida, a number of citizens became interested in buying land on the far side of Pontchartrain.

Among these was Pierre Philippe de Marigny de Mandeville, the only son of that Antoine Philippe de Marigny de Mandeville who had quarreled with Governor Kerlerec and been deported by him to France. The father returned to the colony despite the fact that it had been transferred to Spain. Pierre Philippe got along very well with the new rulers, particularly as his wife was a d'Estréhan and Bernardo de Gálvez became his brother-in-law by marrying into the same family. The ancestral home was a plantation just beyond the Esplanade on the downriver side of the Vieux Carré. Here an enormous house stood at the end of an avenue of trees that ran from the levee. To this concession obtained under the French regime, the young Marigny added large concessions from the Spanish. He also bought up deserted plantations above the city on the river front. He was soon the greatest landowner of New Orleans and the richest resident.

Gálvez made him a colonel of militia and put him in command at Gálveztown, on the Iberville Passage, during the war with the English. Marigny scouted and fought in the country north of the lakes. He grew enamored of it and ended by purchasing a wooded tract on Pontchartrain opposite the Bayou St. Jean. The name he gave it was Fontainebleau. He built a low, rambling wooden mansion, cottage style, where he passed the summer months with his family and a retinue of servants.

In St. Bernard Parish below the city, between Lake Borgne, the river and the Gulf, the Chalmette, Villeré and De la Ronde families cultivated magnificent plantations. These, like the Marigny holdings, were to figure in the annals of the region. They were signs of the general impulse toward expansion.

Trade boomed at New Orleans from the moment the war ended, with Spaniards and Americans both profiting and keeping on the friendliest terms for a short while. The treaty had conceded free access to the Mississippi, "from its source to the ocean," to the British as well as to the victorious parties. But that proved to be empty verbiage. The British no longer had any territory adjoining the Mississippi, and it was simple to create reasons for squeezing out their shipping. In five years New Orleans gained 2,200 inhabitants. Contemporary reports state that there were often as many as forty seagoing vessels—Spanish, Yankee and French—lying at the wharves on the river, and from ten to fifteen at the Bayou St. Jean. Such figures spelled prosperity.

At the end of five years occurred the first of the two great fires that led to the rebuilding of New Orleans along more imposing lines. It was early in the afternoon of Good Friday, March 21, 1788, when an altar candle in a chapel in the military treasurer's home set alight the draperies of the altar. The flames quickly devoured the wooden building and spread to others. There was a strong breeze blowing in from the river, and while this saved most of the structures on the water front, the greater part of the rest of the town was destroyed. The story goes that because it was Good Friday the clergy would not allow the church bells to be used for a general alarm. The Cathedral and the priests' house were among those swept away, as were government buildings with their records. Losses were estimated at about $2,500,000.

The year following this disaster would hardly seem to have been psychologically right for an attempt to introduce the tribunal of the Holy Inquisition. Yet, it was attempted. A Capuchin friar, Antonio de Sedella, who had landed inconspicuously from Spain, wrote the governor to say that he had been appointed commissary of the Inquisition, and that he might soon need the services of soldiers in carrying out his orders. That very night soldiers appeared at his door, but it was to place him under arrest and hurry him aboard a ship about to sail for Cadiz. Miró had given another example of the liberalism that had marked the course of every Spanish governor of Louisiana, and which is the more impressive when contrasted with Spanish bigotry at the same period elsewhere. Miró wrote to Madrid:

"When I read the communication of that Capuchin, I shuddered. His Majesty has ordered me to foster the increase of population in this province, and to admit to it all those that would emigrate from the banks of the rivers which empty themselves into the Ohio. . . . The mere name of the Inquisition uttered in New Orleans would not only be sufficient to check immigration, which is successfully progressing, but would also be capable of driving away those who have recently come. I even fear that, in spite of my having sent Father Sedella out of the country, the most fatal consequences may ensue from the mere suspicion of the cause of his dismissal."

This priest returned to the colony in 1795, became the pastor of the Cathedral, and served for thirty-four years as the beloved Père Antoine. The Inquisition was something he never mentioned again.

The second fire to devastate New Orleans broke out in a courtyard on Royal Street, December 8, 1794. One-third as many buildings were burned as in 1788, but these included important shops and warehouses which had escaped previously, and the financial loss was held to be larger. The French colonial town no longer existed, and many of the early Spanish homes were gone, too. On Dumaine Street, just outside the limits of the fire, a single house that had been erected under Bienville survived. Known as "Madame John's Legacy," it can still be seen, a plantation-style dwelling of some charm. Quite a number of the one-story French cottages were restored. But the core of New Orleans was rebuilt in the Spanish manner, and the city gained thereby. The new architecture was better suited to the climate. Its beauty was undeniable: thick walls pierced with noble arches, the fanlight windows above the doors, the high-ceilinged rooms, the wrought-iron balconies of many designs, the patios, the arcaded streets. The Vieux Carré that we know was created at that time, and the next three generations simply carried forward the idea with greater splendor.

The quick replacing of the public buildings after the two fires was due to the munificence of Don Andrés Almonester y Roxas, a rich Spaniard. He paid for a new *casa del cabildo,* cathedral and priests' house on their original sites facing the Place d'Armes, restored the hospital and public market, and built a chapel for the Ursuline nuns.

American border intrigues, including the plot of James Wilkinson to detach Kentucky from the Union and join it to the Spanish Louisiana, had an effect upon the life of New Orleans. The frontiersmen swarmed down in their flatboats laden with the produce of the West, and lingered at the port they planned someday to conquer. But a deeper mark was left by the French Revolution and its offshoot, the successful slave rebellion in Saint Domingue. Refugees from both terrors were given haven, and they brought ideas with them. In 1792 a company of stranded actors, headed by Louis Tabary, who had been playing in the French West Indies, opened a theater on St. Peter Street where they gave the first professional dramatic shows the city had seen. Two years later a Saint Domingue fugitive, Louis Duclot, commenced the publication of *Le Moniteur de la Louisiane,* the colony's first newspaper.

Governor Carondelet began in 1794, and completed before the end of the next year, the excavation of a basin or inland harbor adjoining Congo Square just outside the ramparts, as well as a canal connecting the basin with the Bayou St. Jean and Lake Pontchartrain. He had intended to continue the waterway through to the Mississippi, utilizing the short existing ditch which is now Canal Street. But the people rioted in opposition to this plan, their spokesmen pointing out the real likelihood that when the river rose in spring to a much higher level than Pontchartrain the city would be drowned. Carondelet deferred to their opinion and merely enlarged the basin. The capacity of the port to accommodate small craft was vastly increased. Smugglers and even pirates took advantage of the improved route. Because contraband goods seized from them were stored at the elbow of the bayou and canal, the lovely plantation house of the period that still stands there is commonly called the Spanish Custom House.

The momentous success of Étienne de Boré in refining sugar in commercial quantities occurred the same year, 1795. Iberville on his first visit to the site of New Orleans had stuck cuttings of cane in the swampy earth. It was the habit of explorers to carry samples and experiment with valuable plants wherever they went. We hear of no results from Iberville's try. Nor did anyone else in Louisiana give a thought to sugar cane until 1751, when the Jesuits imported some from Saint Domingue and raised a small crop. After that several planters dallied with sugar as a side issue. The trouble was that they knew no way of causing the molasses to granulate.

It took the Saint Domingue exiles, fresh from a land where sugar had been the great bonanza, to excite real interest. Boré converted his indigo plantation to cane. He hired an expert from the islands, the only professional refiner then in New Orleans, and at the end of the first season produced $12,000 worth of excellent crystallized sugar. He was hailed as a miracle worker. Yet he had done no more than gamble boldly and corner the available talent. It made him rich. Others rushed to imitate him, and the era of fortunes from sugar in the delta got under way.

The young Duc d'Orléans (one day to be King Louis Philippe) and his two brothers, who had fled the France of the Revolution, came to New Orleans in 1798. They were house guests for three months of the lordly Marigny, who entertained them with a complete disregard of expense both at his mansion on the edge of town and at Fontainebleau. They passed a few days with Boré also, and attended banquets and balls given in their honor by every family with social pretensions. Marigny made them a cash loan of staggering size just before they sailed from the Balize.

This quasi-royal visit is the favorite topic of the contemporary memoirists. They preferred its glamour, naturally, to the yellow-fever epidemics that marked the decade, but they would have performed a more useful service if they had carefully charted the course of the disease. Yellow fever was one of the prime molders of history in the lands about the Caribbean Sea and the Gulf of

Mexico. It is first mentioned under that name in Louisiana in 1767. But we do not hear of its having ravaged New Orleans until 1796, when the Spanish intendant reported that it had long been present. He added: "It attacks foreigners in preference to natives, and, what is singular, it seems to select the Flemish, the English and the Americans, who rarely recover, and who generally die the second or third day after the invasion of the disease. Such is not the case with the Spaniards and the colored people."

The malady, under other names, had been a scourge from the beginning. A French boat which had stopped en route at Havana had brought it to Bienville's pioneers at Biloxi and Mobile in 1704. On that occasion two-thirds of the whites had caught the fever and half of these had died. The French firmly believed that it originated in Spanish countries; they blamed O'Reilly for bringing it again with his army of conquest. From the 1790's on, there was open-mindedness, though it took a century to solve the true nature of yellow jack. It will be dealt with in greater detail in a subsequent chapter.

After the peace of 1783 the Spaniards had not only annexed West Florida, but had laid claim to a strip of land on the east bank of the Mississippi north of the ancient French holdings. Thus they occupied the sites of present-day Vicksburg and Memphis. It had led to resentment and long negotiations by the Americans. In 1795 Spain signed a treaty under which she yielded the east bank above the thirty-first degree of latitude. This meant giving up Natchez and surrounding territory which indubitably had been part of Louisiana. When it came to the point, the governor in New Orleans procrastinated, for Natchez was regarded with a good deal of sentiment. An American mission that was half diplomatic and half a guerrilla raid appeared in 1796, stimulated revolt among the residents and harried the Spanish garrisons.

Two years later Natchez was surrendered and the border established at the thirty-first parallel. This was but another sign of the faltering of Spain's imperial power in both hemispheres, as the sands of the eighteenth century ran out.

Chapter 7

"By the Eternal!"

EVEN as Louisiana had been secretly transferred from France to Spain in 1726, so was it recovered behind the scenes by its former owner. Napoleon, the new colossus, bestrode his world, and the weak King Charles IV was in absolute terror of him. The Treaty of San Ildefonso in 1800 contained private agreements by which Spain got the little Italian principality of Etruria, and in exchange would turn back Louisiana whenever France was ready to receive it. Superficially there were muddled motives and hesitation, as in the original deal. But the lucid mind of the First Consul knew exactly what it was about. The Peace of Amiens brought an uneasy truce to Europe. Now, if ever, was the moment to recapture Saint Domingue and other Caribbean islands lost in the slave revolution, and, if that were successful, to raise the French flag once more on the North American continent.

Napoleon sent his brother-in-law, General Charles Victor Emanuel Leclerc, to Saint Domingue with a magnificently equipped army in the first days of 1802. The blacks were overwhelmed in the field, but a yellow-fever epidemic of unexampled virulence killed so many of the French soldiers that the issue became doubtful. In March 1803 Pierre de Laussat arrived in New Orleans as colonial prefect, announced that the transfer would shortly take place, and started to prepare for the coming of General Victor as captain general with a large body of troops from France. The Creole population was delighted. But already things had taken an evil turn. England was evidently about to renew the war, and her command of the seas would make it impossible for Napoleon to reinforce the Saint Domingue expedition or to maintain Victor in Louisiana. The Corsican decided to drop both phases of his American project.

Meanwhile, Thomas Jefferson had said: "By taking this port [New Orleans] France has committed an act of hostility. She forces us to ally ourselves with the English fleet and nation." He voiced the sentiments of the western States which had been on the point of initiating a coup to wrest New Orleans from Spain, and which could not bear to see the mouth of the Mississippi in Napoleon's strong hands. Jefferson had sent Robert R. Livingston to Paris to help Monroe negotiate for the purchase of New Orleans. It seemed like a hopeless effort. Then suddenly Napoleon conceded more than they had dreamed of asking, and explained himself to his own ministers with glittering and ruthless logic.

"The English have twenty ships of war in the Gulf of Mexico," he declared. "I have not a moment to lose in putting Louisiana out of their reach. They [the American commissioners] only ask of me one town, but I already consider the colony as entirely lost." A day or two later, strolling in the garden of St. Cloud, he apprised Barbé-Marbois: "Well, you have charge of the treasury! Let them give you one hundred million francs, pay their own claims, and take the whole country." The minister ventured a remark about the rights of the colonists. "Send your maxims to the London market," Napoleon retorted. Finally, on April 11, 1803, he told the full cabinet: "I am aware of the value of Louisiana. I give it up with extreme reluctance. To insist on keeping it would be folly. If I were to set my price at what this vast territory is worth to the United States, there would be no limit to the indemnity. I shall be moderate because of my obligation to sell."

The price actually agreed upon was 80,000,000 francs, out of which 20,000,000 were to be applied to claims of American citizens against France. The cash cost of the Island of Orleans and all the vast province west of the Mississippi as far as the Rocky Mountains was 60,000,000 francs, $12,000,000 at par, the best real-estate bargain in history since it works out at four cents an acre. But there was no question then of taking West Florida from Spain. Napoleon was selling the Louisiana that Louis XV had bandied about, and not the section that had been ceded to England

and then conquered by Gálvez. The line through the Iberville Passage and the lakes was once more to be an international frontier.

On November 30, in the hall of the Cabildo at New Orleans, the Spanish governor handed over the keys and other symbols of state to Laussat. The people were declared absolved of their allegiance to Spain. The red-and-gold standard came down in the Place d'Armes, and the French tricolor was raised. Twenty days later, the ceremony was repeated with variations. William C. C. Claiborne, of Virginia, and General James Wilkinson received the province from Laussat, and the Stars and Stripes went to the head of the flagstaff. Claiborne was appointed territorial governor. On both occasions the young Creole magnate, Bernard de Marigny, acted as special military aide to Laussat. The latter had been a guest in his house, a circumstance to which reference will be made in a later chapter.

New Orleans at the time of the transfer had a population of about 10,000, whites being in a slight majority. It was rapidly becoming one of the chief ports in North America. The previous year 265 merchantmen, 158 of them American, had loaded exports worth $2,000,000; 4,500 hogsheads of sugar, 2,000 barrels of molasses, 34,000 bales of cotton, 2,000 hogsheads of tobacco; peltries, rice, indigo, lumber, etc. The combined tonnage of the vessels was 31,241, the equivalent of one large ocean liner today. But this was big business at the start of the nineteenth century. Imports worth $2,500,000 had been handled. Planters and merchants had had prosperous times, and thousands of seamen had earned a good livelihood.

An early guidebook gives a picture of the heart of the city which cannot be improved on. The following was ostensibly based upon word-of-mouth accounts at one remove from actual witnesses of the transfer:

"Here, in front of the Place d'Armes, everything was congregated—the Cathedral church of St. Louis, the convent of the Capuchins, the government House, the colonial prison and the government warehouses. Around the square stretched the leading *boutiques* and restaurants of the town; on the sides were the markets where not only meat, fruits and vegetables were sold, but hats, shoes and handkerchiefs; while in front was the public landing. Indeed, here was the religious, military, industrial, commercial and social center of the city; here the troops paraded on fete days, and here even the public executions took place.

"Here, on holidays, all the varied, heterogeneous population of the town gathered: fiery Louisiana Creoles, carrying rapiers ready for prompt use at the slightest insult to their jealous honor; rude trappers and hunters, *voyageurs* and *coureurs-de-bois,* fresh from Canada; plain, upstanding Acadians from the Attacapa, arrayed in their homemade blue cottonades and redolent of the herds of cattle they had brought with them; lazy nobles, banished to this new world under *lettres de cachet;* yellow sirens from Santo Domingo, speaking a soft bastard French, and looking so languishingly out of the corners of their big, black, melting eyes that it was no wonder they led both young and old astray and caused their proud white sisters many a jealous heartache.

"Here were staid and energetic men from the German Coast up the river, with flaxen hair and Teutonic names, but speaking the purest French, come to the city for supplies; haughty Castilian soldiers, clad in bright uniforms; dirty Indians of the Houma and Natchez tribes, some free, some slaves; Negroes of every shade and hue from dirty white to deepest black, in as little clothing as the somewhat loose ideas of the time and country permitted; and lastly the human trash, ex-galley slaves and adventurers, shipped to the colony to be gotten rid of.

"Here, too, in the Place d'Armes the stranger could shop cheaper if not better than in the *boutiques* around it, for half the trade and business of the town was itinerant.* Here passed peddling mer-

---

* Berquin-du-Vallon, a French traveler at the same period (1803), noted that he found no booksellers in New Orleans, "and for a good reason, that a bookseller would perish of hunger there in the midst of his books, unless these taught the fascinated reader the art of doubling his capital in a year's time."

chants, mainly Catalans and Provençals who, instead of carrying their packs upon their backs, had their goods spread out in a coffin-shaped vehicle which they wheeled before them; colored women selling cakes, and milk and coffee women carrying their immense cans well balanced upon their turbaned heads. All through the day went up the never-ceasing cries of the various street hawkers, from the *'Calas tout chauds!'* in the early morning, to the *'Belles chandelles!'* that went up as twilight deepened from the sturdy Negresses who sold the only light of the colony: horrible, dim, ill-smelling and smoky candles, made at home from the green wax myrtle. . . .

"Almost up to the year 1800 the women of the city, with few exceptions, dressed with extreme simplicity. Little taste was displayed either in the cut of their garments or in their ornaments. Headgear was almost unknown. If a lady went out in summer, it was bareheaded; if in winter, she usually wore a handkerchief or some such trifle as the Spanish women delight in. And at home, when the men were not about—so, at least, said those who penetrated there—she even went about barefooted, shoes being expensive luxuries. A short round skirt, a long basque-like overgarment, the upper part of their attire of one color and the lower of another, with a profuse display of ribbons and little jewelry—thus dressed, the mass of the female population of good condition went about visiting, or attended the ball or theater.

"But even three years had made a great change in this respect; and in 1802, for some reason that it would be difficult to explain, the ladies of the city appeared in attire as different from that of 1799 as could well be imagined. A surprising richness and elegance of apparel had taken the place of the primitive and tasteless garb of the few preceding years—a garb which, had it been seen at the ball or theater in 1802, would have resembled to the critical feminine eye a Mardi Gras disguise. At that period the natural charms of the ladies were heightened by a toilette of most captivating details. Their dresses were of the richest embroidered muslins, cut in the latest fashions, relieved by soft and brilliant transparent taffetas, by superb laces, and embroidered with gold. To this must be added rich earrings, collars, bracelets, rings and other adornments. This costume, it is true, was for rare occasions, and for pleasant weather; but it was a sample of the high art in dress that had come just in the nick of time to greet the fast-approaching American occupation."

There had been scarcely time to print the terms of the transfer when the Americans came with a vengeance. They swarmed in by right, and as there was place for only a few of them in the Vieux Carré they began to build up their own section just above Canal Street. The site had once been the Jesuit plantation. A dozen houses stood there in 1803, and it was called the Faubourg Ste. Marie. Six months later it was unrecognizable. It had become a typical frontier boom town. There began the feud between Latins and Anglo-Saxons which was to last in New Orleans for several generations. The first group made no distinction between French and Spanish blood; all were Creoles, extremely resentful of the threat to their dominion. The newcomers fought back in a more happy-go-lucky spirit, extolling raucously the merits of their brand of democracy.

It took eleven years of turmoil, culminating in Andrew Jackson's defeat of the British on the city's outskirts, to convince the entire community that it formed part of the American Union in fact as well as in name. During those eleven years occurred Aaron Burr's conspiracy, the arrival of the main flood of *emigrés* from the West Indies, the West Florida revolution, the admission of Louisiana as a state, the rise and fall of the Barataria pirates, and the War of 1812.

Burr visited New Orleans in 1805 and plotted with Wilkinson and others in furtherance of his scheme to found an empire in the Southwest. But when he attempted to return with followers under arms, he got no further than Natchez. Wilkinson had betrayed him. He was arrested and taken north, to be tried for treason. The Creoles were lucky not to become involved in Burr's fantasy at the very moment when they were being peacefully and unexpectedly reinforced.

By 1810 the population of New Orleans doubled, and the largest gain was not scored by the Anglo-Saxons, as logically would have been the case. Their number had indeed jumped from a few hundred to 3,000. But there had landed more than 8,000 whites, free persons of color and Negro slaves from countries adjoining the former French colony of Saint Domingue. Why had these delayed so long, seeing the black insurrection had ended in 1803 with the establishment of a republic? The answer was simple. The dispossessed planters had taken refuge in Cuba, Jamaica and other islands under foreign flags, biding their time, hoping that France would yet reconquer Saint Domingue. Many of them had started new plantations or gone into business. Probably they would never have moved on if Napoleon, already at war with England, had not deposed the king of Spain and set up his brother Joseph as monarch in Madrid. The position of the Saint Domingue exiles had become difficult. They were regarded as enemy aliens, particularly in Cuba where the majority had congregated. There was a sudden movement toward Louisiana as the most desirable place of refuge and the only one sure to be permanent.

In the late spring of 1809, thirty-four vessels from Cuba set ashore in New Orleans more than 5,500 immigants, about one-third of whom were white. This was the great rush. A few had trickled in previously. Others came afterward from Jamaica, Puerto Rico, Cuba again, Guadeloupe and Martinique which France would eventually regain. Money and household goods were brought by some, while a considerable proportion arrived penniless. They caused a housing shortage; rents and food prices rose sharply. The Creoles of Louisiana welcomed the West Indians and helped them in every manner to get adjusted, for clearly they would be allies politically and socially.

The Americans, on the other hand, resented what they called the invasion. Governor Claiborne begged the United States consuls in Havana and Santiago de Cuba to halt it. A Spanish regulation forbidding the importation of slaves was raked up. Free persons of color, whether recently landed or not, were ordered to get out of Louisiana. But not one of these measures proved workable. The Saint Domingue Creoles merged with the rest of the French-speaking population. Incidentally, their Negroes brought with them the practice of the voodoo cult.

This was to be the last accession of strength that would come to the Creoles. The recruitment of the Americans would continue without limit, and, perceiving the point, maybe, they stopped complaining. Events in West Florida were more than enough to feed their enthusiasm.

It will be recalled that the United States had forced the hand of Spain and acquired Natchez by treaty. The justification, apart from the urge to expand westward, had been the wishes of the inhabitants. But the territory on the Mississippi just south of the thirty-first degree of latitude was fully as American in feeling as Natchez. Colonists who had filtered in from the north and east bemoaned the fact that their lands had not been included in the Louisiana Purchase. Why, they asked, should Spain be allowed to cling to a last foothold on the river at Baton Rouge? Spasmodic rioting and attempted coups took place from 1804 to 1809. The following year a rumor spread that Napoleon intended to seize all of Florida. Nothing more improbable could be imagined, and one can only suppose that the canard was invented for a purpose. It undoubtedly united the English-speaking malcontents at the western end of the province. They revolted under Isaac Johnson and Philemon Thomas, and seized the fort at Baton Rouge in the only serious fighting that occurred.

On September 26, 1810, the Republic of West Florida was proclaimed, with its capital at St. Francisville. Its eastern boundary was the Pearl River; in other words, it was composed only of the modern Louisiana parishes which lie east of the Mississippi and north of Lake Pontchartrain. The flag adopted was blue with a single white star. Fulwar Skipwith, a polished Virginian who had married a Flemish countess, became chief executive with the title of governor. A commissioner was appointed to go to Washington and seek annexation.

Before the Spaniards could do anything about it, President Madison announced that all of West Florida to the Perdido had actually formed part of the Purchase, and so had belonged to the United States since 1803. He instructed Governor Claiborne in New Orleans to occupy the province, and Claiborne at once moved to obey. No more highhanded act has ever been committed by an American President; that is to say, from the standpoint of strict legality. But it came as a relief to the timid Spanish governor, who wrote Madison early in December from Mobile asking that agents be sent to negotiate the proposition. Skipwith and his cabinet at St. Francisville were more resentful than the Spaniard, for although they had talked annexation they seemingly wanted to enter the Union as a tidy little state and not as part of a Federal territory. They were ignored. Claiborne raised the American flag at St. Francisville and then at Baton Rouge. The republic ended after a life of seventy-four days. It was attached intact to Louisiana. The rest of West Florida was divided between Mississippi and Alabama.

The exploits of Jean Lafitte, chief of the Barataria pirates, constitute an oft-told tale which must be summarized here, however briefly. An understanding of the climax on the Plain of Chalmette would be difficult without it. There were two Lafittes, the brothers Jean and Pierre, Frenchmen from the neighborhood of Bordeaux, who came to New Orleans in 1806. A treasured story has it that they operated a blacksmith shop on Bourbon and St. Philip Streets (Isn't the old building, turned into a café, proof enough?). It remains difficult to believe that either Lafitte would have engaged in such irksome labor. They indubitably ran another kind of shop on Royal Street where they dealt in smuggled merchandise of every description, but mainly luxuries for the feminine trade: perfumes, embroideries, fine silks. The theory has been advanced that the smithy was a blind. In those riotous early days they needed no blind, and soon they became so notorious that their safety lay in having powerful protectors.

Smuggling had changed its character. Foreign ships could no longer evade the customs regulations on the river. But the bayou country to the southwest was an unknown wilderness to the American authorities. Illicit traders and some pirates maintained a rendezvous in Barataria Bay, where they unloaded and sold to middlemen. The middlemen took the goods to New Orleans in small boats, using various waterways known only to themselves. At the end of two years the Lafittes were the most prosperous brokers and retailers in the business. They were not corsairs, and probably had no idea that they would ever engage personally in piracy. Governor Claiborne had heard of them and their kind, but saw no way of coping with them. "Occasionally, in conversation with ladies," he reported, "I have denounced smuggling as dishonest, and very generally a reply, in substance as follows, would be returned: 'That is impossible, for my grandfather—or my father, or my husband—was, under the Spanish Government, a great smuggler, and he was always esteemed an honest man.' "

On January 1, 1808, the slave trade was abolished by Federal statute, and that made a tremendous difference, particularly as England also, had outlawed the traffic. Negroes had figured among the goods handled through Barataria Bay, but not conspicuously. Now they were in great demand, and they quadrupled in value. For this and other reasons, intense jealousy developed among the contrabandists. Foreshadowing the racketeers of a later day, they broke up into warring cliques and passed from price-cutting to the cutting of one another's throats. The Lafittes regarded it as intolerable. They decided to take over the business and reorganize it along efficient lines. Without going into details, it may be said they were completely successful. Pierre remained in New Orleans as manager of the store. The more brilliant Jean moved to Barataria Bay, where he became the unquestioned leader at the headquarters he built on the islands of Grande-Terre and Grande Isle. Gambling casinos, bordellos and cafés, as well as warehouses, sprang up; visitors who came to shop were lavishly entertained.

Jean Lafitte now yielded to the temptation to sail on cruises of doubtful virtue. But it was not until 1810 that he rated as a habitual pirate. In that year revolution came to a head in Spain's South American colonies. The temporary republic of Cartagena was established in the coastal region of New Granada. It issued letters of marque to privateers to prey on Spanish shipping. This was a marvelous opportunity for all freebooters. They met the easy requirements at Cartagena and thereafter could claim that they were within the law. Jean Lafitte invited the privateers to dispose of their prizes at Barataria Bay. He went out himself, and though honest merchantmen flying other flags than the Spanish disappeared with regrettable frequency, the loot he and his fellows brought back had been seized, invariably, from citizens of Spain. Dominique You, Lafitte's most energetic and popular lieutenant, came to Grande-Terre in 1810 with his two brothers. They were Frenchmen who had been living in Guadeloupe. René Béluche, a Creole, rated as the next best aide.

The Baratarians enjoyed their greatest affluence from 1810 to 1813, though even in that brief space of time they had their ups and downs. In 1811 there was a slave revolt in St. John the Baptist Parish up the river, and when this was traced to Negroes bought from the Lafittes a cry arose that the mart at Grande-Terre should be suppressed. The alarm soon died down. The outbreak of war with England in 1812 afforded a fresh stimulus. With American letters of marque afloat as well as those of Cartagena, it was possible to cover up almost any deed of violence on the high seas. Also in 1812, Louisiana attained statehood, and Claiborne was elected the first governor, a circumstance unfavorable to the pirates, for Claiborne was getting sick of them.

In October 1813 a revenue officer seized some smuggled goods near the city, but his party was fired on by Jean Lafitte, one of his men wounded and the goods recaptured. Further bloodshed occurred over a consignment of illicit "black ivory." Claiborne posted a proclamation throughout the city, offering $500 for the arrest of Jean Lafitte. The latter instantly countered with an offer of $1,500 for the governor's person delivered at Grande-Terre, and the waggish document was displayed as prominently as Claiborne's had been. In the middle of 1814 grand jury indictments were returned against all the prominent Baratarians, charging them with piracy. Pierre Lafitte's long immunity ended. He was thrown into jail, along with Dominique You, who chanced to be in town. Jean promptly engaged the two most prominent lawyers in New Orleans, one of them being Edward Livingston, a former mayor of New York, brother of the Chancellor Robert R. Livingston, who had negotiated in Paris for the purchase of Louisiana. Following devious machinations, Pierre and his companion "escaped" from prison and joined Jean at Grande-Terre.

Such was the situation of the outlaws in the fall of 1814 when the danger loomed that the English were planning a serious attempt to capture New Orleans. Peace negotiations had already started at Ghent, Belgium, but no one knew what turn they were taking and they might drag out for months. English and Canadian newspapers, meanwhile, made no secret of the fact that a large expedition had sailed from Plymouth and an Irish port for Jamaica. The troops aboard were veterans of Wellington's Peninsular campaign. The command had been offered to Wellington himself, but on his refusal it had been given to his brother-in-law, Sir Edward Pakenham.

The assembling of this force at Jamaica could have only one meaning. Spain had been England's ally in the final phase of the European wars, and there could be no intention to molest her near-by colonies, while all the French Caribbean islands had already been seized. The objective must be Louisiana. By way of defense, the Federal Government had four companies of regulars at New Orleans under Colonel George T. Ross, and half a dozen gunboats on the river commanded by Commodore Daniel T. Patterson. In Southern Alabama, General Andrew Jackson was on a punitive foray against the Creek Indians; new orders extended his authority over the whole Gulf Coast. Louisiana was advised to add a thousand men to its militia.

New and ever wilder rumors circulated. Then suddenly the English showed their hand—to Jean Lafitte of all people. Captain Nicholas Lockyer of the Royal Navy came in a brig to Barataria, landed with two other officers, and delivered several letters from his superiors. The documents comprised an appeal to the population to revolt against American rule and accept a British protectorate, a threat to the Baratarians in particular that if they did not join they would be treated as pirates and exterminated, and a personal offer to Jean Lafitte. This last was the most interesting. It contained an admission that New Orleans was about to be attacked, and it promised Jean the rank of captain in return for his aid.

Jean countered that he would need a fortnight in which to think the matter over. Lockyer agreed to this and said he would be back for his answer. Promptly the Baratarian leader sent the papers to Livingston in the city and asked him to make a deal with the authorities. If all indictments were quashed and the freebooters given the standing of citizens, he, Lafitte, would bring his men to the defense of New Orleans. The reply was a raid by Commodore Patterson with his six gunboats and an armed schooner. Grande-Terre and Grande Isle were bombarded, their buildings leveled, their population dispersed. Many of the pirates were killed and some captured. Lockyer, who had been hovering near by, slipped beyond the horizon.

Patterson, feeling very righteous, announced that the Lafittes had been trying to hoax him, and that he had cooked their goose for good. But Livingston went on insisting that the documents placed in his hands were genuine. Among those who took his view was General Jacques Philippe Villeré, the ranking officer of the Creole militia, son of the Villeré who had perished resisting O'Reilly.

Andrew Jackson had been reinforced in Alabama by a Tennessee brigade. He chose first to attack Pensacola in Spanish Florida, on the grounds that it was harboring British naval units. The forts there were reduced with ease. The exploit has been counted among Old Hickory's laurels, but it was sheer luck that the delay involved did not prove fatal to his larger responsibility. He had no information about the movements of the main enemy expeditionary force, and the latter almost succeeded in getting to Louisiana ahead of him. He set out by land for New Orleans on November 21. Three days later a great British fleet under Admiral Sir Alexander Cochrane, consisting of fifty warships and transports, assembled in Negril Bay at the west end of Jamaica, and sailed at dawn.

The route followed by Jackson was along the north shore of Lake Pontchartrain to a point opposite the Bayou St. Jean, or St. John as it will be appropriate to call it henceforth, the name having become permanently Anglicized. He crossed in small boats and landed on December 2 at the old Spanish fort which stood at the mouth of the bayou. Alexander Walker, one of his early biographers, writes that on that day his complexion appeared "sallow and unhealthy, his body thin and emaciated like that of one who had just recovered from a lingering and painful sickness. But the fierce glare of his bright and hawklike eye betrayed a soul and spirit which triumphed over all the infirmities of the body." He had suffered severely from fevers in the campaign against the Creeks.

He has been accused of despotic behavior on his arrival in New Orleans, but it amounted to his enforcing martial law in the face of a crisis, and this it was his duty to do. The legislature had been dilatory about raising troops. He went over its head and made an appeal for volunteers, to which not only the Americans but the Creoles and the free men of color responded ardently. He roughly bossed Commodore Patterson no less than Colonel Ross. General Coffee was summoned from Baton Rouge with his 2,000 men.

Word came that the British fleet had been sighted off Cuba some days previously, headed straight north. It had the choice of two obvious approaches. It could either attempt to force the Mississippi, which was inadequately defended by one small fort about twenty-five miles up the river; or it could enter Lake Borgne to the east and land soldiers for a march of fifteen miles across flat but swampy land. An attack by way of Barataria Bay seems to have been discounted, though if Lafitte had taken the English side it is not inconceivable that he could have guided the foe, undetected, through the maze of bayous. Perhaps that was why Lockyer's move to enlist him had been attempted in the first place. We do not know.

Jackson, however, did take the precaution that appears far-fetched to the modern student. To guard against British warcraft from Canada sneaking down the Mississippi and entering the lakes to assault New Oreans from the rear, he ordered the closing of the Manchac as far as its junction with the Amite. That was done by sinking a boat in the entrance, and then filling in the bayou with such thoroughness that the Iberville Passage was abolished. It has never been reopened. The nature of the lakes was modified by cutting them off from the inflow of water at floodtime from the Mississippi.

Anticipating from further reports that the objective of the British fleet was Lake Borgne, Patterson sent five gunboats, one tender and a dispatch boat under Lieutenant Thomas Ap Catesby Jones to watch for it at Pass Christian. It was sighted on December 10, and Jones retired into Lake Borgne and took up his position in shallow water near the Malheureux Islands. The enemy armada anchored off the Chandeleur Islands in the Gulf, beyond which its larger units could not go. The morning of December 14, the British sent out 45 launches and barges, each mounting one gun and with 1,200 men aboard; the commander was Captain Lockyer. In opposition the Americans had only the five gunboats, with a total of 23 guns fit for action and 204 men.

There ensued for two hours what is known in naval annals as the Battle of Lake Borgne. It was too unorthodox and one-sided, really, to be dignified as a battle. The British closed in stubbornly, took heavy losses which they could afford, captured a gunboat by boarding and turned its cannon against the others. The maneuver was repeated until all were forced to surrender. Both Jones and

Lockyer were seriously wounded. The American casualties at 60 all told were relatively larger than those of the British at 300. It had been a brave but foolish gesture on the part of Jones to accept action. He had been given orders to save his vessels if they were threatened, and this he could have done by falling back on the fort called Petites Coquilles (later rebuilt as Fort Pike) at the entrance of the Rigolets. He could then have worked his way into Pontchartrain and been of use in reporting on the subsequent landing operations of General Pakenham. As it was, the English preserved for a while longer the element of surprise in their domination of Lake Borgne.*

Jackson was vague about the details of what had happened. But he sensed a desperate situation. At that late date he worried about a possible invasion by the Mississippi route and provided for a last-ditch defense of Fort St. Philip. He did not know that the mass of the British expeditionary force had been put ashore on Pea Island (now Pearl River Island) on the north shore of Lake Borgne. His call for a general mobilization in New Orleans required every able-bodied man to take up arms.

It was at this juncture that Jean Lafitte calmly presented himself to Jackson and renewed his offer to throw the Baratarians into the fight on the American side. Let bygones be bygones, he said: the charges of piracy, along with the destruction of Grande-Terre and Grande Isle by Commodore Patterson. The recruits would number a couple of hundred at the most, but among them would be expert gunners. Dominique You had been an artilleryman in the Napoleonic armies. Jackson, who had once called the Baratarians "hellish banditti," needed every seasoned man he could get, and he accepted without making binding promises. It is easy to over-romanticize this business. A company was formed with Dominique You as captain and René Béluche as his chief lieutenant. The names of Jean and Pierre Lafitte do not figure on its rolls. Ac-

---

* In 1931 children playing on Shell Beach, Lake Borgne, picked up coins dated in the early 1800's, of Spanish and United States mintage, half buried among the shells. The money is believed to have been lost in the naval fight between Ap Catesby Jones and Lockyer.

cording to strongly supported tradition, nevertheless, Pierre was a combatant and Jean rendered valuable services as a liaison officer.

East of New Orleans a neck of flat land separates Lake Pontchartrain from Lake Borgne. In the southerly bend of the section, between Borgne and the river, were located the Villeré, De la Ronde and Chalmette plantations, and still closer to the city the Marigny plantation, all referred to in the preceding chapter. The low-lying peninsula was intersected by several bayous. One of the largest of these, the Bayou Bienvenue, could be entered from Lake Borgne, and by following a branch waterway the Villeré house could be reached.

Jackson had placed a small picket at the mouth of Bienvenue. But on the morning of December 23 the first wave of Pakenham's army arrived in small boats from Pea Island, overwhelmed and seized the members of the picket. Redcoats hurried down the canals and surrounded the Villeré plantation, which was named Béka. General Villeré and several officers were taken prisoner. One member of the staff, Major Gabriel Villeré, the general's son, escaped by jumping out of a window and sped to the neighboring De la Ronde plantation.* There he found his friend, Colonel Pierre Denis de la Ronde, who had been in command at the Chef Menteur pass and had just ridden in with news of the British advance.

The two men went posthaste to New Orleans. They saw Jackson at his headquarters on Royal Street and blurted out their narrative. Old Hickory listened in glowering silence until they had finished, then stood up, banged with his fist on the table and swore his famous oath:

"By the Eternal, they shall not sleep on our soil!"

---

* Its name was Versailles and it was one of the show places of Louisiana. Some ten years earlier, Pierre Denis de la Ronde had indulged the grandiloquent dream of founding there a city and port on the Mississippi which, since it would be closer to the mouth of the river, might end by taking precedence over New Orleans. He planned to connect it rearward, by means of a broad highway, with Lake Borgne, where he would father another city to be called Paris. Nothing came of this except the road, which he began. It is known today as Parish Road, and the residents imagine that this designation signifies a thoroughfare built by the local authorities. Actually it is a mistranslation of "Chemin de Paris."

The general, in fact, marched out that day at the head of 2,000 troops composed of Coffee's Tennesseans, a detachment of marines, various militia companies under Major Plauché and others, Saint Domingue free men of color under Major D'Aquin, and Choctaw Indians. It was impossible literally to fulfill his vow, but he checked the vanguard of the invaders in a sharp engagement on Gentilly plain just beyond the Marigny plantation and saved the city from becoming a battlefield.

This preliminary action is often underplayed in popular accounts, though it was of vital importance. Maneuvering for position followed, during the course of which the British made two determined attempts to break through, but were repulsed. The ship of war *Louisiana* and the naval schooner *Carolina,* under Patterson, played a useful part, firing from the Mississippi until the *Carolina* was blown up by an enemy shot and the *Louisiana* disabled. Cannon from the latter were then put ashore and employed as a battery.

Jackson's final position was behind the Rodriguez Canal, a dry grass-grown ditch twenty feet wide and four deep, running from the river to woods and swamps. Coffee's forces were on his left, those of Carroll at the center, and the Louisiana regiments on his right. The British were on the far side of the Plain of Chalmette, which stretched between the two armies. The American breastworks were in part composed of cotton bales daubed with mud to solidify them, while the British had masked their guns with barrels of sugar.

At first light on the morning of January 8, 1815, Pakenham threw his red-coated columns into a charge on Jackson's center. It was an application of the formal methods of European warfare on a terrain where these were an absurdity, and against men whose forte was a deadly marksmanship. The American guns plowed furrows through the serried ranks of the foe, and as the Red Coats came stubbornly nearer the sharpshooters picked off individuals by the score. The British behaved with the utmost gallantry, but were simply blasted from the field. Pakenham, two of his generals and several other high officers fell. Meanwhile an assault along the levee had been stopped at the very bastion. The success of a small British troop in crossing the Mississippi and breaking up an American position on the west bank was of no lasting avail. By 8:30 the infantry fire had ceased, and at 2:00 P.M. the guns fell silent as those of the invaders who had not surrendered withdrew out of range.

With a few short of 4,000 men, among whom had been the Baratarians and hundreds of freshly-arrived Kentucky marksmen, Jackson had routed the British army of 12,000-odd. The disproportionate losses amounted to 2,017 in all categories for the enemy; seven killed, six wounded, and a few missing on the American side.

Andrew Jackson became one of Louisiana's heroes for all time. In general orders he paid special tributes to the local troops, including the pirates. The latter were given full pardons by President Madison for their previous offenses. But lasting reform was not for them. Jean Lafitte's short essay at respectability bored him. He set up a new establishment on the Texas coast near Galveston, engaged in privateering for a few years and then vanished, probably a victim in an obscure sea fight. It is not known how Pierre ended. Béluche joined the revolutionary forces in Venezuela, and commanded a ship for Simón Bolívar. Only Dominique You among the Baratarian leaders settled in New Orleans, where he played politics unsuccessfully and died poor. The epitaph on his tomb, in French, credits him with resembling the Chevalier Bayard, "without reproach and without fear."

Louisiana State Museum

TYPICAL MISSISSIPPI RIVER FLATBOAT

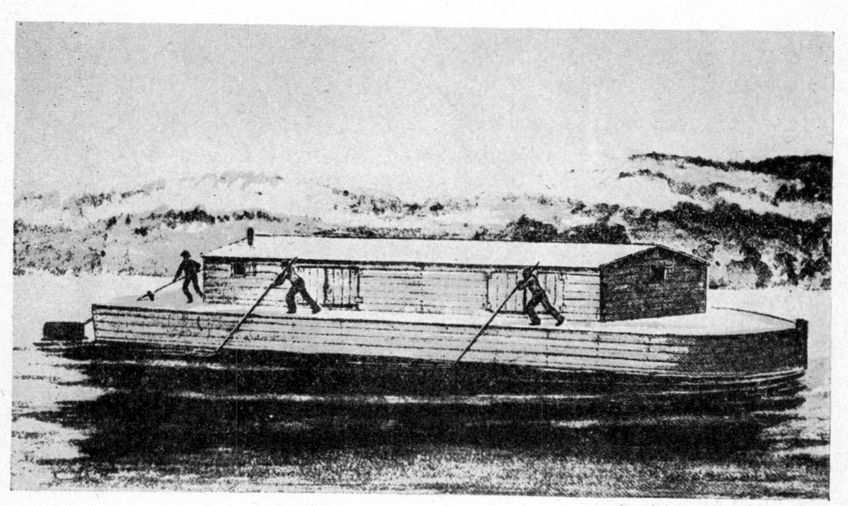

Louisiana State Museum

OHIO RIVER KEELBOAT

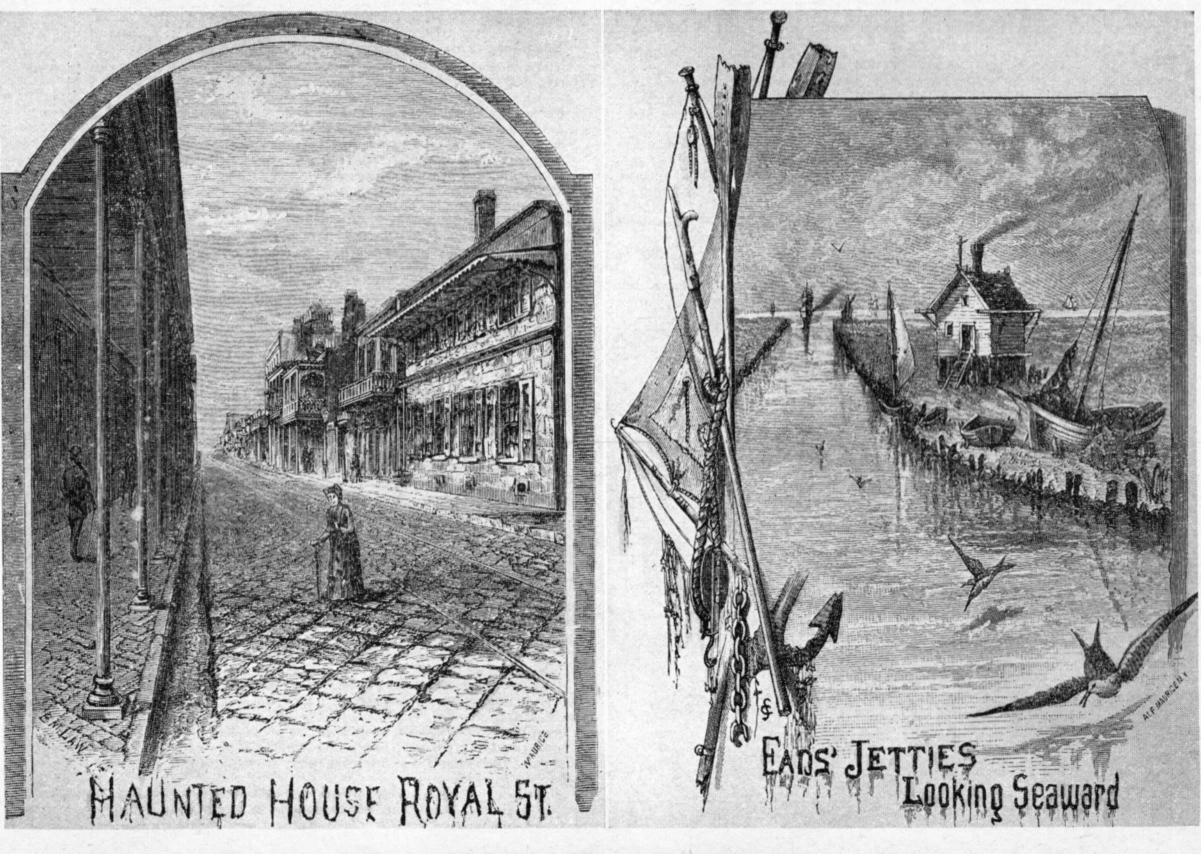

FROM AN OLD GUIDEBOOK

Part II

A CENTURY OF ROMANCE

Chapter 8

Steam Comes to River and Lake

Up to this point a somewhat detailed story of events has been told. It seemed the best way to show how the lake became important to modern man through the growth of the city on the Island of Orleans. Several volumes would be required to treat the busy nineteenth and twentieth centuries in the same fashion. So hereafter special aspects will be chosen for attention, and with less emphasis on political history. When it is preferable to dispose of a theme in any given chapter by pursuing it far into the future, this will be done. Generally speaking, however, the structural plan will be chronological.

On a small-scale map Lake Pontchartrain looks fairly oval. A detailed chart shows an irregular outline that bears a curious resemblance to the stomach of a beast distended across the middle and pinched at one end, with appropriate outlets like a gullet and an intestine. This may not be the most elegant of comparisons, but it has the merit of being accurate. To the west Pontchartrain connects with little Lake Maurepas, which has much the same silhouette but which instead of lying at the same angle is tilted on the map from northeast to southwest. At the eastern end—the pinched one—Pontchartrain is linked with Lake Borgne. The latter is an open-mouthed lagoon, purse-shaped, which bites into the land in the direction of the Mississippi and creates a peninsula between itself and the big lake. The peninsula would be an isthmus if it were not for the Rigolets, the familiar channel at its north end. But there are further variations: a smaller natural canal called the Chef Menteur which runs due south from Pontchartrain to Borgne, and an inlet known as Lake St. Catherine on the Pontchartrain side of the peninsula. The reader can get a clear mental picture only by studying the chart.

We have noted that when Andrew Jackson closed the Manchac which gave access to the Amite and Lake Maurepas, he blocked off the lakes from the Mississippi and brought about conditions which changed them. This must be clarified. The north shore of Pontchartrain dates back to the glacial period, while the south shore is of comparatively recent formation. The intervening basin is covered with a glacial deposit of gravel and sand, to which has been added the residue of ages upon ages of marine life. All have been smoothed and rounded to fine particles by the restless waters. The bottom is not even, but is a corrugated pattern of sand dunes molded by the contrary action of storms and floods. The storms go on as before, while the floods are not what they used to be. In the old days, when the Mississippi went on a real rampage its waters fairly poured through the Bayou Manchac and over the flat country on both sides until they reached the lakes. Even in ordinary years there was some overflowing of the river at the chief point of ingress each spring. The plugging of the bayou and the subsequent raising of levees stopped this, save at long intervals, and the effect was to stabilize the bottoms of both Maurepas and Pontchartrain.

The hurricane of 1915 and the two occasions on which the Bonnet Carré Spillway was opened, in 1937 and 1944, to deflect Mississippi floods, were major disruptions, of which more in the proper place. It is a fact, however, that soundings of the basin are less variable than they would have been if the Bayou Manchac had remained open.

Professor Reinhard A. Steinmayer, geologist, of Tulane University, has said that because the dominant storm winds blow from the southeast, Pontchartrain tends to wear away its northern shore, and to become broader while shrinking lengthwise. Also, its total area dwindles. The process, needless to say, is so slow that it is of no practical importance to the next ten generations of mankind. But the streams that now empty into Pontchartrain are inadequate to maintain so large a body of water forever.

The naval phase of the War of 1812 had been fought entirely by sailing ships, though steam, which was vastly to increase the trade of New Orleans, had already made its appearance. Robert Fulton's first experiments had proved successful several years before the war. In 1809 Nicholas J. Roosevelt, who was associated with Fulton, made a trip down the Mississippi in a steamboat to determine whether the invention could be employed on swift-flowing rivers. The doubters had predicted that he would come to grief in the currents. He made a favorable report to his backers, and the *New Orleans* was built on the upper reaches of the Ohio in 1810-1811. She arrived at the city for which she had been named on January 10, 1812, several months before the outbreak of war, the pioneer of a revolutionary passenger and freight service. The Louisiana *Courier* described the event as follows:

"The steam-boat called the *New Orleans* arrived from Pittsburgh on Friday last. The captain says that she was only 259 hours from Pittsburgh to this place, which is at the rate of about eight miles an hour. This steam-boat was built at Pittsburgh for the Ohio Company, to which Messrs. Livingston & Fulton of New York ceded a part of their privilege. She appears to us as long as a frigate, is about 405 tons, and intended as a regular trader from this place to Natchez. We are assured that she can go at the rate of five knots an hour against the current, which promises the most happy results to this valuable and useful discovery."

The *New Orleans* barely reached Natchez on the return trip and had to be scrapped. Two new steamships were seen on the lower Mississippi in the next few months: the *Comet,* which did not hold up, and the *Vesuvius.* In December 1814 the *Enterprise* came to New Orleans, bringing munitions for Andrew Jackson. She was owned by Captain Henry Shreve, the genius who was to fix the type of paddle-wheel steamers best suited to the river, to launch a prosperous fleet and have his imitators by the score.

Men of large affairs still did not think much of steam. "Our harbor," writes Governor Claiborne in March 1815, with the British scarcely two months gone, "is again whitening with canvas; the levee is crowded with cotton, tobacco, and other articles for exportation." Why, indeed, should the conservative have faith in steam at that stage of the game! Though the new craft descended the Mississippi at a sensational clip, none of them was able to buck the current going north until 1816, when Captain Shreve did it. The traffic then developed swiftly.

The year 1816 was noteworthy for two other things: the election of General Jacques Villeré as governor to succeed Claiborne, and the flooding of the rear suburbs of New Orleans as a result of a break in the levee at Carrollton. The Creole victory at the polls inaugurated a seesaw arrangement under which the races alternated in high office for the next two decades. Fears that the city could never be made really safe were aroused by the flood waters, which took twenty-five days to disappear. An early historian remarked in astonishment that that twelve-month turned out to be the healthiest in a period of forty years. Yellow fever had been dreaded, since it was supposed to be caused by the miasmas of swamps. From what science now knows, it seems plausible that the flood, which occurred in May, destroyed the larvae of mosquitoes that might have carried the disease in July.

J. G. Flügel, a German, came to the United States in 1803 and remained until 1818. For a number of years he was engaged in trading along the Mississippi. In 1817 he made a round trip during the course of which he traveled part of the way on the second *New Orleans*. His description of the craft, taken from his journal, is as follows:

"This steamboat *New Orleans,* finished for navigation, cost $65,000. She was built at Pittsburgh in 1815 under the direction of one Hardinger (a German) and Captain Gale—for a company at New York, Messrs. Rosewalt [Roosevelt], Fulton and Livingston, the same company that built the old *New Orleans* in 1810. She was built after Fulton's plan and construction—her machinery alone cost $20,000. She carries, exclusive of her machinery, 200 tons. Her length in keel is 140 feet, and breadth in beam 28 feet. She carries no sails, runs from 3 to 4 miles against the stream in an hour, and downstream 9 to 10 miles.

"The ladies' cabin is below deck, it being the most retired place. It is elegantly fitted up. The windows are ornamented with white curtains and the beds, twenty in number, with red bombazette curtains and fringes and mosquito bars, besides sofas, chairs, looking glasses, etc., and an elegant carpet ornaments the floor. This cabin is 30 feet in length. Above deck is an elegant round-house of 42 feet in length and 28 in breadth for the gentlemen. This room for the convenience of passengers is provided with 26 berths in 13 state rooms, with mattresses of Spanish moss (in which the woods of Louisiana abound). Other necessary bed-clothes are handsomely flowered. Each berth has a window. Sofas or settees and chairs, two large tables, a large gilt framed looking glass, several elegantly finished recommendation cards and regulations of the boat in gilt frames—all these adorn the room, and finally an elegant carpet covers the floor.

"The Captain's room is on the starboard side and is tolerably large. Forward of the round-house, adjoining the same, on the larboard side, is the bar-room fitted up equal to a coffee house and the present keeper, Louis Roach, is a very accommodating, pleasant man. Above the water-wheel on the larboard side is the clerk's office and lodging. He receives the freight, weighs and measures it, keeps the accounts, etc. On the starboard side ranging with the former is a room for the head engineer and the bar-keeper. Further on the deck forward of the engine is the kitchen and forward of this is a room for the mate and the pilot. This appears to me to be an excellent plan, as these two officers are placed where they are the most available in case of alarm. Forward of this, immediately under the prow below deck, is the forecastler's lodging with 12 berths, seats and a table for the hands in general.

"I find that the engine effects 18 revolutions per minute. This, however, cannot be an exact calculation. The Captain is very particular with her boiler (for I observed him this afternoon stuffing up several holes), it being very old, the same that sank in the old *New Orleans* about two years ago. He is daily expecting a new copper boiler from New York. When he gets the same on board he tells me the engine will perform 22 revolutions per minute. Consequently, it will give the boat much greater velocity through the water. This boiler, now on board, contains 8 tons of water. She consumes 6 cords of wood in 24 hours, which is taken in along the coast where the inhabitants have it in readiness at $2.50 per cord (8 feet long, 4 high, and 4 broad). The vessel can be stopped in an instant if there is any danger, and with facility she can be brought to shore, or turned in any direction. Near the forecastler's watch-way is a large bell by which the servants are awakened.

"Captain Gale told me that dragging the small boats (which the vessel carries), he had discovered, was injurious to the vessel, as well as impeded her progress. Therefore, he had obtained cranes by which the small boats were hauled up. This is effected as the boat is proceeding. On the lar-and-starboard sides of the bow are two anchors, a provision used only in case of a storm, for commonly they make use of a large cable, which after it has been used is regularly coiled up. As the climate is exceptionally hot and would scarcely be endurable in the summer months on board a steamboat where the heat of the fire and the boilers would be sufficient to prevent persons from traveling or, at least, would render them uncomfortable when traveling, the boat is completely covered with awning at that time, and above the round-house is an elegantly decorated walk with iron railings and nettings (made by Henry, a German sailor). There the gentlemen passengers sit comfortably and have a commanding view over the boat, river, and land, and enjoy the cool breeze. The awnings, the Captain tells me, have no tendency to impede progress.

"The sight of these swimming volcanoes on water is very agreeable. They generally have colors at their poop and the American eagle and stars give a very handsome effect. A swivel-gun is carried to signalize their arrival and departure. It is generally fastened at the middle of the bow. The one on board this boat is a little 4-pounder."

Flügel gives the annual payroll, starting with $2,500 for the captain and totaling $9,720. He goes on: "Maintenance is very costly in this part of the country since everything, especially provisions, are high; for one pays from $20 to $45 per month for board in New Orleans. The expenses in case of damage to machinery, which now and then occur, no one can state, but the final and total expenses are very great. The income obtained is proportionately great, for the Captain told me that on one trip from New Orleans to Natchez, the net proceeds amounted to no less than $4,000. There is within the bounds of knowledge no business in any part of the globe which is more lucrative than this, but it will not be so in a few years hence, for I know the enterprise of the Americans, and the rivers as far as they may be navigable will be crowded with steamboats. . . .

"Way passengers up stream pay 12½ cents per mile and down stream 6¼ cents. The freight she receives for Bayou Sara is paid at the rate of 30 cents per square foot, and so for a barrel measuring five square feet, $1.50, and for heavy articles such as iron, lead, etc., 75 cents per cwt."

The diarist tells of noticing upstream "a large white cloud, which seemed to me something unusual." It turned out that the boiler of the *Constitution* had burst, a few minutes after she had challenged another steamboat to a race. Twelve passengers were scalded to death. But Flügel refrains from worrying about the boiler on his own boat, which he had seen the skipper industriously patching.

Steam came more slowly to Lake Pontchartrain than to the river. This was natural, because the brigs, schooners and sloops in the coastal traffic through the Sound and the Rigolets were well suited to the shallow waters of their route. They did not have a current to contend with in either direction. The advantages of greater speed were balanced against the cost of engines, and for several years the sailing craft remained unchallenged. Then the Louisiana *Courier* announced in its issue of October 19, 1818, that competition was being planned. The report was dated from Philadelphia the previous September 17, as follows:

"The elegant Steam Boat *Maid of Orleans,* intended to ply from Mobile to New Orleans, through Lake Pontchartrain, will be launched from the shipyard of Messrs. Vaughan and Bowers, Kensington, at 3 o'clock P.M. today."

The maiden voyage of the *Maid of Orleans,* a Captain Morrison on the bridge, occurred in February 1819. She appears to have been the first steam vessel to enter the lake. Her tonnage is not given, but she must have been quite small, as she is sometimes referred to anomalously as a steam schooner. She may have been fitted with masts for the emergency use of canvas. For many months after her advent she is listed in the *Courier's* shipping notices as the only one of her kind amid a host of sailing craft to and from Mobile. Then we find the announcement that "the *Maid of Orleans,* or other steamboat," will make the trip in one direction or the other.

Progress in steam navigation on Pontchartrain continued to be retarded through the 1820's, mainly because a port with good docking facilities was essential. It took a startling enterprise to meet the need. This will be described in another chapter. But New Orleans was stimulus enough for the flotillas that sought the Mississippi, doubling and trebling in size each year.

The boom in commerce which the ships symbolized went hand in hand with an accelerated growth of population. The American quarter, or Faubourg Ste. Marie, beyond Canal Street was already overcrowded three years after the close of the War of 1812. It had been built haphazard on the old Jesuit plantation and the swampy lands of Jean Gravier. Its water front, which then came up to Tchoupitoulas Street, was excessively marshy and difficult to improve with quais. Unless the quarter was reorganized and extended still farther to the southwest, a new location would have to be developed. The leaders of the American businessmen who took up the problem were Samuel Jarvis Peters, a well-known merchant; James H. Caldwell, an actor-manager; and William H. Sparks. They felt that a downriver site would be preferable. The anchorage off the Marigny plantation was excellent, and the marginal lands were more solid than in the Faubourg Ste. Marie. Therefore, they approached the opulent Bernard with an offer to buy what remained of his estate. This was in the middle 1820's.

Much fanciful stuff has been written concerning the incident we are about to note. Usually it is made to appear that Marigny had never before contemplated the breaking up of his plantation. But in 1805 the Louisiana Territorial Legislature passed an act authorizing Bernard de Marigny, then a minor, "jointly with his guardian," to "sell and lease all or any" of the lots to be laid out in his lands adjoining the city. As a result, a large number of parcels were immediately sold. In 1809 the proprietor advertised 650 lots in the Louisiana *Courier,* and in 1819 James Hepburn, acting as his agent, announced in the same paper that "purchasers of lots in the new Faubourg Marigny are hereby notified that the distribution thereof will take place by lot" on a specified date.

Peters and his associates, therefore, were seeking to expand a going township. All accounts agree that Bernard said he liked the plans of the Americans for a big hotel, a theater, cotton presses, gas and waterworks plants, warehouses and shops on his domain, and that after driving a hard bargain as to the price he agreed to sell. The papers were drawn up, but when the parties met in a notary's office to sign them Marigny asked for an indefinite postponement. Under Louisiana law his wife's signature was necessary along with his, he explained, and Madame de Marigny had refused to attend because she had not made up her mind whether the sale was in her best interests.

This was regarded by the American syndicate as an evasion. Peters, a forthright, domineering character who was not accustomed to being crossed, berated Marigny and accused him of intending to steal the idea and attempt the promotion himself. Tearing up the deed of transfer, Peters shouted, "I shall live, by

God, to see the day when rank grass chokes up the gutters of your *faubourg*."

The fact that New Orleans spread so enormously up the Mississippi instead of down it was decided by this episode. The syndicate turned back to the existing American section and transformed it. Peters, the head of the largest wholesale grocery in the South while still in his twenties, was especially devoted to public affairs; he fathered libraries and schools. Caldwell, who had staged the first play in English in New Orleans, built two theaters, designed hotels, and branched out into the gas business. A new suburb beyond Howard Avenue was called the Garden District because of the spaciousness and beauty of its American-style homes. All this was not accomplished in a day, but by 1830 the Faubourg Ste. Marie was a rival on even terms with the Vieux Carré.

Meanwhile, Bernard de Marigny had done exactly what Sam Peters had suspected he had in mind. The rest of the great plantation that started at the Esplanade on the edge of the old city was cut up into building lots, with the exception of a small area surrounding the ancestral home. Bernard planned the streets and named them himself. Everything was to radiate from a broad avenue which he ambitiously called the Champs-Élysées, but which never lived up to his expectations and was soon translated into Elysian Fields Avenue. There was a Marigny Street and a Mandeville Street. Most of his other names were delightfully colorful. They included Bons Enfants, Grands Hommes, Amour, Desire, Bagatelle—and Craps! The story goes that the game of craps played with dice was brought to New Orleans by the young Louis Philippe when he and his two brothers were the house guests of Bernard de Marigny's father in 1798. The family took it up, and it became a mania among the members of the Creole *haut monde*. Bernard was particularly fond of it; another version is, that he was the real inventor, but ascribed it to the French prince as a joke. Anyway, the rue de Craps figures on the early maps. Its identity was lost when it was made into an extension of Burgundy Street.

The Faubourg Marigny proved relatively unsuccessful. The lots were in good demand—purchasers drew straws for them—but they served mainly to house an overflow of the less prosperous Creoles. Few pretentious mansions were erected. Business was slow to adopt the splendid sites offered, for the merchants of the Vieux Carré had no reason to move, and new American capital almost invariably followed the bandwagon south of Canal Street. Later a combine of planters and brokers built the great Levee Cotton Press at a cost of $500,000 in the Faubourg Marigny, but the Faubourg Ste. Marie topped it with the Orleans Cotton Press at $750,000 and several minor presses.

The rivalry became acridly political as well as commercial, with the two French quarters hanging together against the American. The Creoles were still able to elect a majority in the City Council when, in the middle 1830's, the state legislature adopted a curious compromise to meet the complaints of the Americans that ordinances discriminating against them were being jammed through the council. The charter was withdrawn and a new one issued which divided the city into three municipalities. Each of these was to be ruled by a board of elected aldermen, presided over by a recorder. There was also to be a fourth board, headed by the mayor, which would deal only with problems of common interest. The Vieux Carré was renamed the First Municipality, the Faubourg Ste. Marie the Second Municipality, and the Faubourg Marigny the Third Municipality. In practice, the general council had very little authority, and the mayor became a figurehead. The recorders were the men who framed politics for their units and spent the public funds.

Both races plumed themselves on the arrangement. The Creoles had despaired of preventing the rise of the outlander tide, but believed (Bernard de Marigny dissenting) that their two municipalities would always give them the advantage in the city as a whole. The Americans held that their superior aptitude for trade and their driving force would, if unhampered, make their quarter a virile stepmother whose authority the wayward would be obliged to accept in due course. Events proved that the tripartite government was wasteful and unnecessary. The Faubourg Ste. Marie won. At the end of sixteen years a single municipality was reestablished and the seat of administration shifted from the old Cabildo to a city hall of Greek Revival architecture on Lafayette Square.

Chapter 9

City of Pleasure

NEW ORLEANS has always been a city moved by a spirit diametrically opposed to puritanism in any form. The catch phrases used to describe the place are illuminating, whether it be the "Paris in America" of the French and Spaniards, the "good-time town" of the river boatmen and the whole tribe of roustabouts and sailors, or "the city that care forgot" and the "wide-open New Orleans" of later days. No other big city in these states has the flair for colorful gaiety that makes Mardi Gras the great event of the year, or is able to combine good Catholicism with the absolutely uninhibited "continental Sunday." It is taken for granted there that life was meant to be enjoyed. A superior cuisine and wines that do it justice are part of the philosophy; they have never been lacking. Song and dance, horse racing and all sorts of public amusements are considered necessities, and the few attempts to censor them have simply been laughed out of court.

Along with this, of course, has gone a toleration of the vices. Your true Orleanian regards the term "vice" as exaggerated, anyway. If one of the natural appetites is involved, there is a reason for it in the scheme of things. He is willing to admit, however, that sordid manifestations are evil, and there have been plenty of these in the long history of the community. Much has been written about local gambling, drunkenness and whoring, and some attention paid to the lust for bloodletting at certain periods. They are strands in the pattern. The practice has been to lump them together without a due apportioning of emphasis, as though they were of equal significance!

On the sporting side New Orleans has been first and foremost a gambling town. The frenzy for taking chances on games, contests and lotteries has put other venial sins in the shade. It arrived with Bienville's pioneers, and even in the rakish eighteenth century men remarked with astonishment how especially prone to cards and dice the Louisianians were. The authorities have limited the expression of the urge at times, but have never come anywhere near to suppressing it. Liquor, yes; the saloon survived even under Prohibition. Women, yes. But both these have been regulated without excessively annoying the patrons. The very character of the city would have changed if gambling could have been outlawed to the extent that it is in, say, New York or Chicago.

The Spaniards were capable of bursts of austerity. Thus Governor Miró decreed that Sunday must be strictly observed, and that even the dances of the slaves permitted that day of the week in Congo Square must not begin until after vespers. He forbade white men to have colored mistresses, and ordered the free women of color to array themselves modestly with the *tignon* as a prescribed headdress to mark their social position. He barred gambling. The restrictions were flouted, except that vividly-striped Madras kerchiefs, artfully arranged, proved more attractive than any hat in contrast with golden skins and were adopted by the quadroon beauties as a cachet. When the first theatrical troupe arrived from Saint Domingue the shows were closely watched for sacrilege and subversive political ideas. In the early days of the American regime there was a brief spell of concern about the morals of the theater. Interference with any of these matters for the next hundred years consisted of the emptiest of gestures.

The original public ballroom of New Orleans was on Condé Street (now a continuation of Chartres Street), between St. Ann and Dumaine. It was an unpretentious wooden structure opened around 1790, its floor some eighty feet wide and with tiers of boxes on both sides. Dances were held there each winter by the *haut monde*. Strolling companies gave plays and operettas. The earliest fencing exhibitions, a sport over which the city was to become impassioned, took place in this crude arena. So, too, did every kind of gathering that would attract large crowds, the serious one night, the equivocal or frankly indecorous the next. It was the scene of political rallies, and of masked routs promoted by the underworld. Most picturesque were the so-called quadroon balls, which began there but reached their apogee decades afterward in more gorgeous surroundings; they were dances held by the guardians of well-bred free colored girls who sought to place their wards advantageously as concubines. No man of Negro blood was allowed to attend these affairs. White women obviously would not have dreamed of going. The Creole blades made little secret of the fact that they found them more entertaining than the average society ball.

In 1808 the St. Philip Theater was completed, a far more pretentious building than had housed the Saint Domingue troupers, in fact the first real theater in New Orleans. The *haut monde* promptly moved over, leaving the Condé Street place to the quadroon balls and the rowdies. But the St. Philip was unfortunate. It had been in existence only five years when John Davis, the Saint Domingue entrepreneur, built the magnificent Théâtre d'Orléans a few blocks away, and alongside it the Salle d'Orléans with gaming rooms on the ground floor and a ballroom one flight up that was reputed to have the best dance floor in the United States. Suffice it to say that St. Philip languished by slow degrees and ended, ironically, by installing a permanent floor and becoming the Washington Ballroom, the favored resort of a demimonde more vulgar than that which had patronized the old hall on Condé Street.

The Théâtre d'Orléans had a beautiful exterior with Doric colonnades. Inside it was arranged like an opera house, its boxes luxurious and its loge seats adorned with lattice or iron grillwork. Davis set out to offer amusement on a prodigious scale. The bill would often start with a vaudeville at 6:00 P.M., followed by a comedy, and on top of that a serious drama which might run until two o'clock in the morning. But music was what charmed the aesthetic side of John Davis' nature. By engaging roving foreign singers and organizing his own stock company for the supporting cast, he introduced New Orleans to opera, its great and most lasting artistic love. After his death, his son Pierre carried on. Grand opera arrived in 1837 with Mlle. Julia Calvé in repertoire. She married Charles Boudousquié, the associate manager of the theater, who presently took over from the younger Davis. At the Orléans until 1859, and then at the French Opera House, which he built, Boudousquié was the impresario who set a standard that even New York did not equal for many a day. His work was ably continued by Placide Canonge. "Nowhere outside of Italy," says an old commentator, "was the opera ever so powerful or popular as in the Creole city."

James H. Caldwell erected the American Theater in the Faubourg Ste. Marie in 1823, the city's first building to be lighted with gas. He completed the St. Charles Theater in 1835. The English drama was developed at these two houses, and before long they had rivals. As in so many other things, New Orleans fell into separate camps where the stage was concerned. The American side of town did best with the legitimate theater, and the Vieux Carré with opera.

The chief interest of John Davis, to be sure, was gambling. His Salle d'Orléans had a rather plain façade. The rooms were finished with hardwoods, and in all the larger ones hung crystal chandeliers. Paintings and statuary regarded at the time as good, and in any event expensive, were lavishly displayed. The ballroom had a lofty ceiling, tastefully furnished loges, a balcony overlooking the garden close of the St. Louis Cathedral, and a stairway connecting with a courtyard where refreshments were served. Here the quadroon balls attained their full splendor. Officially they were called the Bals du Cordon Bleu. Few Louisiana historians have dealt with them candidly, but foreign visitors made penetrating comments, and now and then a Northerner glimpsed the truth that lay below the surface.

Bernhard, Duke of Saxe-Weimar Eisenach, writing of his travels in 1825, remarked that he had attended both the quadroon affairs and subscription masked dances given by white society, and that he found the former "much more decent." Yet the writer has seen him misinterpreted in print to the effect that he praised his first quadroon ball, was noncommittal about his second, and condemned his third as a "den of ruffians." Saxe-Weimar applied that epithet to the St. Philip Theater in its days of decadence, and on the occasion of a mixed masquerade which was followed by a fight. Harriet Martineau, in the middle 1830's, referred to the institution with sympathy for the colored girls, expressed as follows: "They are highly educated, externally, and are, probably, as beautiful and accomplished a set of women as can be found. Every young man early selects one and establishes her in one of those pretty and peculiar houses, whole rows of which may be seen in the Ramparts. . . . The quadroon women are rarely known to form a second connection. Some men continue the connection after marriage."

In the 1850's Frederick Law Olmsted wrote of these free women of color, in his *A Journey in the Seaboard Slave States:* "Their beauty and attractiveness being their fortune, they cultivate and cherish with diligence every charm or accomplishment they are possessed of. Of course, men are attracted by them, and, not being able to marry them legally, and with the usual forms and securities for constancy, make such arrangements 'as can be agreed upon.' When a man makes a declaration of love to a girl of this class, she will admit or deny, as the case may be, her happiness in receiving it; but, supposing she is favorably disposed, she will usually refer the applicant to her mother. The mother inquires, like a Countess of Kew, into the circumstances of the suitor; ascertains whether he is able to maintain a family, and, if satisfied with him in these and other respects, requires from him security that he will support her daughter in a style suitable to the habits she has been bred to, and that if he should ever leave her he will give her a certain sum for her future support, and a certain additional sum for each of the children she shall then have. . . . I do not mean that love has nothing at all to do with it; but love is sedulously restrained and held firmly in hand until the road of competency is seen to be clear, with less humbug than our English custom requires about it."

The negotiations described by Olmsted usually started at the balls held in the Salle d'Orléans, and also, when he wrote, in the Globe Ballroom, an advertisement of which he cites. There are almost no references to them in the newspapers of the times, for they functioned by tolerance and white women would have been offended if the affairs had been treated as legitimate news. They deteriorated and died slowly after the War between the States. In the early 1880's they were being held in the hall on Bienville Street, between Burgundy and Dauphine, and run—always with decorum—by a well-known procuress named Hermina. The late Lyle Saxon, a gifted and liberal writer, was an exception among Louisiana chroniclers in his effort to recreate sympathetically the atmosphere of the quadroon balls and their reason for being.* By a quirk of fate, the Salle d'Orléans has been since 1881 a convent for colored nuns.

Davis' gambling casino in connection with the salon was at its gaudiest from 1827 on to the 1840's. It operated around the clock, including Sundays when a banquet was served to all patrons gratis. Roulette was the favorite game. Davis also opened a scarcely less pretentious establishment on the Bayou St. John a short distance out of the city, and we shall note that he and Bernard de Marigny co-operated in bringing the thrills of chance to Mandeville. He had a host of emulators, some of whom were very successful without quite achieving the glitter which the old master knew so well how to capture. Hewlett's, in the former Bourse de Maspero on Chartres Street, was perhaps the next most famous palace of luck. St. Cyr's and Pradat's were liked by the elite. Harvey Elkin had run a gaming hall on Canal Street for Americans before he moved to Spanish Fort.

* Lyle Saxon, *Fabulous New Orleans* (New York: Century Co., 1928).

It is impossible to estimate the number of cheap places that flourished at any given period. There has been no end to them. A century ago the mob played faro, blackjack and keno by preference. Then they took up roulette and dice, and before long they went crazy over poker, the American game *par excellence.* Rules have been altered in some cases to step up the excitement, and mechanical innovations have crept in. But generally speaking the old pastimes continue to have the edge today.

Rich Orleanians often played as heavily in their homes as in the casinos. That great elegant of the 1830's and '40's, Antoine Julien Meffre-Rouzan, merchant and art collector, held regular sessions in his mansion on Dauphine and Esplanade. Before the guests arrived it was his custom to fill a Sèvres bowl, which stood inconspicuously on a table in an anteroom, with banknotes of all denominations. If any gentleman was embarrassed by losing the money he had brought, he stepped over to the bowl and took whatever he felt he needed to remain in the game. He could make as many such trips as he pleased, leaving his I.O.U. each time, of course. If still in the red when the play ended, he sent his messenger around the next morning with the sum owed. Meffre-Rouzan neither counted nor checked. In answer to a question, he once said with hauteur that he had never had reason to suppose that he had been taken advantage of.

Though Bernard de Marigny would bet anywhere and on any hazard, most of his ruinous play was done in private circles. He died at eighty-three, the owner of one small house on Frenchmen Street in his *faubourg,* where he had been living for several years hard pressed for ready cash. Colonel John R. Grymes, a leader of the bar from the first days of the Louisiana Purchase and a big money-maker, gambled so incessantly and with such bad luck that he, too, died poor. He once estimated his losses over the tables at $50,000 a year. There was scarcely a single prominent Orleanian, at least up till modern times, who did not pay his tribute to the blind goddess. Even the shrewd Judah P. Benjamin, marvelously successful attorney, political conjuror, the so-called "brains of the Confederate cabinet" in which he was Secretary of State, did not escape the infection.

Benjamin took pride in being a philosophical epicurean as well as a man of affairs. He practiced a cult of pleasure, on the theory that he—and not his appetites—was the master. He ate and drank as a gourmet. Though loyal in catering to the needs and whims of a selfish wife, he did not ignore the charms of other women. Notoriously, as he himself admitted, when it came to cards his control was often unseated. Benjamin, a model of inscrutable poise at his desk while the Confederate Government was tottering, found relaxation in winning and losing large sums in Richmond's clandestine salons.

Gambling on the Mississippi steamboats was an American phenomenon of such proportions that a literature of respectable size is devoted to it. George Devol, perhaps the most celebrated of the sleight-of-hand artists who prospered at the racket, described in a spicy book of memoirs his experiences of forty years. He boasted that he had "fought more rough-and-tumble fights than any man in America, and was the most daring gambler in the world." He and some of his colleagues took occasional flurries ashore, but oddly enough no casino in New Orleans opened by a river shark ever did well for long. A little professional gambling occurred on the lake boats; the field was too limited to appeal to the big-timers.

If grand opera was the medium through which New Orleans made its obeissance to art, and gaming was the city's pet vice, the imaginative impulses of an adventurous people much given to laughter seized upon the ancient practice of Carnival and shaped it into a unique instrument of fun. Every Catholic country celebrates this festival on the eve of Lent, culminating on Mardi Gras, the Tuesday before Ash Wednesday. The milder the climate, the more public the merrymaking. That is why there are elaborate carnivals at Naples and Nice, but none at Warsaw. It would be impossible to stage street revels in flimsy costumes amid the snows of a Polish winter. A literal translation of Mardi Gras into English is Fat Tuesday, but the French word *gras* carries other connotations than those of fat. It means good cheer, and to a certain extent license. The day is the last, until forty days afterward, on which the devout may eat meat and allow themselves certain other luxuries.

Iberville and Bienville entered the mouth of the Mississippi on March 2, 1799, which that year was Mardi Gras. The fact that they named a connecting waterway through which they passed the Bayou Mardi Gras shows that they brought the festival in their hearts. From the earliest times in Biloxi, Mobile and New Orleans the day was remembered, and when conditions in the colony became more settled it was always marked by feasting and spontaneous jollity outdoors. The first king and queen of Louisiana carnivals were inspired by a current fairy tale, and were called *Le Roi et la Reine de la Fève*. The *fève* was a sort of large bean. Masquerades became more and more common. The Spaniards, however, enforced a law against masking, chiefly because criminals were perverting the custom; too many men had been stabbed or robbed by individuals who escaped unrecognized behind their masks. This regulation was maintained for a long time after the Purchase, though not strictly. In 1824 carnival masquerades were advertised, and by 1827 they were legal once more.

That year a number of young Creole gentlemen, some of whom had just returned from college in Paris, organized the first grand street procession on Mardi Gras. There were sporadic repetitions during the next decade. In 1837, 1838 and 1839 the marchers filled the principal streets of New Orleans, and from then on public reveling of one kind or another was a fixture. The *Commercial Bulletin* wrote of the 1838 affair: "A delighted throng followed on the heels of the cavalcade as it marched through our city and suburbs, and wherever it went the procession raised a perfect hubbub and jubilee. The exhibition surpassed anything of the kind ever before witnessed here . . . carriages superbly ornamented—bands of music, horses richly caparisoned—personations of knights, cavaliers, heroes, demigods, chanticleers, punchinellos, etc., etc., all mounted." Confetti-throwing had not yet come in, but little boys carried bags of flour and dashed handfuls upon selected victims.

The idea of presenting scenes on floats originated in Mobile, where associated groups of celebrants called themselves Cowbellions de Rakin, because they had started out by making a hilarious racket with borrowed cowbells, rakes and other implements. It reached New Orleans in 1857 when the Mistick Krewe of Comus, organized above the Gem saloon on Royal Street, staged an elaborate pageant. That was the inception of the type of Mardi Gras that the Crescent City has made famous. The dozens of "krewes" that have since been born acknowledge Comus as their father. One and all have been, and are, secret societies which plan to astound and dazzle the public on the climactic day. A reporter of 1857 described the first Comus tableaux, *The Demon Actors in Milton's Paradise Lost,* as follows:

"This Krewe, concerning whose identity and purpose there had been such tortures of curiosity and speculation, made their *début* before the public in a very unique and attractive manner. They went through the streets at nine o'clock with torchlights, in a guise as much resembling a deputation from the lower regions as the mind could possibly conceive. The masks displayed every fantastic idea of the fearful and the horrible, their effect being, however, softened down by the richness and beauty of the costumes, and the evident decorum of the devils inside.

"After going through the principal streets and calling upon Mayor Waterman, for the purpose, we suppose, of obtaining a license to 'raise the supernatural' in the Gaiety Theatre, they proceeded to that elegant establishment in order to entertain the hosts of guests they had summoned. The interior of the theatre was decorated with a profusion of hanging wreaths and festoons of flowers. In a short time the doors were thrown open; all the space inside, apart from the floor and stage, was jammed with an audience composed of the elite of Louisiana and the adjacent States—none being in mask but the Krewe.

"In due time the Mistick Krewe appeared on the stage in the full glare of the lights. If we may so speak, they were beautiful in their ugliness—charming in their repulsiveness. There were upward of a hundred of them, and no two alike, whilst all were grotesque to the last degree. They represented the different characters with which religion, mythology and poesy have peopled the Infernal Regions, and which Milton has aggregated in his *Paradise Lost.*

"Four tableaux were given. The first represented Tartarus, the second the Expulsion, the third the Conference of Satan and Beelzebub, and the fourth and last the Pandemonium. At the conclusion of the tableaux the barriers were removed, and the brilliant audience crowded upon the dancing floor. The Mistick Krewe disbanded, dispersed among the crowd and joined in the dance in a manner which showed them to be very gentlemanly and agreeable devils."

The general scheme then adopted has been enlarged, owing to the multiplicity of carnival societies, but remains the same in essentials. Rex came on the scene in 1872 as the first King of Carnival, and offered the novelty of a pageant in daylight. The yearly competition for his post and that of his queen is terrific behind the scenes. Mardi Gras was made a legal holiday in 1875, and Rex has ever since been entitled on that day to issue proclamations which nominally take precedence over the city ordinances. The Negroes, who had always been employed as torchbearers for the parades, claimed an independent part with their Zulu organization in 1910. Bizarre comedy marks the antics of King Zulu.

Carnival was suspended during the four years of the War between the States, suppressed once in the Reconstruction period, halted again for two years in World War I, and four years in World War II. Mordant political satire has permeated the tableaux at times. Thus, in 1873, when the theme was *The World of Audubon,* the oppressors of the South were caricatured as beasts, birds and reptiles. The New Orleans Mardi Gras has been called "the most conspicuous survival of the medieval fete." It has also been said that no one, even though he be a native Orleanian, can understand all the ramifications of Mardi Gras unless he is a member of one of the older societies. Behind the mask of folly power has been exercised.

To meet the demands of an upsurging prosperity two hotels were built in the late 1830's which may be said to have set a standard that the rest of the country quickly adopted. The St. Charles and the St. Louis, of New Orleans, were the first great American hotels, antedating the famous Astor House of New York, one of the earliest buildings of that type in the North. They were more than caravansaries. Some of the city's most vital business was conducted in their rotundas. Indeed, they were commonly known as the St. Charles Exchange and the St. Louis Exchange. They were also the political centers of the state, the American faction rallying at the St. Charles, and the Creoles at the St. Louis. The tides of pleasure swirled about their banquet rooms and bars.

Promoted by James H. Caldwell and others in 1835, the St. Charles was built on the street of the same name and on the site where its modern successor stands. It had a portico of Corinthian columns and a high, white cupola said to be second in size only to the dome of the Capitol in Washington. A native rhapsodized as follows: "The traveler journeying this way, whether steaming up the Mississippi or whirling cityward from Lake Pontchartrain, could distinguish this dome from afar, resplendent under the rays of a Southern sun, like Henry of Navarre's famous white plume at Ivry. It was visible indeed fully forty miles away; was the first view the traveler got of the Crescent City, the last object that faded away in the dim horizon when cars or steamboats bade New Orleans adieu. In every town there is some representative building whose career is in itself a history of the city it adorns and beautifies. Such is the Parthenon to Athens, Notre Dame to Paris, and St. Mark's to Venice."

Hyperbole apart, there can be no doubt that the St. Charles was imposing against the dead level of the Mississippi delta. Lady

Wortley, making an American tour, called it the finest piece of architecture she had seen anywhere in the New World. There being no sugar or cotton exchanges, it was adopted by the merchants in those lines as their clearing house. The growth of the entire Faubourg Ste. Marie was stabilized around it as a core.

But the St. Louis, situated in the Vieux Carré, was really the more artistic building. Pierre Soulé, eminent lawyer and statesman, headed the company that erected it. Three or four years after the opening it was burned to the ground and promptly reconstructed along even more splendid lines. There was a wide, pillared arcade in front, and one entered the hotel between tall granite columns with capitals of cast iron. The rotunda was paved in varicolored marbles and decorated with murals by the younger Canova. The enormous dome, so low that it was necessary to stand back more than a block to see it, constituted the main architectural novelty. This dome weighed one hundred tons and was ingeniously composed of earthen cylinders fitted together by a method that had not been used since the Middle Ages. Auctioneers made the rotunda their headquarters. On the right side was a raised platform from which choice slaves were sold to the highest bidders.

The most successful of the early managers of the St. Louis was James Hewlett, who transferred to it many of the activities of his near-by exchange on Chartres Street. This included gambling, to which several suites on an upper floor of the hotel were devoted. Hewlett inaugurated a long series of subscription balls, which society patronized ardently. He staged a ball and supper in honor of Henry Clay, for which 200 persons paid $100 a ticket. The whole $20,000 is said to have been spent for food, rare wines, music rendered by the orchestra of the opera company at the Théâtre d'Orléans, flowers and decorations. In those days the sum was regarded as immense for a single entertainment.

A carpetbag government took over the St. Louis in 1874 and proclaimed it the Statehouse of Louisiana. It served that purpose for two years, during the course of which its furnishings were wrecked and befouled by vandal politicians. After a long period of neglect it was done over and renamed the Hotel Royal. But its popularity could not be recaptured. It was an empty shell when an anti-rat drive by Federal officials, in 1916, decided the owners to demolish it.

In addition to hotels, the 1840's brought the first modern apartment buildings to New Orleans. Therein lies a tale with a dramatic background. It will be recalled that the rich Spaniard, Don Andrés Almonester y Roxas, had restored the Cathedral, the Casa del Cabildo and other public structures after the two great fires that occurred toward the end of the eighteenth century. He was the owner of valuable lots on both sides of the Place d'Armes. Late in life he married into the De la Ronde family and had one daughter, Micaela, who inherited everything.

Micaela at sixteen became the wife of Joseph de Pontalba, a family connection, and the couple went to live in Paris. There were several children, but the marriage proved unhappy and a legal separation was had, vastly to the mortification of the husband's father and head of the family, the Baron de Pontalba. On a day of unsolved mystery, Micaela conferred with the old man behind locked doors. Pistol shots were heard, followed by silence. Servants had to break down a door. Pontalba was found with his brains blown out, a gun still clutched in his hand. The woman lay insensible, desperately wounded, a ball having passed through her breast. To the end of her life she never explained what had happened.

Although divorced, she assumed the courtesy title of Baroness de Pontalba. Her estate had reverted to her, and she managed it competently, holding her agents and attorneys to the strictest accountability. She was a terror to her lawyers, whose bills she always disputed. The mansion which she built in Paris was a show place. But she never lost her interest in New Orleans, or the admiration she had had as a young girl for Andrew Jackson. She talked politics like a man, truculently declaring herself a royalist in France, but a democrat in America. "Don't talk democracy to my son," she once said, "for he is a Frenchman, and Frenchmen are no more prepared for democracy than so many monkeys. Talk democracy to me, for I am a Jackson Democrat."

The 1848 revolution alarmed the baroness, and she concluded it would be wise to absent herself. Now was the time to revisit New Orleans and look after her property there. The sleepy old Place d'Armes struck her as being in need of a thorough renovation. First she persuaded the city fathers to chop down the fine old trees, some of which had stood for a century, a few perhaps from the time of Bienville, and she would landscape the ground at her own expense. Place d'Armes was an outdated name, anyway, she felt. So she got the state legislature to pass an act changing it to Jackson Square. Busily she started a fund to raise a bronze equestrian statue to the general, and of course gave a large subscription. The result is the figure by Clark Mills, frozen in a posture perilously close to lost equilibrium and flourishing a cocked hat for the birds to nest in, which has become the city's unofficial emblem. The fact that identical copies stand in front of the White House and in Nashville, Tennessee, has not prevented New Orleans from taking it to its heart.

Micaela's project for her own buildings was more original. Small Spanish buildings faced the north and south sides of the square. No doubt they were picturesque, but they could not hope to survive much longer in so prominent a location. Micaela tore them all down and erected in their place two four-story blocks of flats, designed by James Gallier, Sr., the ablest architect of his day. They still stand, charming examples of the Renaissance tradition, adapted to the locality by deep balconies with elaborate cast-iron grillwork, the brick of which they are built softened to an old rose by the years, the roofs covered with slates. The first and second stories have immense, high-ceilinged rooms, and the windows are proportionately tall. Known as the upper and lower

Pontalba buildings, they have become state property and fortunately are being preserved.*

They had just been completed in 1851 when Jenny Lind, the "Swedish Nightingale," arrived in New Orleans under the management of P. T. Barnum to sing at the St. Charles Theater. The Baroness Pontalba had the central apartment of her building on the St. Peter Street side specially furnished, staffed it with servants, induced the renowned chef Boudro to come there temporarily from Milneburg, and tendered it to Miss Lind free of charge. Rarely has there been so great a furor over an artiste, even in the warmhearted Creole city. Seats for the first concert were auctioned off, the initial sale being for $240. The Nightingale's carriage could scarcely make its way through the adoring crowds in the streets, and her receptions were crushes of the elite. Her engagement was prolonged to a month. Micaela de Pontalba reveled in the perspicacity that had led her to play hostess to so glittering a star; but following the *coup d'état* by Louis Napoleon in 1852, Paris once more appealed to her and she returned to pass the rest of her life by the banks of the Seine.

Those early '50's were remarkable for other theatrical prodigies. In 1853 Adelina Patti appeared as a child wonder on the same program with the violinist Ole Bull, and seven years later made a sensation in major roles at the French Opera House. Also in 1853 the dancer Lola Montez, who had been mistress of the King of Bavaria, filled the Varieties Theater for three months and divided the public into two camps. Her supporters won a clamorous victory for her over the minority who objected to her scarlet past.

Of cruder forms of entertainment there was no lack in New

---

* There is a story that before Micaela married Pontalba, her hand was sought unsuccessfully by John McDonogh, an American merchant. When she was planning her apartment buildings, she asked McDonogh's permission to use a narrow strip of land he owned in the the rear. Believing he had consented by word of mouth, she went ahead—and was promptly sued for damages by her old swain. McDonogh was one of three rich New Orleans eccentrics who left the bulk of their fortunes in benefactions to the public, the others being Alexander Milne and Judah Touro. All were bachelors, dressed shabbily and had the reputation of being "tight" with their money.

Orleans. Gaëtano's Circus, from Havana, set up its tents year after year in Congo Square during the early part of the nineteenth century, until raided one summer night by flatboat men from the Mississippi on a drunken spree. Dog fights, contests between wild beasts, and ratting matches were among the cruel sports patronized up to the period of reform in such things that followed the War between the States. An advertisement in 1853 announced that for twenty-five cents one could see a champion jackass named Rough and Ready tackle three large bulldogs. A serious attempt was made to introduce the classic Spanish bullfights. Cockfighting, of course, had a host of followers, the mains at lake-shore resorts being renowned.

A. Oakey Hall, *bon vivant* and wit, who later was elected mayor of New York, paid a visit to New Orleans in 1846-1847 and wrote a volume of light essays about it.* His fancy, emphatically, was for the American side of town. He called the St. Louis Hotel "the headquarters of Creole loaferism," and was irked by the mustaches he noted there. The St. Charles delighted him. He commented lyrically on "oysters and lunches, juleps and punches." He had a good word for the opera. But in a mood of unwonted solemnity, he complained as follows:

"The theatres and the opera are open of a Sunday night; bulls are sometimes baited in the Third Municipality of a Sunday afternoon; aeronauts ascend from shouting crowds, under the eaves of a well-filled church; cavalry in active exercise deaden the eloquence of a popular preacher; firemen in parade jostle returning congregations; infantry are at target practice on the Bayou Road; crowds of merchants throng the post-office lobbies at noontime. But so conspicuous is the excellence of the public *morality* that these things, which appear singular and reprehensible to a stranger, are little regarded by the great body of churchmen in the city."

---

* A. Oakey Hall. *The Manhattaner in New Orleans* (New York: Redfield, 1851).

New Orleans never has been known to change its Latin ways because of a visitor's admonition. It is by temperament less an American town than the capital of a Caribbean country. And the Anglo-Saxons who have become naturalized there have seemed to prefer it as it is.

CIVIL WAR SUBMARINE AND INVENTOR

This boat is one of the experiments of Captain Horace Lawson Hunley. He was greatly encouraged by the planter, Ruffin R. Barrow who was his principal financial backer.

Louisiana State Museum

GENERAL P. G. T. BEAUREGARD

Chapter 10

City of Terror

PHYSICAL setting and the mixed composition of the people worked together to give New Orleans a dark side. The number of crimes of violence was abnormally high at most periods of the city's history. Lawlessness was perhaps at its worst immediately after the Purchase, when the keelboatmen and flatboatmen of the middle frontier came down the Mississippi as traders and ran wild along the water front. The Creoles called them Kaintocks on the assumption that they were all from Kentucky, the territorial name which for some reason had registered. As the American section of town grew, a red-light district and gambling center of singular depravity was established to cater to these Kaintocks. The Vieux Carré also developed a sordid night life, side by side with its elegant extravagancies. Robbery under arms flourished in both camps, and murder was a commonplace. Other writers have dealt extensively with this phase of New Orleans life. It is not intended to rehash it here.

But the part played by disease—particularly the fantastic scourge of yellow fever, and in a lesser degree malaria—has not been adequately treated. To be sure, the chroniclers have reported lurid details. They have failed to give due emphasis to the point that the city's notoriety as a plague spot deterred many brilliant men from settling there, and its recurrent epidemics took a tremendous toll of those who ventured it. The digging of the Erie Canal and the building of the transcontinental railroad systems from east to west are not the only reasons why New Orleans dropped behind in the race to be the chief port of North America. Yellow jack is also to blame. And when the grim actor lost his role in the drama at the beginning of this century, ambition for the future was freed of a serious limitation.

Iberville, the discoverer, who had planned to return to Louisiana, died of yellow fever at the end of an expedition that had taken him to Havana. Tonty of the Iron Hand and Sauvole were among the pioneers who succumbed to the same malady on the Gulf Coast. A Spanish Governor, Gayoso de Lemos, was a victim, though some accounts say he dug his grave with his teeth. The mortality among soldiers and immigrants mounted to fifty percent in some years. On the negative side, Henry Clay as a young lawyer was offered a splendid connection, but refused to live in New Orleans because he feared the fever.

The disease is one of the oldest ills of mankind in the New World. It was known to the Aztecs, and Humboldt asserts that there are records of it dating from the eleventh century. Oviedo, the Spanish historian, tells of the great number of deaths among the followers of Columbus in 1494. During the following century Mexico was decimated by an epidemic. Père Dutertre and Père Labat, priestly memoirists of the French West Indies, both described the symptoms and progress of yellow fever, being the first to identify it for European physicians. Their work ranged from 1640 to 1706. Père Labat called the fever the *mal de Siam,* because he supposed that it had been brought on a ship arriving in Martinique from Siam. He evidently confused it with what he had heard about bubonic plague. But as the vessel in question had called at Brazilian ports en route, there is small doubt about the true source of infection. His name stuck briefly. It was as "the Siam disease" that the scourge reached Biloxi and Mobile in 1704.

Yellow fever caused the French expedition led by Pointis and Du Casse to abandon Cartagena in a hurry after the city had been looted in 1697. The English under Admiral Vernon were paralyzed for the same reason and before the same fortress in 1741. Campaigns, indeed whole wars, as well as large peacetime enterprises, have failed in the American tropics because of the intervention of yellow jack. The outstanding instance was in Saint Domingue, where the disease tipped the scales in favor of the revolutionists, first by ravaging the English troops that had been sent to aid the planters, and then—more sensationally—by reducing to impotence the French army under Napoleon's brother-in-law, Leclerc, on the heels of its sweeping reconquest of the island. Spain might have suppressed the Cuban insurrection of 1895-1898 if she had not lost 100,000 soldiers by death or invalidism to yellow jack, a larger army than the patriot cause ever had in the field. The French attempt to dig a canal at Panama in the 1880's was thwarted by an annual death rate in excess of 150 per thousand, even more than by managerial blundering and wastefulness.

But the perennial tragedy was the breaking out of epidemics in populous cities. The hot months of the year never passed without a number of communities being stricken somewhere around the Caribbean Sea and the Gulf of Mexico. The most afflicted port in the United States was New Orleans. The malady was as good as certain to appear there each summer, though fortunately it seldom reached epidemic proportions.

Yellow fever attacked the blood and the liver, then spread to the digestive tract, the kidneys and brain. It gave the skin a jaundiced color, hence the name. But the chief symptom was a black vomit, and the Spaniards called the evil *el vómito negro.* It ran its course in seven days, at the end of which time the patient either died or began to mend. For the first four or five days, however, there had simply been lassitude and mild pains. The sufferer had been able to move about, and usually persuaded himself that nothing was seriously wrong. At last he would be smitten with devastating fury. To this may be ascribed the many stories of persons being seen in "perfect health" one day and dying the next.

The scientific nature of yellow fever need not detain us. The disease is caused by a microscopic organism hostile to man which gets into the system, as with malaria, typhoid and other fevers. A fortuitous, original case must have been a rare occurrence. The calamity was that the infection could be transmitted from one ill individual to scores of others, and an endless chain built up. There was a sole means of transmission, the variety of mosquito named Stegomyia Calopus; but until the riddle was solved by United States Army Surgeons Reed, Carroll, Agramonte and Lazear in Havana, in 1901, humanity did not know that. Earlier generations were firmly convinced of the following errors: that yellow fever sprang from miasmas wherever there was foul water and heat, notably in the vicinity of tropical swamps; and that it was contagious.

Bizarre variations of these beliefs held sway. Pathetic, bungling methods of combating the scourge were practiced. A Dr. Wilson maintained in the 1840's that decaying wood was the cause. Some authorities held that bilge water in the holds of ships was supremely malignant. Certain houses where victims had died were thought to have become impregnated with the disease; they were "yellow-fever houses," and subsequent tenants were sure to fall ill. A building that got this reputation was destroyed. Rooms in which deaths had occurred were always fumigated by the prudent. Bed clothing and mattresses were burned. Frequently there was an effort to purify whole sections of towns by lighting bonfires in the streets, by burning chemicals and barrels of tar, and even by discharging cannon loaded only with gunpowder. Masks soaked with disinfectants were worn to prevent the inhaling of the poison.

Observers noted odd contradictions. During the blockade of the coast on both sides of Vera Cruz in the Mexican War, frigates that had become extremely dirty were spared the fever, while it developed aboard clean ones. At times, of course, it was the other way around. A hospital was placed on a small coral island, perfectly dry and healthy, yet men who had not been off it for weeks were attacked. On the ships and on the island, a single phenomenon had been constant. When strong and uninterrupted breezes blew from the mainland, the fresh cases had been numerous, and breezes from seaward had had the opposite effect.

Analyze the above points, and it will be seen that they all had a bearing on the simple but elusive truth. Where there was rotten wood and other forms of decay, there would be stagnant pools for mosquitoes to breed in. A house where several deaths had taken place was, likely as not, badly located from a health standpoint. Burning, fumigation and disinfectants killed a certain number of the insects, though far from enough to halt an epidemic. Offshore winds brought the Stegomyia to ships and islands, clean or unclean.

Dr. John Hastings, United States Navy, satisfied himself that yellow fever was not contagious. Writing in 1848, he declared that he had "slept for a considerable time, on repeated occasions, under the same roof and in immediate contiguity with patients laboring under every stage of the disease, from the very first day of the attack to the last hour of existence. I have also cut myself with a scalpel, when handling black vomit and other fluids and tissues of patients who died of yellow fever; and still suffered not the least inconvenience from this contact and exposure." He cited a Dr. Firth, who had inoculated himself harmlessly with serum drawn from a patient. But the worthy physicians had doubtless been exposed to mosquitoes during the course of their experiments. They had proved immune. Had they contracted yellow fever in the circumstances, they probably would have accepted the contagion theory. Which goes to show what a muddle science was in, lacking the key fact.

Even the mosquito had been weighed as a factor. Dr. Nott, of Mobile, Alabama, wrote in 1848, the same year as Dr. Hastings, that he had noticed the prevalence of mosquitoes wherever there was yellow fever, and that he believed it was due to the insects. Dr. Louis Daniel Beauperthuy, born in Guadeloupe, was more specific. In a scientific paper published in 1853, he stated: "The disease develops under conditions which favor the development of mosquitoes. The mosquito plunges its proboscis into the skin and introduces a poison which has properties akin to that of snake venom. . . . Marshes do not communicate to the atmosphere anything more than humidity, and the small amount of hydrogen they give off does not cause in man the slightest indisposition in equatorial and inter-tropical regions renowned for their unhealthiness. Nor is it the putrescence of the water that makes it unhealthy, but the presence of mosquitoes."

What Beauperthuy failed to account for correctly was the source of the virus with which the mosquito infected man. He thought that it was taken from extraneous decomposing matter; it did not occur to him that it might come from the blood of a previous human sufferer. Only as to the means of transmission was he clear, and in this he ran far ahead of his times.

New Orleans was helpless, through ignorance, under its many visitations before the darkness lifted. Reading the evidence, one is astonished that a city subject to such terrors was not abandoned. It would surely have been, but for the circumstance that those who recovered from yellow fever could regard themselves as exempt. Very rarely was a person hit twice by this disease. Also, the native-born were unlikely to contract it. The fortune seekers provided the mass of victims, and danger not yet experienced has seldom deterred men from taking chances.

In the last decade of Spanish rule there was only one year in which New Orleans had no yellow fever. Exact records were not kept until 1817, when 80 cases were listed. The malady raged violently in the summers of 1822, 1824, 1827, 1828, 1829 and 1830. It assumed a virulent form in the last four years. Almost a thousand died out of a population of about 75,000 in 1829, and the mortality in 1830 was equally heavy. A respite was had the following season. Then came the black years of 1832 and 1833 when the city was stricken by both yellow fever and Asiatic cholera.

The Reverend Theodore Clapp, a Presbyterian clergyman of New England birth who spent thirty-five years in New Orleans and passed through twenty epidemics, has given in his autobiography some of the best eyewitness accounts that we have. He was a man of unflinching courage and devotion to duty. The minister he succeeded had died of yellow fever, but Clapp seemed to have no fear for himself and never caught it. He writes:

"A fatal yellow fever had been spreading destruction in the city six weeks before the cholera commenced [September 1832]. Thousands had left it to escape this scourge. So that, at the time of the first cholera, it was estimated that the population did not exceed 35,000 inhabitants. . . . The same epidemic broke out again the following summer, in June 1833. In September of the same year the yellow fever came back again. So, within the space of twelve months we had two Asiatic choleras and two epidemic yellow fevers, which carried off 10,000 persons that were known, and many more that were not reported."

Decidedly cholera was the more serious factor in those two years. It had swept around the world, and New Orleans was one of the many places that suffered. But yellow fever, the ancient enemy, returned alone and did frightful damage in 1837, 1847 and 1853. Clapp says:

"The two most fatal yellow fevers which I have witnessed were those of 1837 and 1853. In the former year there were 10,000 cases of fever reported, and 5,000 deaths. The epidemics broke out about the middle of August and lasted eight weeks. . . . On the day of my arrival it rained incessantly from morning till night. In the space of twelve hours the interments were over 300. The same day I visited two unacclimated families belonging to my own church, who were all down with the plague. In these families were nine persons; but two of them survived. I knew a large boarding house for draymen, mechanics and humble operatives, from which forty-five corpses were borne away in thirteen days. A poor lady of my acquaintance kept boarders for a livelihood. Her family consisted of eight unacclimated persons. Every one of them died in the space of three weeks.

"Six unacclimated gentlemen, intelligent, refined and strictly temperate, used to meet once a week to enjoy music, cheering conversation and innocent amusements. They had been told that it was a great safeguard, in a sickly summer, to keep up good spirits and banish from their minds dark and melancholy thoughts. They passed a certain evening together in health and happiness. In precisely one week from that entertainment five of them were gathered to the tomb. One of the most appalling features of the yellow fever is the rapidity with which it accomplishes its purpose.

"There is some difficulty in arriving at the true statistics touching the epidemic of 1853. It was supposed by the best informed physicians that there were 50,000 or 60,000 unacclimated persons in New Orleans when the epidemic began, about the 1st of July. From that time to the 1st of November, the whole number of deaths reported were 10,300. Of these 8,000 died of the yellow fever. The physicians estimated that 32,000 of those attacked this year were cured. Of course, if this calculation be true, the whole number of cases in 1853 was 40,000.

"The horrors and desolations of this epidemic cannot be painted; neither can they be realized, except by those who have lived in New Orleans and have witnessed and participated in similar scenes. Words can convey no adequate idea of them. In some cases all the clerks and agents belonging to mercantile establishments were swept away and the stores closed by the civil authorities. Several entire families were carried off—parents, children, servants, all. Others lost a quarter, or a third, or three-fourths of their members, and their business, hopes and happiness were blasted for life. The ravages of the destroyer were marked by more woeful and affecting varieties of calamity than were ever delineated on the pages of romance. Fifteen clergymen died that season—two Protestant ministers and thirteen Roman Catholic priests. . . .

"The physiognomy of the yellow fever corpse is usually sad, sullen and perturbed; the countenance dark, mottled, livid, swollen, and stained with blood and black vomit; the veins of the face and the whole body become distended, and look as if they were about to burst. . . . Think, reader, what it must be to have one's mind wholly occupied with such sights and scenes for weeks together; nay, more—for months, for years!"

Mortality figures apart, the 1853 epidemic is generally held to have been the most gruesome of them all. August 31 that year was "Black Day," on which 230 deaths from yellow fever were reported. Incidentally, only 57 native-born Orleanians perished of the disease in 1853.

There were severe visitations in 1858 and 1867. But the next major disaster did not occur until 1878. Fortunately, too, this was the last that reached such huge proportions. Thereafter improved drainage served to keep down the number of mosquitoes. In 1878 children seemed abnormally susceptible. A single city block had 105 cases among the very young, with an average of five deaths a day. The total fatalities were almost 4,000. It was a bad year everywhere in the Mississippi Valley. Memphis had an epidemic that was relatively much worse than the one in New Orleans. The population of the Tennessee community was only 45,000, of whom 14,000 were Negroes; 17,000 were stricken and 5,000 died. The deaths of whites exceeded those of blacks in a ratio of more than four to one. Greenville, Mississippi, lost 400 of its 2,300 inhabitants.

The problem of the disposing of corpses during those seasons of terror may well be imagined. New Orleans had always had trouble with its cemeteries. The delta soil was so saturated with moisture that at a depth of three feet a grave began to fill with water. So vaults were built above ground, the pretentious ones containing shelves on which the caskets were placed, while others—the so-called ovens—were brick structures with horizontal cells into which the coffins were thrust from the outside and the open ends sealed. In an epidemic it was impossible to provide enough vaults. Trenches had to be dug and the human remains sunk in the mire. Even this crude procedure often proved inadequate, due to a shortage of coffinmakers and gravediggers.

In 1853 there were weeks when 300 funerals a day should have been held. This could not be managed. Mortuary carts went up and down the streets, the drivers shouting: "Bring out your dead!" The corpses, sometimes encased in the flimsiest manner, were loaded on top of one another, taken to the cemeteries and dumped out to await their turn for a grave. The New Orleans *Bee* furnished a glimpse of the conditions on August 9 that year: "Upon inquiry yesterday we ascertained that the festering and decaying bodies which had been deposited in the Lafayette Cemetery had at last been consigned to mother earth. The eyes will no longer be pained and the nostrils offended by the further continuance of the horrible neglect. The Mayor of our City, though absolutely destitute of all direct authority, upon learning the facts on Sunday, secured the labor of the chain gang and set them immediately to work."

People who could not regard themselves as acclimatized had only one recourse when a yellow-fever epidemic started. If their business permitted, they fled to the country for the hot months, and in any event they sent away their families. The favored refuges were the north shore of Lake Pontchartrain and the gulf coast of Mississippi. The deadly Stegomyia was to be found in those localities, and sporadic cases of fever occurred. Yet the infection never became a general menace among the pines or along the sandy beaches. Why? We must suppose that it was because the inhabitants were widely spaced, and a mosquito which had bitten a patient had few opportunities to transmit the virus.

Harriet Martineau remarks that she observed children who had been displaced so often and so suddenly that it had had a bad effect upon their nerves. The flippant Oakey Hall, recovered from a dose of yellow fever himself, describes a stampede of the unexempt, from merchants to pickpockets, on a July day when the Board of Health admitted that the scourge was in the city.

Obviously there was another side to the picture, or men would have gone mad. The Reverend Mr. Clapp quotes a doctor who declared that the native-born had greater freedom from ordinary diseases than urban dwellers in the rest of the country. Show him a Creole who had confidently sat out the 1833 terror, this doctor said, and he'd show you one of the heartiest men on earth. Let a person adopt the habits of the old population, and he should be insured at as small a premium as in any part of the United States. Clapp goes on: "I received this statement then with utter incredulity, but now I can cordially subscribe to its correctness. During eight months of the year New Orleans is blessed with an extraordinary degree of health. From the first of October to the ensuing summer the weather is generally more agreeable and salubrious than that of any other place with which I am acquainted."

In 1881 Carlos Finlay, a Cuban physician of Scots ancestry, struck closer to the truth than Beauperthuy had done. He told the Academy of Sciences, Havana, that mosquitoes conveyed yellow fever from man to man. In just what circumstances, he did not know. The theory was as good as ignored for twenty years. When Drs. Reed, Carroll, Agramonte and Lazear started their experiments for the American army of occupation, Finlay offered advice, and after every other approach had been tried they gave his a thorough test. They discovered that only the female Stegomyia transmitted the disease, that she incubated the germ only if she had sucked the blood of a patient within the first three days of his illness, and that she could pass it on only after a delay of from twelve to twenty days. The rest was easy. Treat the surface of stagnant water with oil and you destroy the unhatched larvae of Stegomyia. Fumigate with sulphur to get those on the wing. The carrier could be exterminated in a single season. This was done throughout the American tropics, and yellow fever sank into insignificance.

New Orleans was backward in adopting the measure. A mild epidemic occurred in 1905, and this stimulated the authorities to act. The Catholic archbishop, Chapelle, was a victim. There were 105 sufferers from the fever on August 12, but after that the situation cleared up rapidly. There has never been another outbreak, and the number of isolated cases in the past forty years could be counted on the fingers of both hands.

Malaria is less dramatic than yellow jack. A first attack is rarely fatal, but it can become chronic in the system, render the victim susceptible to other ills, and in the long run cause as many deaths as its notorious cousin. Some forms are more malignant than others. For example, the first Mrs. Jefferson Davis, who was a daughter of President Zachary Taylor and a sister of General Richard Taylor, C.S.A., died shortly after her marriage of a virulent malaria contracted in New Orleans.

In places where the environment is suitable, malaria is present during the hot weather every year. It may become epidemic, but because its progress is slow the public is inclined to underestimate the peril. New Orleans was plagued by it from earliest times. A variety of Anopheles mosquito is the carrier, a fact established in India by Surgeon Major Ross of the British Army, in 1897. He showed that the parasites absorbed with the blood of a human sufferer underwent further development in the mosquito, which itself became infected. Then when the malarious mosquito bit a healthy man, it infected him.

The Anopheles can be combated in precisely the same way as the Stegomyia. But the species is so numerous that the task of destroying it in any given section is prodigious. Since the early years of this century malaria has been brought under control in New Orleans. It has not yet been eliminated.

Chapter 11

The Code Duello

THE seigneurs and officers who led in the colonization of Louisiana came with arms at their sides and the tradition that the only way for gentlemen to settle their quarrels was in single combat. At the same time the duel had passed its peak at home, and serious attempts to suppress it were being made by the French Court. During the reign of Henry IV (1589-1610), it is estimated that some 4,000 men of the upper classes were killed in duels. Cardinal de Richelieu, the great minister in the next reign, struck resolutely at the habit and even went so far as to execute a nobleman and one of his seconds for having taken part in a fatal private contest. Louis XIV set up courts of honor before which offended parties were ordered to lay their cases, and he provided the severest penalties for those who took such matters into their own hands. Nevertheless, duels were being fought *sub rosa* all over Europe, and the Louisiana pioneers inevitably broke the law more freely than they might have ventured to do in France. The custom established itself firmly in New Orleans during the eighteenth century, under both the French and Spanish regimes, but it was not practiced to excess. After the Purchase it grew suddenly to be a mania, and for almost sixty years it was a most serious factor in the life of the community.

The fact that a usage—the duel with swords—which the modern mind regards as typically Latin should have flourished, as never before, among Creoles who had just come under Anglo-Saxon rule is not so surprising as it may seem at first blush. The Americans of that period also were mad about dueling, though they generally employed pistols. It was a natural temptation for the Creoles, resentful as they were of the change of sovereignty, to pick quarrels with the newcomers in such circumstances that the old resident was the one challenged and could fix the conditions. Many Americans were killed at the start because they had been maneuvered into fighting with swords. Then, as if to show that they were not mere assassins of strangers, the Creoles became more touchy over points of honor among themselves. The next phase saw the Americans taking up swordsmanship and the natives practicing with firearms. Presently contests were being waged with every kind of weapon, including sabers, rifles and shotguns. The elite, however, consistently preferred the rapier. It ceased to be a racial matter and was accepted as a New Orleans institution; if you lived in that city you took it for granted that you were not likely to get by without a few duels.

Certain moralists and religious persons, of course, were active in opposition. They succeeded in 1848 in having a constitutional clause adopted, disfranchising participants in affairs of honor. No dead letter was ever more completely stillborn. The clerk in charge of a voting booth who would have dared to bring this up against a gentleman presenting himself did not exist. But the Creoles were offended at the prohibition being in black and white. They protested bitterly that it was an attempt to drive men of courage from the state. Their representatives raised such an uproar in the legislature for four years that the clause was repealed in 1852. It took the vast bloodletting of the War between the States to cause a reaction against dueling.

Much has been written about the code that governed these encounters. At first it was very simple. If a man felt he had been affronted by another of his own social standing, he either challenged on the spot or sent a friend to demand satisfaction. There was no such thing as the other party explaining away the offense. He could offer an apology, but it was only the rare individual who would lay himself open to a suspicion of cowardice by apologizing, whether in the wrong or in the right. Seconds would be appointed, and these would arrange the details of the meeting. Occasionally they attempted to find a formula which would permit the principals to be reconciled without fighting. On the field it was the duty of the seconds to propose a reconciliation after one of the parties had been wounded no matter how slightly, or, in a duel with firearms, if there had been an exchange of shots with no hits. They were empowered to halt the affair if their principal had received a dangerous hurt—unless, as was often the case, the articles called for a fight to the death.

The impromptu bout came to be thought *déclassé*. There must absolutely be conferences in advance and a setting of the time and place. A French authority named Châteauvillard had drawn up an elaborate code to which the best opinion adhered. Governor John Lyde Wilson of South Carolina furnished embellishments with particular reference to the use of pistols. José Quintero, a Cuban, included every variation of punctilio in a book of rules that was the final word on the subject.

For example: The showing of resentment by means of a blow that inflicted, or was intended to inflict, injury was unpardonable. A man guilty of such crude behavior need not be challenged, but could be horsewhipped publicly by the offended person or his agent. A symbolic blow—usually given by flicking the face with a glove or handkerchief—avenged an insult, and if a duel were then sought it must be by the one receiving the blow. Should an individual decline a challenge from an equal he could be "posted" as a coward, by means of a signed statement affixed in public places, or a card in a newspaper. But it was allowable to refuse a challenge from a minor, if you had not made an associate of him; one who had been posted; one who had been publicly disgraced without resenting it; one whose occupation was unlawful; or one who was in his dotage, or a lunatic.

All of the above regulations were at times ignored. But generally the Louisiana code duello set standards of honor and courtesy that were held in scrupulous respect. There can be no doubt that with a threat of the kind hanging over them men were far more polite in their ordinary social relations than is the case today. The trouble was that they drew the point too fine. The smallest breach of etiquette, even unintentional; an awkward gesture; a slight hint of irregularity in a business deal—such trifles could and did result in the offender being called out.

Under the Spaniards a good many quarrels that originated in the Condé Street ballroom were settled right there. A space was cleared among the merrymakers, and the friends of the principals formed a ring to protect them while they fought. The police found this outrageous, as it surely was. So it became the custom to go to the garden behind the Cathedral. Later disputants at the St. Philip Theater and the Salle d'Orléans repaired to this same garden, which remains unaltered except that it is enclosed with an iron fence and is not open to the public. A great many encounters sprang from jealousy over some beauty at a quadroon ball, especially during the period when those unique social affairs were enjoying their greatest glory in the Salle d'Orléans.

As the duel became more formalized the meetings were held on the Fortin plantation to the northeast of the Bayou St. John, about where the New Orleans race track known as the Fair Grounds is now located. In 1834 the hotheads shifted to the Allard plantation, west of the bayou, because they had taken a fancy to the grove of oaks at the end nearest the city. This developed into the most celebrated dueling ground in America. The turf beneath three great trees called the Sisters was especially favored. Creoles spoke casually of settling their differences *"sous les chênes d'Allard,"* while Americans used the catch phrase "under the Oaks." The original trees draped in Spanish moss are to be seen today in City Park, which was created from the old plantation.

In the 1830's and 1840's, when the mania was at its height, an average of twelve duels a week were fought in the shade of Allard's Oaks. The record for a single day is believed to have been four. Nor was this the only meeting place. Large "galleries" of spectators were attracted to the well-known site. So parties who valued privacy would select some quiet spot on the shores of Lake Pontchartrain, or would cross the lake and do battle in the vicinity of Mandeville.

To keep in trim for the always imminent test, men practiced assiduously in the fencing academies. New Orleanians were addicted anyhow to swordplay as an art, or sport. But it is inconceivable that so many *salles d'escrime* would have prospered, had it not been for the stimulation afforded by dueling. Around 1840 there were between fifty and sixty academies, concentrated mainly in the four blocks of narrow Exchange Place running from Canal Street to St. Louis Street, and spilling over into Conti, Royal and Chartres. They were supported by the not more than 20,000 adult males of the upper classes then living in New Orleans. Some of the masters were immensely popular. In fact, they were the idols of the day, only to be compared with a matador in Spain, an Italian tenor, or a modern Hollywood star. Members of the Creole aristocracy accepted them as friends, at least in masculine circles. Young bloods imitated their mannerisms.

An early outstanding master was L'Alouette, an Alsatian, almost as renowned for his own affairs of honor as for his teaching. He killed a colleague named Shubra under the Oaks. Montiasse, another Alsatian, was a Napoleonic veteran. There were Cazères and the Rosière brothers, all from Bordeaux. Gilbert Rosière, called "Titi," had come to New Orleans to be a lawyer, but had spent his patrimony roistering with the gay blades he met, had turned to the foils to make a living and proved a great success. Most of the masters were French. The names of Labourette, Thimécourt, Dauphin, Bonneval, Reynaud and Monthiarch should be mentioned. Italians and Spaniards also figured. Poulaga, an Italian, made quite a stir. Pepe Llulla from the Balearic Islands had the reputation of being the leading all-around expert, with firearms as well as swords, among the masters who practiced in New Orleans.

Notable, considering the prejudices of the time and country, was the fact that several colored men competed on even terms with the white masters. The first was Black Austin, a free Negro, whose skill with the colichemarde (the type of rapier locally favored) gave him much prestige. Then came Robert Séverin, a mulatto, who fell in a duel while traveling in Mexico. But the greatest of them was Bastile Croquère, also a mulatto though of light complexion, whose personality and career were legendary. He had a good mind, had studied in Paris, and was as polished as any *boulevardier*. In addition to being strikingly handsome, he indulged a dandyism that would have been thought insufferable in any other man of color. His clothes, of somewhat eccentric cut, were made by the best tailors, and for jewelry he wore cameos: rings, bracelets and breastpins. His swordsmanship was so excellent that many regarded him as the supreme teacher. Croquère had fought and won duels in France, but that was the sole privilege denied him in New Orleans. Blades of the old families were willing to learn from him, or invite him to champagne parties; they never would have accepted his cartel.

It should be realized that before the War between the States, or more properly Reconstruction, the New Orleans attitude was not one of hatred or scorn of the Negro race. There simply was a sense of feudal superiority. The free persons of color formed an intermediary class, relations with which were governed less by taboos than by circumstances. The talent of Bastile Croquère made all the difference in the world. So did the comeliness and good breeding of some girl at a quadroon ball.

Accounts of actual duels are the best means of illustrating the grim melodrama and freakishness of the custom. Claiborne, the first American governor, had his troubles from the start. The Creole press attacked him mercilessly. He ignored printed stories to the effect that he was dissipated and uncouth, that he gambled at private houses and delighted the next morning in fining professionals $50 a head. Then, after he had been barely a year in office, his beautiful young wife died. There appeared a flowery prose poem, entitled "A Dream," which it was plainly hinted that the ghost of Mrs. Claiborne roamed the official mansion, lamenting the ill-treatment that had driven her to the grave. It was signed "Fidelis." Micajah Lewis, the governor's secretary and brother-in-law, investigated and found that "Fidelis" was one Robert

Sperry, no Creole, yet a bitter political opponent. A challenge was sent. They met with pistols, and at the first exchange Lewis was shot through the heart. He muttered, "I believe——" and fell dead. What that proved as to the significance of Sperry's "dream," nobody was able to figure out.

The following year, 1806, Daniel Clark, the territorial delegate in Congress, quarreled with the governor over rumors connected with the Burr conspiracy. Clark's language was so offensive that although Claiborne felt that as chief executive he should not set the example of dueling, he slipped off to a secret meeting. He was shot through the right thigh and lay disabled for over a month.

Bienaimé de Lauzon, the only son of a prominent *emigré* family from Saint Domingue, via Jamaica, took his sister to a ball at the Salle d'Orléans shortly after its opening. In those days it was customary for the ladies to return at the end of each dance to their places in a row of chairs against the wall. The room was jammed. To provide his sister with a chair, Lauzon passed one over the head of a young woman already seated. This person jumped up, clapped her hand to her heart, and gasped as if in alarm. Lauzon started to apologize, when the other's escort appeared and asked him icyly to step out onto the balcony for an explanation. Only ill-mannered fellows frightened women by passing chairs over their heads, the escort said. Lauzon resented the words and tone. Seconds were appointed. The ladies were not told about the challenge. The next afternoon Mme. de Lauzon, seated at a window, overheard a passer-by say, "That is sad about Bienaimé." His companion questioned, "What is sad?" and the reply came: "Shot dead in a duel. They are bringing home his body." The mother fainted. The sister was away visiting and actually went to another ball that evening in ignorance of the facts.

As with so much else in the history of nineteenth-century New Orleans, it is impossible to write about dueling and not bring in the name of Bernard de Marigny. He was a clever swordsman and somewhat of a fire-eater. Far more bouts are credited to him than he could conceivably have fought, but some fifteen appear to have been authentic. The details even of these are obscure, because he was too much the grand gentleman to make a show of his private quarrels. There is a story that while he was a member of the state legislature he took offense at the remarks of a fellow member named James Humble, a blacksmith by trade, and sent him a challenge. The other stipulated that the encounter should "take place in Lake Pontchartrain in six feet of water, sledgehammers to be used as weapons." As Humble was nearly seven feet tall and Marigny less than five feet eight inches, the Creole had no choice but to laugh it off. Not a bad story, and one that has found its way into a dozen books. Unfortunately the rolls fail to show that there ever was a Louisiana legislator named Humble. Nor would Bernard de Marigny have dropped a challenge once issued. He would have appealed the nonsense about six feet of water and sledge hammers to a court of honor, obtained a verdict and forced the blacksmith either to fight according to the code or let himself be horsewhipped out of public life.

Another tale concerns the two duels in which his brother-in-law, the attorney Alexander Grailhe, was a principal. Marigny called Grailhe to account for making too free with property in the name of the attorney's wife. The dispute ended "under the Oaks," when Marigny thrust his opponent through the body, inflicting an injury which thereafter caused Grailhe to walk with his head and shoulders bent forward. The sequel, as ordinarily reported, is that they fought again (motive not given) and that Bernard said, "This time I shall try to straighten him!" Lo and behold, the lawyer's new wound caused him to lose his forward bend, but gave him a backward one. The truth seems to have been still more curious, an amazing example of the working of luck.

An abscess had formed inside the chest cavity close to the spine, as a result of the thrust Grailhe had received from his brother-in-law. The surgeons of that day did not dare operate. The lawyer went around stooped and emaciated, obviously a doomed man. In a café one afternoon he got into an argument with an acquaintance—not Marigny—felt that he had been insulted and required satisfaction. The other answered, courteously and with justice, that he would be accounted a murderer if he fought an opponent in Grailhe's physical condition.

"You are thinking of swords," snarled Grailhe. "Of course I can't hold a sword, but I'm just as capable of aiming and firing a pistol as I ever was."

Still the other demurred, but the crippled hothead was so insistent that he had to be given his way. His antagonist's ball pierced his chest, and in its passage literally shot out the abscess. The loser soon recovered his health, whereas if he had not fought that duel he would almost certainly have died within a month or two.

Some versions of the incident hold that the first encounter was with Numa Augustin and the second with Bernard de Marigny. You may take your choice. Grailhe ran afterward for the mayoralty, losing to John T. Monroe, whose firm conduct in City Hall when New Orleans was captured by the Federals won lasting celebrity.

In the 1840's a young Creole caused a sensation by meeting a French officer on horseback with broadswords. Space and a clear field were needed, so they chose the Plaine Raquette, an amusement ground in the Faubourg Marigny. An eyewitness is quoted as follows: "It was a handsome sight. The adversaries, stripped to the waist, were mounted on spirited horses. They rode up, nerved for the combat; the Frenchman heavy, somewhat ungainly, but with muscles like whipcords and a broad, hairy chest, which gave every evidence of strength and endurance; the Creole, lighter in weight, admirably proportioned, counterbalanced with youthful suppleness his adversary's rigid strength. A clashing of steel... and the Creole, by a rapid half-circle, and by a *coup de pointe à droite* plunged his blade through the body of the French officer."

In another cavalry duel, Colonel Schomberg of the United States Army met Alexandre Cuvilier on D'Aquin's green, near Carrollton, and escaped with his life because Cuvilier's broadsword missed him by a hair and killed his horse instead.

Those 1840's saw high tide for the duel, and also the spread of extravagant variations which were to bring the whole business into disrepute. Nothing could have been worse for the dignity of the code than the affray forced upon Alcée La Branche by an editor named Hueston. La Branche was a prominent Creole, a Democrat who had been the first United States chargé d'affaires to the republic of Texas, and then Speaker of the lower house in his own state. He had already been involved in a fantastic clash. While sitting as Speaker one of his rulings had incensed old John R. Grymes, the famous lawyer, *bon vivant* and gambler. Rushing down the aisle, Grymes drew a pistol and fired at La Branche. The latter promptly produced a weapon of his own and returned the fire. Neither man was hit. This is sometimes called La Branche's "first duel," but it was in no sense an encounter the code would have recognized. Nor did it lead to a challenge. Oddly enough, La Branche had never had occasion to send or receive one. Then, in 1843, he ran for Congress from a New Orleans district.

All the Whig papers assailed him, naturally. Hueston, in his Baton Rouge *Gazette,* surpassed all bounds by advising the voters not to disgrace themselves by electing a man so craven that he had managed not to have a record on the field of honor. When La Branche next ran into Hueston there was an unseemly brawl, followed by a challenge. The editor insisted on double-barreled shotguns loaded with ball, a barbarism that threw off the marksman's aim. There were two exchanges without damage. La Branche was willing to call it quits, but Hueston clamored that he had come there to kill or be killed. On the third exchange the editor was wounded slightly, and on the fourth he was fatally blasted through both lungs. La Branche escaped without a graze.

During that same political campaign, United States Senator George A. Waggaman was killed by Denis Prieur, the man who had served longest as mayor of New Orleans, ten years. A few years afterward Prieur's nephew, George W. White, was forced into a grotesque duel. One P. Le Blanc became furiously offended at some insult he believed had been offered him by the managers of a public ball. He made up his mind that he would compel at least one of the managers to give him satisfaction, so he put all the names in a hat and drew one, that of White. Meeting his man a little while after on the street, he abused him grossly and was challenged. Le Blanc was the more experienced duelist. But White fired the instant the signal was given and wounded him mortally. Le Blanc's pistol went off in the air as it dropped from his hand.

The hunting rifle was occasionally employed. One of the most sensational of these clashes took place in the pine woods near Mandeville, in the early 1840's, between Colonel S. L. Oakey, of New Orleans, and an Englishman named Wright who had recently arrived from Savannah, Georgia. Both were in the cotton business, Oakey being a large commission merchant and Wright a buyer for interests in the North and abroad. For some time a series of unsigned letters which cast aspersions upon the methods of New Orleans cotton houses had been appearing in the *Sentinel* of Vicksburg, Mississippi. That the author lived in the Crescent City seemed probable from interior evidence; it was thought despicable that he should launch his attacks in an out-of-town newspaper, as if hoping thereby to evade the consequences.

Oakey conducted an investigation, learned that Wright was the person responsible and challenged him. The Englishman blustered and bluffed. He chose rifles and let it be known that he was a dead shot. Oakey was not very familiar with the weapon. It was even said that he had never fired a rifle, but that may be discounted. He did tell his seconds that he felt there was nothing to be gained by practicing at a range in the short time left to him. On the appointed day a large party crossed the lake and massed on both sides of the forest clearing that had been selected. The opponents stood only forty paces apart. At the word Wright blazed away like a novice, and missed. Oakey fired once, dropping his man with a bullet through the heart.

Sometimes affairs of honor were amiably conducted. The New Orleans *Delta* of February 3, 1860, reports: "A hostile meeting took place yesterday morning at the Half-way House between two young Creoles of this city; and it was all about a girl. We have not had the pleasure of knowing the young lady, but have it on the best authority that she is 'divinely fair,' and as good as she is fair. Were she to know what went on yesterday on her account, her humiliation and sorrow would have been unbearable. Fortunately, however, no great damage was done. The weapons were small-swords. At the second pass, one of the duelists received a flesh wound in the arm. After the affair, the successful duelist treated all the parties to the affair to a breakfast at the Half-Way House, during which much champagne was put away."

Tradition has it that women fought duels now and then in old New Orleans. The serious encounters of this kind, if any, were effectively hushed up. But in 1844 the *Picayune* reported that "two girls of the town, with their seconds, who were also girls, were arrested by the police when about to fight a duel." The party was cornered near the Bayou St. John with pistols and bowie knives in its possession. All the women were held for trial before a magistrate.

It may seem a bit absurd or lacking in humor for fencing masters to have been the persistent duelists that they were in New Orleans. Some of their bouts were over trivialities. Gilbert Rosière, for instance, was once weeping copiously during a favorite aria at the opera. A young man in the audience laughed at him. "If I weep, I can also fight," said Rosière, and in the morning he proved it by pinking the youth neatly. But on the whole the masters treated combat as so much publicity for themselves, and as a means of thinning the ranks in a crowded calling.

At a grand exhibition of masters in 1840, Thimécourt outpointed the Italian, Poulaga, with the broadsword. Poulaga had had the reputation of being unbeatable with that arm. He was so mortified that he demanded and obtained a renewal of the test on the field of honor the next day. It proved one of the most terrible and bloody fights ever staged in the city. Thimécourt wore down the Italian, who refused to surrender, and was finally compelled to kill him. On another occasion the master Monthiarch challenged Thimécourt with little better success. When his chest was laid open and his antagonist declined to meet him for another reprise, Monthiarch stuffed his ghastly wound with a handkerchief, and brushing the surgeon aside he left the field, complaining bitterly that the times were becoming soft.

The most relentless killer of the lot was José (Pepe) Llulla. His vivid personality and odd name made a hit with writers, who gave him a good press, and as a result he is one of the best remembered figures. Pepe reached New Orleans about 1840 and became a bouncer in a sailors' boardinghouse. He impressed L'Alouette with a demonstration of his natural skill, and the old master accepted him as a pupil. Soon he was the biggest drawing card at L'Alouette's academy. After he had opened his own place, he developed into a bully around town and stood ready to fight with every imaginable weapon. He is said to have sent twenty men to their graves. Proclaiming himself a Spanish royalist, he hounded Cuban refugees in New Orleans, forced several into unequal contests and slew them. He received a decoration for this from the Spanish government. Logically enough, on retiring from the arena he became the manager of a cemetery.

All journalists, but notably critics, were men who had to be careful what they wrote. Emile Hiriart, dramatic critic of the *Delta,* had to fight three duels on three successive days in 1859, because he had cast aspersions on the artistic talents of a Mlle. Bourgeois of the Opera and referred sarcastically to "the lady's admirers among the dilettanti." Two of the contests were inconclusive. He shot dead his third opponent.

Dueling rapidly declined after the War between the States. By 1880 the practice was downright unfashionable. The last recorded meeting was in 1888, when five shots were exchanged harmlessly between André L. Roman, editor, and Emile Ribore, business manager, of a French language newspaper.

Chapter 12

Cruelty and Black Magic

In April 1835, a celebrated English visitor in the person of Harriet Martineau, the writer, came to New Orleans. She was the first foreigner of importance to arrive by a steamer on the lake route from Mobile. Her leisurely tour of about a year through the United States resulted in two books, *Society in America* and *Retrospect of Western Travel,* which were very widely read on both sides of the Atlantic. Miss Martineau was one of those busy, fluent authors capable of turning out a couple of best sellers each year, who are undeservedly forgotten because of the topical nature of their work. The next generation regards them as outdated reporters, ignoring the point that if we wish to learn the truth concerning a given period there is no sounder guide than a good contemporary journalist. Harriet Martineau brought certain antipathies in her intellectual baggage, notably a detestation of slavery. But it is admitted that she gave an unbiased account of that institution as she saw it in practice. Her style is lucid, and her books are as readable as though they had been written yesterday.

She describes the impression made on her by a first glimpse of the Gulf of Mexico under a torrential rain with rolling thunder and sheets of lightning, and goes on: "It soon grew dark; before morning we were in Lake Pontchartrain, so that this stormy view of the gulf was the only one we had. We amused ourselves in the morning with tracing the dim shores. . . . About nine o'clock we arrived in sight of the long piers which stretch out from the swamp into the lake, the mudcraft, the canoes with blacks fishing for crabs; the baths, and the large Washington Hotel with its galleries and green blinds, built for coolness, where gentlemen from New Orleans go to eat fish and bathe. Next we saw the train of railroad cars waiting for us; and, without the loss of a moment's time, we were whirled away to the city, five miles in a quarter of an hour."

A few days later she took a carriage drive in the contrary direction, and this is what she has to say about the route: "To the lake on a fine afternoon. This road winds for five miles through the swamp, and is bordered by cypress, flowering reeds, fleurs-de-lis of every color, palmetto, and a hundred aquatic shrubs new to the eye of the stranger. The gray moss common in damp situations floats in streamers from the branches. Snakes abound, and coil about the Negroes who are seen pushing their canoes through the rank vegetation, or towing their rafts laden with wood along the sluggish bayou. There is a small settlement, wholly French in its character, where the ancient dwellings, painted red and with broad eaves, look highly picturesque in the green landscape. The winding white road is thronged with carriages driven at a very rapid rate and full of families of children, or gay parties of young people, or a company of smoking merchants going to the lake to drink or to bathe. Many go merely as we did, for the sake of the drive and of breathing the cool air of the lake, while enjoying a glass of iced lemonade or sangaree. It was along this road that Madame Lalaurie escaped from the hands of her exasperated countrymen about five years ago."

The chief reason for introducing Harriet Martineau is the fact that she reported the case of the notorious Madame Lalaurie. Dozens of others have dealt with it. There are few books on New Orleans which do not retell the story of the cruel mistress who tortured and killed her slaves in what became the "haunted house" on Royal Street. But the ghostly element has been overdone, and at the same time there is a tendency in some versions to make out that her character never was so black as it had been painted. Extenuating circumstances are advanced in her favor. It is argued that members of her immediate family were massacred in a slave revolt, and that thus her reason had been affected. A few apologists go so far as to maintain that the business was a canard designed to bring her into disrepute; she was a good woman, really, and her prominent connections should not be embarrassed by the old gossip.

Truth is all that matters, especially more than a century after the event, when the contention that the feelings of living persons might be hurt no longer has weight. Early aspects of the affair reached the courts, and although there was no trial for murder to bring everything to light, the newspapers of the day give frank reports of the closing scene. Also, there is the testimony of Harriet Martineau. Her second book, *Retrospect of Western Travel,* quoted above, was published in 1838, which accounts for her statement that Madame Lalaurie escaped "about five years ago." The actual date was April 10, 1834. Miss Martineau was in New Orleans just one year later, and it is difficult to believe that a conscientious writer like her would have set forth mere sensationalism which she had failed to investigate. At the very least, she was recording what she was told by Creole friends who would have been unlikely to slander a member of their own race to a foreigner. She says that she was asked not to publish the story "as exhibiting a fair specimen of slaveholding in New Orleans, and no one could suppose it to be so; but it is a revelation of what may happen in a slaveholding country, and can happen nowhere else."

Madame Lalaurie had been born Delphine Macarty, a descendant of the pioneer French-Irish family into which Don Esteban Miró, the Spanish governor, married. Before Lalaurie she had two husbands, a Spaniard named Ramón de López and a rich New Orleans banker and legislator named Jean Blanque. She had one daughter by López, and a son and three daughters by Blanque. Perhaps significantly, both these men died suddenly. It would add to the macabre fantasy if research should one day prove that Delphine had started as a husband-poisoner. She took her third mate, Dr. Louis Lalaurie, in 1825, when she was about forty-five. Little is known about him except that he was of French birth and manifestly not rich, since it was Delphine herself who purchased the site and erected the house he is credited with having built for her at an approximate cost of $100,000. The structure now to be seen at the corner of Royal and Governor Nicholls (formerly Hospital) Streets is of three stories, French Empire style, with classic scrollwork, arabesque figures and an unusually beautiful doorway. It is said to be a faithful restoration, though architects think that the top floor has probably been enlarged from an attic.

The Lalauries moved into the house in 1832. They were to be there only two years, which was a short space of time in that leisurely age for the development of a hostile public opinion against a carefully guarded private household. But let Harriet Martineau be the chronicler.

"It had been long observed," she writes "that Madame Lalaurie's slaves looked singularly haggard and wretched, except the coachman, whose appearance was sleek and comfortable enough. Two daughters by a former marriage, who lived with her, were also thought to be spiritless and unhappy-looking. But the lady was so graceful and accomplished, so charming in her manners and so hospitable, that no one ventured openly to question her perfect goodness. If a murmur of doubt began among the Americans, the French resented it. If the French had occasional suspicions, they concealed them for the credit of their faction. 'She was very pleasant to whites,' I was told, and sometimes to blacks, but so broadly as to excite suspicions of hypocrisy. When she had a dinner-party at home she would hand the remains of her glass of wine to the emaciated Negro behind her chair, with a smooth audible whisper, 'Here, my friend, take this; it will do you good.'

"At length rumors spread which induced a friend of mine, an eminent lawyer, to send her a hint about the law which ordains that slaves who can be proved to have been cruelly treated shall be taken from the owner and sold in the market for the benefit of the State. My friend, being of the American party, did not appear in the matter himself, but sent a young French Creole who was studying law with him. The young man returned full of indignation against all who could suspect this amiable woman of doing anything wrong. He was confident that she could not harm a fly, or give pain to any human being.

"Soon after this a lady, living in a house which joined the premises of Madame Lalaurie, was going upstairs when she heard a piercing shriek from the next courtyard. She looked out and saw a little Negro girl, apparently about eight years old, flying across the yard towards the house, and Madame Lalaurie pursuing her, cowhide in hand. The lady saw the poor child run from story to story, her mistress following, till both came out upon the top of the house. Seeing the child about to spring over, the witness put her hands before her eyes; but she heard the fall and saw the child taken up, her body bending and limbs hanging as if every bone was broken. The lady watched for many hours, and at night she saw the body brought out, a shallow hole dug by torchlight in the corner of the yard and the corpse covered over.

"No secret was made of what had been seen. Inquiry was instituted and illegal cruelty proved in the case of nine slaves, who were forfeited according to law. It afterward came out that this woman induced some family connexions of her own to purchase these slaves and sell them again to her, conveying them back to her premises in the night. She must have desired to have them for purposes of torture, for she could not let them be seen in a neighborhood where they were known.

"During all this time she does not appear to have lost caste, though it appears that she beat her daughters as often as they attempted in her absence to convey food to her miserable victims. She always knew of such attempts by means of the sleek coachman, who was her spy. It was necessary to have a spy, to preserve her life from the vengeance of her household; so she pampered this obsequious Negro, and at length owed her escape to him.

"She kept her cook chained within eight yards of the fireplace where sumptuous dinners were cooked in the most sultry season. It is a pity that some of the admiring guests whom she assembled round her hospitable table could not see through the floor and be made aware at what a cost they were entertained. One morning the cook declared that they had better all be burned together than lead such a life, and she set the house on fire. The alarm spread over the city; the gallant French Creoles all ran to the aid of their accomplished friend, and the fire was presently extinguished.

"Many whose curiosity had been roused about the domestic proceedings of the lady, seized the opportunity of entering those parts of the premises from which the whole world had been hitherto carefully excluded. They perceived that, as often as they approached a particular outhouse, the lady became excessively uneasy lest some property in an opposite direction should be burned. When the fire was extinguished they made bold to break open this outhouse.

"A horrible sight met their eyes. Of the nine slaves, the skeletons of two were afterward found poked into the ground, the other seven could be scarcely recognized as human. Their faces had the wildness of famine, and their bones were coming through the skin. They were chained and tied in constrained postures, some on their knees, some with their hands above their heads. They had iron collars with spikes which kept their heads in one position. The cowhide, stiff with blood, hung against the wall; and there was a stepladder on which this fiend stood while flogging her victims, in order to lay on the lashes with more effect. Every morning it was her first enjoyment after breakfast to lock herself in with her captives and flog them till her strength failed.

"Amid shouts and groans, the sufferers were brought out into the air and light. Food was given them with too much haste, for two of them died in the course of the day. The rest, maimed and helpless, are pensioners of the city.

"The rage of the crowd, especially of the French Creoles, was excessive. The lady shut herself up in the house with her trembling daughters, while the street was filled from end to end with a yelling crowd of gentlemen. She consulted her coachman as to what she had best do. He advised that she should have her coach to the door after dinner, and appear to go forth for her afternoon drive, as usual; escaping or returning, according to the aspect of affairs. It is not told whether she ate her dinner that day or prevailed on her remaining slaves to wait upon her. The carriage appeared at the door; she was ready and stepped into it. Her assurance seems to have paralyzed the crowd. The moment the door was shut they appeared to repent having allowed her to enter, and they tried to upset the carriage, to hold the horses, to make a snatch at the lady. But the coachman laid about him with his whip, made the horses plunge, and drove off.

"He took the road to the lake, where he could not be intercepted, as it winds through the swamp. He outstripped the crowd, galloped to the lake, bribed the master of a schooner which was lying there to put off instantly with the lady to Mobile. She escaped to France and took up her abode in Paris under a feigned name, but not for long. Late one evening a party of gentlemen called on her, and told her she was Madame Lalaurie, and that she had better be off. She fled that night, and is supposed to be now skulking in some French province under a false name.

"The New Orleans mob met the carriage returning from the lake. What became of the coachman I do not know. The carriage was broken to pieces and thrown into the swamp, and the horses stabbed and left dead upon the road. The house was gutted, the two poor girls having just time to escape from a window. They are now living, in great poverty, in one of the faubourgs. The piano, tables and chairs were burned before the house. The featherbeds were ripped up and the feathers emptied into the street, where they afforded a delicate footing for some days. The house stands, and is meant to stand, in its ruined state. It was the strange sight of its gaping windows and empty walls, in the midst of a busy street, which excited my wonder and was the cause of my being told the story the first time. I gathered other particulars afterward from eyewitnesses.

"The crowd at first intended to proceed to the examination of other premises whose proprietors were under suspicion of cruelty to their slaves; but the shouts of triumph which went up from the

Bureau of New Orleans News

AMERICA'S FIRST APARTMENTS

The Pontalba Apartments were built over a century ago by the Baroness Pontalba, daughter of Don Andres Almonester y Roxas. Of especial note are the exquisite iron railings with their frequent repetition of the monogram A-P.

Bureau of New Orleans News

JACKSON SQUARE

The old Place d'Arms of Bienville's time is now known as Jackson Square. From left to right are the Cabildo, Saint Louis Cathedral, the Presbytere and the Pontalba Apartments.

ADAH ISAACS MENKEN

whole Negro population of the city showed that this would not be safe. Fearing a general rising, the gentlemen organized themselves into a patrol, to watch the city night and day till the commotion should have subsided. They sent circulars to all proprietors suspected of cruelty, warning them that the eyes of the city were upon them. This is the only benefit the Negroes have derived from the exposure."

Miss Martineau's account appears to owe something to a contemporary news story in *L'Abeille* of New Orleans, which has been characterized as an early example of yellow journalism. But she also cites "friends" and eyewitnesses" in terms that are weighty coming from a writer of her standing. She is guilty of a few errors of fact. For instance, Madame Lalaurie did not catch a boat directly to Mobile from the Bayou St. John, but crossed to Mandeville on the north shore of Lake Pontchartrain, where a week later she and her husband are known to have been the guests of one Louis Coquillon. The Lalauries then went to Paris together, and lived there unmolested until Delphine's death in 1842. If the husband's attitude seems to have been singularly tolerant, it must be remembered that it was the wife who had the money. Miss Martineau's assertion that the two unmarried daughters—Pauline and Laure Blanque—had been reduced to poverty is unbelievable; this, like the tale of the mother's degradation in France, could have been based only on hearsay afterward when the book was written.

However, the body of Harriet Martineau's report holds up. Even the apologists admit that slaves were found chained in their quarters at the time of the fire, and that an indignant crowd smashed the premises. It would have taken abnormal severity toward bondfolk to upset the public of that day. Madame Lalaurie was a sadist, and small doubt about it. Soon her deserted dwelling became *the* haunted house of the Vieux Carré, though there were others to which tales of the supernatural had clung from earliest times. After it was rebuilt it passed through the hands of several owners, then became in succession a school, a gambling house, a social welfare institution, and an apartment building. Always there have been tenants who vowed that they saw ghosts there, the favorite story being that of the little Negro girl re-enacting her leap to death from the roof to the courtyard.

The second most celebrated haunting in the city is supposed to take place atop the roof of a house on Royal Street near Orleans Street. The specter of a nude quadroon girl walks back and forth wringing her hands on certain nights in winter, those laying claim to "second sight" aver. She had been the mistress of a Creole blade. When she tried to induce him to marry her, he promised flippantly that she would have her wish if she proved her love for him by spending the night on the roof, naked and alone. Why this would prove anything, especially love, is not clear. It was December and unusually cold. The girl took him seriously. Within a few hours she had frozen to death. One might think his spirit would find it harder to rest than hers.

To return to the lake—a form of the miraculous has been closely linked with the shores of Pontchartrain. This is voodoo, a primitive animist cult of Dahomey on the West Coast of Africa, which was first brought by slaves to the French colonies in the West Indies, and introduced into Louisiana at the time of the black revolution in Saint Domingue. There had been talk of it earlier as a menace. Governor Bernardo de Gálvez had forbidden the importation of slaves from Martinique, because the cult was rife among them. The matter became serious when refugee planters and their families began to arrive, in many cases accompanied by faithful Negroes. Included among the latter were numbers of voodooists. Governor Carondelet forbade the admission of any more blacks from Saint Domingue. His orders were evaded. The prefect, Laussat, during the short French restoration of 1803, was the only ruler who actually turned back a shipload of island Negroes. All restrictions were removed by Claiborne, and in the great rush of 1809 thousands landed with their masters. By 1820 voodooism was firmly rooted in the southern part of the state.

As practiced then, it definitely was a religion, as it still is to the illiterate masses of Haiti. That it was mixed up with sorcery and the selling of charms for profit does not alter that fact. Power was exercized by *papalois* and *mamalois,* priests and priestesses, but as is invariably the case with a cult that has no written dogma, it assumed a local form wherever it was established. Thus in the colony of Saint Domingue (later Haiti) it was diabolical, its ritual calling, among other things, for human sacrifices, while at the same period the mild version called obeah was being developed in Jamaica. Louisiana voodooism occupied a midway position. No case of murder, through ritualistic sacrifice or otherwise, ever reached the courts, and while this does not prove that there were no such deaths it implies that at all events they were extremely rare.

An oddity was the rise to chief eminence of a voodoo queen who tolerated none but the most servile *mamalois,* and the relegating of the *papalois* to the lesser status of "doctors." Necessarily, the leaders of both sexes were free persons of color since it was important that they should have liberty of action, but most of the rank and file were slaves. The succession of queens laid claim to an authority almost papal, for each one altered the rites on the grounds that she had been told in a vision to do so.

The first woman known to have been queen was a quadroon from Saint Domingue, who made a pretense of earning her living selling sweetmeats in the Place d'Armes. Her name was Sanité Dédé. In 1822 or 1823 she began to hold nocturnal meetings in an abandoned brickyard in Dumaine Street. A Louisiana planter stated that at the age of fifteen he was taken there by a family slave and witnessed the regulation ceremony of serpent worship. He saw six white men and two white women in the audience. The date was 1825. His torrid descriptions of orgiastic dancing should be taken with a grain of salt, for they appeared in a highly sensational book when he was an old man.* The bare circumstances of the meeting place and the personnel, however, fit in with other evidence.

---

* J. W. Buel, *Metropolitan Life Unveiled, or the Mysteries and Miseries of America's Great Cities* (St. Louis: Historical Publishing Co., 1882).

Nothing significant is known about Sanité Dédé, except that she probably was the one who fixed the night of June 23, St. John's Eve, as the major celebration of the year. The jumbling of voodooism with Catholic feast days and ceremonials occurs in every New World land where the cult is practiced. The Haitians have gone so far as to adopt certain saints into the voodoo hierarchy.

But if Sanité Dédé is forgotten her successor, Marie Laveau, is one of the most widely remembered figures in the history of New Orleans. Creoles and blacks are equally fascinated by her legend, and not all the credulity is on the Negro side. Many facts about her are demonstrably true. The rest is obscurity, beginning with the strong likelihood that instead of one Marie Laveau there were two, mother and daughter, who succeeded in confusing the record and creating the impression that the original queen of that name had lived to a very great age.

Marie Laveau, a free mulatto, was born in New Orleans a year or two before 1800. She married one Jacques Paris, a man of her color, in 1819, the ceremony being performed by the famous Père Antoine. A few years later the husband died and she became the mistress of a light-colored man named Christophe Glapion. He was from Saint Domingue and had fought in the Battle of New Orleans under Major d'Aquin. Several children were born to the voodoo queen and Glapion. One of them was a daughter, Marie, and although the date of the birth is given as 1827 the calligraphy in the register is blurred and it may have been 1835.

The elder Marie had a reputation for great beauty of face and figure. No authentic portrait of her exists, the one in the Cabildo Museum being admittedly dubious. She was a hairdresser who went to the homes of the best families to ply her trade. This enabled her to impress her personality on white people, men as well as women, and she found clients among them when she began to deal as a side line in the amulets and magic powers of the black art. She became an active member of the voodoo organization in the middle 1820's. About 1830 she seized control from Sanité Dédé, by what method we have no way of telling.

With her rise, voodooism became a formidable influence in New Orleans—important to the Negroes, free and enslaved, who regarded Marie Laveau as semidivine and made few moves without consulting her or one of her subservient "doctors"; scarcely less important to certain whites, who pooh-poohed it only in public. Distinguished women consulted Marie privately about their affairs of the heart, employed her to find lost objects, and bought her potions for the cure of maladies. The son of a rich merchant is reputed to have ascribed his acquittal on a serious charge to her intervention, and to have deeded to her as part payment the little house on St. Ann Street near Congo Square where she lived for years.

Marie Laveau was so sure of herself that she held some voodoo meetings openly, to her financial profit, and allowed favored whites to attend even the secret rites, without destroying the sense of awe essential to the cult. Shortly after she became queen she built a house on Lake Pontchartrain between the Bayou St. John and Milneburg. It was whitewashed on the outside, and so was called the Maison Blanche. She hid there off and on for long periods, during the course of which she occasionally saw visitors who were willing to pay high for the opportunity. Very secret voodoo rites for the elect were celebrated at the Maison Blanche, but it is known that Marie used it also as a house of assignation, where she made appointments for white men with comely colored girls.

The beach on both sides was lonely. The biggest voodoo gatherings took place there, but never twice at the same spot. Soon the great St. John's Eve ceremony and the lake shore were associated together in the public mind. Thousands of curiosity seekers went out each year, by carriage and on the Pontchartrain Railroad, hoping to find the celebrants. They rarely came upon them, for at the first warning sound the Negroes slipped back into Alexander Milne's healthful cypress swamps.

The queen, meanwhile, saw nothing incongruous in being also an ardent practitioner of the Catholic faith. She attended mass at the Cathedral. No doubt this gave her valuable ideas, for she adopted the worship of the Virgin Mary into voodooism to a degree unknown even in Haiti. As she grew older she took an interest in the condemned at the Parish Prison, especially murderers. Marie prayed with some of the most notorious killers in their cells up to the morning of their execution. In one case there was a commutation of sentence at the last moment, which of course was credited to her beneficent magic.

The date of Marie Laveau's death was 1881. Her burial in St. Louis Cemetery No. 1 was attended by hundreds, and reported in the newspapers. Yet many believed that she still lived. This was twelve years after she had yielded the crown to Malvina Latour, a dark-skinned mulatto, and retired to the supposed solitude of her cottage near Congo Square. George W. Cable visited her toward the end and wrote a description of her for the *Century Magazine* which falls short of solving the riddle. Cable, a celebrated chronicler of his city, though an expatriate from New Orleans in middle age, declared that, when he saw her, "They said she was over one hundred years old, and there was nothing to cast doubt upon the statement. She had shrunken away from her skin; it was like a turtle's. Withal one could hardly help but see that the face, now so withered, had once been handsome and commanding."

Cable's article was published in 1886. The experience antedated that by almost a decade. Marie at the time of his visit could not have been much more than eighty, and it is improbable that a mulatto would have taken on the appearance of such extreme decrepitude at that age. Besides, he was told that she was over a hundred. Her devotees considered her a very active force around, let us say, 1878, and did not speak of her as an ancient survivor until long afterward. Did Cable really see Marie, or was some anonymous crone palmed off on him?

The original Marie Laveau had, according to the best evidence, abdicated to Malvina Latour only in the matter of the voodoo ceremonials, and had reserved the lucrative business of charms (*gris-gris*) and medicines. This she passed on to her daughter Marie. In private life, the latter had made a mystery of her relationship with the old woman, and had frequently substituted for her in dealing with the voodooists. The funeral was no sooner over than she became the one and only Marie Laveau—not a case of resurrection or rejuvenation, but in some queer fashion the queen herself defying the years. Malvina Latour may have been the titular monarch, but the real prestige was enjoyed by Marie Laveau II. Lafcadio Hearn went to see her at her home on several occasions. Because of his known penchant for colored women, it was reputed that he became her lover. But as she was then in her fifties, the relationship seems improbable. Hearn's love of the exotic, especially with an added sauce of the macabre, is explanation enough of why he should have sought the friendship of a voodoo priestess.

An unsigned article published in 1885* sets the scene for a voodoo gathering under Malvina Latour, as follows:

"On St. John's Eve last year the night was dark, and in the eastern sky hung a black cloud, from which now and then burst flashes of lightning which lit up the road, the bayou and the surrounding swamp with a lurid glow, in fit introduction to what was to follow. The scene on the lake coast from Spanish Fort to Milneburg was one which cannot easily be forgotten. All along the shore, at intervals scarcely more than 300 yards, groups of men and women could be seen standing around blazing pine-knot fires, their dark, copper-colored faces weirdly gilded by the red flames and their black forms thus illuminated appearing gigantic and supernatural against the opaque background of the lake and sky on one side and the mystical darkness just tinged with starlight of the seemingly limitless swamps on the other. Some of the men were stripped to the waist, and all were gesticulating with animation, or seemed to be in waiting for something. Along the road at various intervals were Negresses standing by small tables where gumbo and coffee were dispensed.

"Between Spanish Fort and Milneburg the shore was crowded

---

* *Historical Sketch Book and Guide to New Orleans* (Edited and compiled by several leading writers of the New Orleans Press. New York: Will H. Coleman, 1885). A number of the chapters are known to have been written by Lafcadio Hearn.

with Negroes, who seemed to be enjoying themselves laughing, talking and romping like children, and the music which came from the shanty where a dance had evidently been started sounded like that of an ordinary Negro ball. As soon as the purlieus of Milneburg were left, the way down the lake shore toward the now brilliant bonfires was difficult, for in the darkness one had to pick his steps. Between the lake on the one side and the swamp on the other there was a belt of land not more than fifty feet across, and in some places this was diminished by more than half by the encroachment of Pontchartrain's waves. There was no roadway, but simply a devious bypath which wended around stumps and mud holes in a most irregular manner.

"After some ten minutes' walk there came to the ear the faintest sound as of a drum beaten rhythmically, and on listening a chorus of voices could be heard. The hundreds of small watchfires along the shore twinkled like stars in the distance, and where they were built upon little points of land they were reflected in the water so brightly the duplication added a peculiar weirdness to the scene.

"Pursuing the same path was a party of Creole Negroes, the men carrying musical instruments and the women laden with coffee-pots and buckets of gumbo. They were not inclined to talk, and when asked where the Voodoo dance was to take place answered that they knew nothing about it. Passing around a little willow copse that grew almost in the lake there opened to the view a scene Doré would have delighted to paint. The belt of land here was about 100 feet in width, and in the middle of this little plot was burning a huge fire. Grouped around it were some thirty or forty Negroes, the rising and falling of the firelight giving a grotesqueness to their figures that was as curious as it was entertaining. Their shadows stretched out over the rushes and reeds of the swamp, and their faces looked wild enough to satisfy any lover of the mysterious.

"Built half over the swamps and half on the land stood a small hut or, to give it all its pretensions, a house of two rooms. It was like most of the fishermen's cabins seen along the lake, but rather more roomy. Through the open window there came quite a flood of light, and a song was heard chanted, it seemed by some eight or ten voices. It was almost three-quarters of a mile below Milneburg, and the place was appropriately selected, for certainly no more dismal and dreary spot could have been found. Citywards the swamp, with its funereal cypresses, stretched in gloomy perspective, while in front, lapping the rushes and stumps, the ripples in the lake came in, the water appearing almost black from the vegetable matter held in suspension. . . . The music in the house began with renewed vigor at this time, and there was by general consent a movement thither. It was nearly midnight. The wide gallery on the front was soon thronged, and it was noticed that but few were allowed to enter the large room which formed the eastern side of the building. The door was closed, and a stout young Negress guarded it on the outside."

Events inside the building proved to be a harmless enough rigmarole. Little else could have been expected, since the chief of police, Zach Bachemin, was a member of the intruding party.

Over a long period, dating from the time of the first Marie Laveau, the voodooists called Pontchartrain St. John's Lake. It is easy to see how this came about. The great ceremonial day of the cult was St. John's Eve, and the relationship between the meeting place and the saint was eventually confused. Devotees used to speak of "going swimming in St. John's Lake," to which the proper ritualistic answer was, "Yes, Little John." One no longer hears the appellation.

Malvina Latour dropped out of the picture about 1890, and in 1897 the second Marie Laveau died of heart failure or a stroke in a public ballroom. Voodoo thereafter grew tamer and tamer. The Negroes have corrupted the very name. It is "hoodoo" now, a designation that fits a traffic in fear-producing talismans, luck powders and bottled love, which is about all that remains of the cult.

But New Orleans continues to be vastly interested in Marie Laveau. The question of where her body actually lies is thought an enigma, and this is complicated by the point that people are not sure whom they mean: the first Marie, or the second, or both. There is a story that the authorities forbade the inscribing of the name on any tomb, because they did not want voodoo worshipers to gather there for nocturnal meetings. It is also said that the coffin of the original Marie was secretly moved to an unmarked resting place. No record of her daughter's funeral exists. Blank tablets in several cemeteries are believed to indicate the true grave, the most popular being an "oven" in St. Louis Cemetery No. 2. All of them are visited, notably on St. John's Eve and on All Saints' and All Souls' Days, by scores of the faithful. They scratch crosses and petitions on the stone, pay in advance by pushing coins into chinks, and leave offerings of food. The writer counted forty-six crosses penciled on the St. Louis Cemetery No. 1 tomb on All Saints' Day 1941.

This vault bears the announcement that it is that of "the family of the Widow Paris—*née* Laveau," and that in it reposes "Marie Philomène Glapion, deceased the 11th of June, 1897, at the age of sixty-two." Paris was the legal name of Marie the Elder, and Glapion was the father of the daughter who bore the same Christian name as hers. So where is the great mystery? It would seem that both queens were interred in this vault. Without the privilege of raising delightful goose pimples over its flirting with the occult, however, New Orleans would not be New Orleans.

Chapter 13

Nude Lady of the Lake

EVERY ONCE in a while there materializes a personality without great talent except that of being a personality. In rare instances such a one is remembered beyond the tomb. Generally he has been a mystifier, an exhibitionist as often as not, but almost invariably a dilettante. He seldom makes his mark on the stage, because too many actors go in for mystification and exhibitionism for these traits to seem memorable, and dilettantism is a luxury the stage cannot afford. From New Orleans, nevertheless, came forth a woman who proved an exception. She was a second-rate actress and not remarkably beautiful, except as to certain details of her figure. But by sheer personality she achieved an identity which earns her a niche among the eminent of her period. Her name was Adah Isaacs Menken.

She wanted the world to believe that she had been born on the shores of Lake Pontchartrain, perhaps because that was where Manon Lescaut was supposed to have been buried and it appeared poetic that the dunes which had taken should now give back. Her biggest success was as a naked lady who galloped onto the stage on a black horse, and of course she was not really nude. These were but two of her numberless dramatizations, personal and histrionic. Myths of which she was the heroine were the breath of her existence. She succeeded in confusing the record so thoroughly that it is hard to come at the truth of the simplest biographical details.

On Adah's authority, most accounts say that she was born at Milneburg on June 15, 1835. Careless writers often add that the place was then a substantial suburb, or even a rival of New Orleans. But Milneburg in 1835 was a fledgling community consisting of the Pontchartrain Railroad's station, a landing place for boats, a hotel, and a few villas and hovels on lots recently sold by old Alexander Milne. There is no proof of the birth claim, and it is highly improbable that it occurred there.

The lady was vague about her parentage, contradictory as to her very name. Sometimes her father was James McCord, and sometimes James Campbell, Richard Irving Spencer or Ricardo La Fuertes. All these men had been fairly prominent Orleanians in the 1830's, except that the fourth was plain Fuertes instead of the impossible Spanish combination of "La Fuertes." A favorite version was that James McCord—conveniently deceased—had married a widow with children, of whom Adah had been one, had adopted her and given her the legal name of Adelaide McCord. Again, it would be Campbell who had done as much; she naïvely called him "Sir" Campbell, because he was related to the Duke of Argyll. Needless to say, the local vital statistics show no espousals of the kind contracted by either McCord or Campbell. She also said that her mother was Dolores Adios Fuertes, and that she had received this identical name at her christening.

But when she married the Jewish musician Alexander Isaacs Menken at Galveston in 1856, she declared herself to be Ada Berthe Théodore. It was then that she gave June 15, 1835, as her birth date. The seriousness of the occasion inclines one to believe that she was more likely to have been approximating the truth than at any other time. A search of the registry of births in New Orleans fails to show a daughter born to any McCord, Spencer or Fuertes from 1833 to 1839. However, in 1839 Auguste Théodore, a free man of color, a wheelwright by trade, registered a girl child under the name of Philomène Croi Théodore. His residence was 35 rue Bagatelle (now an extension of Chartres Street) in the Faubourg Marigny. The circumstances are suggestive. If Adah Isaacs Menken was an octoroon light enough to "pass" as white, there was every reason for her to becloud her ancestry. Interracial marriages were illegal in Louisiana, though not in Texas at that period. She might have feared that if she used any but her actual family name the contract would be nullified, yet not have hesitated to alter the Christian names to throw her husband off the track. The incorrect date would have established the fiction that she was old enough to marry without her parents' consent.

Furthermore, this was not the first time she had called herself Théodore. Out of the kaleidoscope of her whimsies, it seems possible to pluck the fact that she and her sister Josephine danced in public in the early 1850's as the Théodore Sisters. Adah maintained that they had been members of the ballet at the French Opera House, an impossibility since that house did not open until 1859. She may have meant the Théâtre d'Orléans, the previous home of opera in New Orleans. Even so, the ballet and a sister act do not jibe. How the girl could dream!

She averred that at the age of twelve she had translated Homer's *Iliad* from Greek into French, and not long afterward had been captured by Indians in Texas from whom she had escaped by the use of romantic wiles. Both these tales are the sheerest bunk. It remains curious that she should have been sufficiently familiar with the *Iliad* to quote from it. We know nothing about her education. She said that she published a book of poems in New Orleans when she was twenty-one. Strange that not a single copy should have come down to posterity. Yet she did contribute verse to American periodicals, and at the time of her death a volume in which Swinburne, Rossetti and Dickens took some interest was on the press in London.

Starting with the marriage to Menken, she can be pinned down to reality, and the story is glamorous enough. She developed a pro-Hebraic complex that lasted until the end. She had herself formally received into the Jewish faith. She adopted Adah Isaacs Menken as her permanent name, it being her notion that the added "h" Hebraicized Ada. Yet despite her sentiment for the man and his religion, the course of true love did not run smooth. Menken accomplished one thing for her. He got her on the legitimate stage in Shreveport, Louisiana, in 1857. Shortly thereafter she left him, and there was a divorce. She appeared in several plays in New Orleans the following year. Then she knocked about the country, north, east and west, alternately in fly-by-night companies and in stock. Between engagements she posed as a model for sculptors. A Shakespearean "ham" of the day yielded to her entreaties and cast her as Lady Macbeth. She forgot her lines and he was forced to prompt her throughout. Later he remarked sadly, "Adah, you should go in for the sensational." The advice sank deep.

In 1859 she married John C. Heenan, the heavyweight prize fighter known as "The Benicia Boy," a colossal roughneck with whom she quarreled incessantly, but who helped to publicize her. They had one child who died soon after birth. When the War between the States broke out, Adah defended secession so vehemently that the authorities picked her up in New York for questioning. But she was no rival of Belle Boyd, "the female spy" of the Confederacy. War or no war, she was about to seize her great chance in the theater.

For more than twenty years an adaptation by H. H. Milner of Byron's poem, *Mazeppa,* had been played as a thriller. It depended on one scene in which a rider bounds across the stage and then takes a perilous leap. The role had been filled by both men and women. A producer decided to try Adah in it, and she contributed two innovations. Others had substituted a dummy for the leap, but she would stay on the horse's back throughout. In the second place, she would wear flesh-colored tights without even a loincloth so as to give the impression of being naked. The show was thus offered in Albany, New York, in June 1861 and made a tremendous hit. It packed the Bowery Theatre, New York City, for weeks. Adah became at a stroke one of the best-known and highest-paid women in the business. Many have achieved that distinction, and are as forgotten today as last year's fireworks. But it was only a prelude for Adah Isaacs Menken. She had a flair that turned notoriety into a sort of fame, chiefly because she perceived the subtlety that her type could live in man's memory only by contact with the genuinely illustrious.

Having discarded The Benicia Boy, she married Robert Newell, alias Orpheus C. Kerr, the popular humorist. It was an odd choice, as she quickly realized. He disappeared from her life somewhere on the long road between New York and San Francisco, where she had gone to present *Mazeppa* most profitably before gaping audiences of Gold Rush pioneers.

Europe, in 1864, was the next step and the decisive one. It is fabulous that a woman with Adah's slight artistic equipment and un-Victorian amorality could have made the stir that she did in four short years. She was booked at Astley's, in London, and soon had the huge, somber metropolis of the Anglo-Saxon world, as it then was, in a turmoil. The young bloods adored her. Long-faced puritans thought her a menace. The critics unanimously reviewed the play not from the standpoint of plot or acting, but in appraisal of Adah's physique and in discussion of whether simulated nudity in the theater was or was not objectionable. She replied sedately in the press that she considered the human body beautiful in itself, that a simple display of it could not be indecent, and that her own poses were no more suggestive than those in classic sculpture. So unoriginal a statement was out of character, and could only have been due to the mutton-and-ale atmosphere of British respectability, which she felt she must placate.

Her later utterances were by no means demure. Soon she was calling herself the "Royal Bengal Tigress," without a qualm at the notion of a great cat of the jungle being billed in an equestrian act. She drove about London in a four-in-hand, her crest a horse's head surmounting four aces, and with silver bells on the harness.

It would be pointless to trace all her goings and comings. Sufficient to note that she captivated Paris in *Mazeppa* and a new melodrama entitled *Les Pirates de la Savane,* that she played Vienna once and oscillated between London and Paris. Midway she visited New York and engaged in her most tragic matrimonial venture. She married James Paul Barclay, a broker and gambler whom she had first met in California. She lived with him for three months in a brownstone mansion on Seventh Avenue, which she named Bleak House after the Dickens novel. Barclay squandered $150,000 on her, fled suddenly to Philadelphia and died in mysterious circumstances, probably a suicide. Adah swallowed poison, with almost fatal results, then had herself carried aboard a ship. It had been a serious error of judgment to interrupt her tinsel glory and her amazing friendships in the Old World.

Regarding her first stay in London her manager, Ed James, wrote: "Adah began to give breakfasts, dinners and reunions that would break a Belmont's heart or purse, or in fact the purse of anyone, if continued long. She never really valued money, and in spite of our efforts to induce her to make provision for a rainy day she laughingly put it off with, 'Ed, when I get so that I have to borrow money I want to die.' "

Charles Dickens was seen at those parties, though he did not warm up. So were William Makepeace Thackeray, William and Dante Gabriel Rossetti, and Charles Reade, the author of *The Cloister and the Hearth.* Reade says of Adah in his *Diary:* "A clever woman with beautiful eyes; bad actress, made hit playing *Mazeppa* in tights; goodish heart." Belle Boyd, who had run the blockade on a mission for the Confederacy, was a guest at least once.

Louis Moreau Gottschalk, the great Creole pianist and composer, himself of New Orleans birth, found his compatriot a bit irritating in Paris. He declared: "Miss Adah Menken, after having driven all the people crazy, has carried away 50,000 dollars. You will easily understand that the chaste muses, sisters of Apollo, can only go astray before the public which is enthusiastic at the nudities of *Mazeppa.*"

But the Naked Lady's supreme conquest was Algernon Charles Swinburne, finest of lyric poets and most erratic of men. It has often been stated, erroneously, that he was an early attendant at her salon, and that she inspired his poem "Dolores," that tour de force of metrical cunning and violent, beautiful imagery which the artistic youth of London chanted in the streets after his *Poems and Ballads* was published in 1866. Swinburne was not the type to dally in a salon; his habits were unsociable, and he was drinking heavily.

"Dolores" had been written some years before. His French biographer, Georges Lafourcade, has proved anyway that Swinburne did not meet Adah until October 1867. That he had seen her on the stage is possible. He may well have been beguiled by the coincidence that she said her baptismal name was Dolores, and that she lived like a reincarnated *Dame des Septs Douleurs.*

Swinburne did not seek her out. Dante Gabriel Rossetti is said to have had the bawdy idea of betting Adah £10—hoping to lose—that she could not become the poet's mistress. At all events, she went alone to Swinburne's lodgings and announced that she was his for the taking. The next morning she raved about his poetry, which she sincerely admired, told him of her own efforts in the art and expressed some theories. Swinburne answered, "Darling, a woman who has such beautiful legs need not discuss poetry." He ended by treating her aesthetic yearnings kindly enough. A few pages of her manuscript bore corrections in his hand. The charge that he wrote any of the ingenuous verse she signed is ludicrous, yet it was made at the time.

Adah's fable of her nativity had now been altered to the effect that her birthplace was an exquisite Louisiana lakeside town called Chatrain. Milneburg had come to have too commonplace a sound. She may have had "Port Pontchartrain" in mind, but erred in the spelling of the contraction she invented. Swinburne, who was a sound French scholar, must have been amused. If she had been erudite or conventional, she assuredly would have bored him. Adah was the only woman with whom he ever admitted having had a love affair. They were photographed together, and he sent copies to his friends. One note referred to her as "my present possessor—known to Britannia as Miss Menken, to me as Dolores (her real Christian name)." After her death the following year he wrote to an intimate: "I am sure you were sorry on my account to hear of the death of my poor dear Menken; it was a great shock to me and a real grief. I was ill for some days. She was most lovable as a friend as well as a mistress."

The business of the pictures, however, had caused him great annoyance. The photographer had surreptitiously sold a number of prints, and some of these were displayed in shop windows. Hostile newspapers poked fun at the small figure of the lyrist portrayed clasping the flamboyant beauty's hand. The rumor circulated that he planned to join her stage company. He was actually relieved when after a few weeks she left for Paris, because with her out of the way the gossip dwindled. Meanwhile Swinburne's publisher, Hotten, had agreed to issue a volume of verse by Adah, and it can scarcely be doubted that this was at Swinburne's request.

In her last year in London her earnings had exceeded £6,000, some accounts say £10,000—between $30,000 and $50,000. The publicity from the liaison with the poet, who was then at the high-water mark of his fame, had helped her financially. Only Patti took more from the box office that year.

But the spendthrift Adah arrived in Paris short of funds and needing desperately to repeat her triumphs. Also, her mercurial fancy had turned toward another literary lion: Alexandre Dumas, *père*. He was sixty-five years old, corpulent and wheezing after a life of self-indulgence, but he was the author of *Monte Cristo* and *Les Trois Mousquetaires*. Before he had been introduced to her, she said that she proposed to be his mistress. The thing was not hard to arrange. He had no sooner heard the rumor than he started to dance attendance. An apartment specially furnished to suit her taste was offered and accepted. Dumas, like Swinburne, was photographed with her leaning on his shoulder, and again the indiscretion was the talk of the town. Parisians, to be sure, were not censorious in the London manner, but they found the alliance bizarre. Paul Verlaine wrote a sarcastic poem, beginning:

> *L'Oncle Tom avec Miss Ada,*
> *C'est un spectacle dont on rêve.*

The robustious old quadroon author, son of a mulatto who had been a French Revolutionary general, and grandson of a Negress of Saint Domingue, did not like that quip about "Uncle Tom."

He eased himself out of the relationship with Adah. Her fantastic life was nearing its close, and with a due regard for drama the gods saw to it that the end should be marked by a note of almost intolerable pathos.

She was rehearsing *Les Pirates de la Savane* for a revival when she collapsed, suffering from what the doctors diagnosed as an internal tumor. It may have been cancer. She lingered for several weeks, inadequately nursed in a second-rate hotel, ignored by the many who had so recently paid her homage, and barely able to meet her expenses. On August 10, 1868, she died, aged thirty-three if the birth date she gave when she married Menken was correct, only twenty-nine if she was the daughter of Théodore, the New Orleans free man of color.

A handful of mourners saw her to a cheap grave in Père Lachaise. But the following year remorseful friends had her body removed to the Montparnasse Cemetery and raised a shaft bearing the words, "Thou Knowest," which she had once chosen as her epitaph.

She never saw her volume of poems, entitled *Infelicia*. It appeared very shortly after her death. The dedication was to Dickens, "by permission." The would-be Whitmanesque style of the more ambitious pieces did not suffice to mask a basic inability to grasp the technique of verse. Yet there were some arresting phrases: "Dim, discolored hours" . . . "The white tent of my youth." Swinburne wrote in his copy of the book a line from his own *Laus Veneris:*

"Lo, this is she that was the world's delight!"

Chapter 14

Chata-Ima, the Poet-Priest

ONE of the powerful literary and moral influences of the early nineteenth century, though he is now largely ignored by English readers, was the Vicomte de Chateaubriand, author of *Atala, René, Génie du Christianisme, Mémoires d'Outre-Tombe* and other works. He invented the so-called "Byronic hero," the victim of destiny, devoured by tragic pessimism, yet wearing an aura of glamour. Flouting the French Revolution, Chateaubriand was a romantic reactionary, an aristocrat and a devout Catholic. Influenced himself by Rousseau, he exalted Nature as against civilization, while identifying it with the religious spirit. His ideas were thin, but his use of historical background adroit, and his sense of stage setting masterly. The picturesque, as fixed by this lush stylist, held descriptive writing in its thrall for several generations. Victor Hugo learned from him. Such dissimilar figures as Longfellow and George Sand owed him a debt.

Nowhere did Chateaubriand have so relatively great an effect as in Louisiana, which he professed to have visited and which he made the scene of several romances. Literate Creoles read him avidly. After all, his *Les Natchez,* of which *Atala* and *René* were the best episodes, was a cycle based upon the massacre at Fort Rosalie in 1729. Local writers fell completely under his spell. It is not too much to say that four-fifths of the early French prose and verse produced by Louisianians was imitation Chateaubriand. Adrien Rouquette, the poet-priest of the Lake Pontchartrain pine woods, and his brother, Dominique Rouquette, stood out among those who were profoundly swayed.

Adrien, or Chata-Ima as the Choctaw Indians renamed him, must have a place in any history of the lake. He was possessed of individual virtues and strength of character. But Chateaubriand had set a mark even upon the form his piety took. The disciple cannot be fully understood unless we know something about the master's connection with America.

François René de Chateaubriand was born a chevalier, the last of ten children, in a narrow street of St. Malo, in 1768. He became a lieutenant in a royal regiment, was a member of the entourage when the King and Queen fled from Paris, but was too young and insignificant to rate the guillotine. In 1791 he contrived a trip to the New World on the visionary pretext of seeking the Northwest Passage. He landed at Baltimore, went to Niagara Falls, traveled through the Alleghenies and down the Ohio River to its junction with the Mississippi. If he crossed to the western bank, he set foot on Louisiana territory as it was then constituted. In his journal and his lectures he said vaguely that he had traversed wide spaces, had followed the whole course of the Mississippi and seen Florida, but this was almost certainly not the case. He returned to France at the end of a few months, and his extraordinary literary and political career started.

There can be no question that the "forest primeval" in America had impressed him deeply, and that he informed himself about Indian lore and French colonization. When the times were calmer under Napoleon, he plucked a tale from his mass of notes, polished it, gave it the title of *Atala,* and issued it in 1801. He won a tremendous success, of the kind that is bestowed when the public takes a new art form to its heart.

What, then, is *Atala?* Characterization and plot are as stilted as can be. An Indian warrior named Chactas (French for Choctaw) is befriended by a Spaniard whose captive he is, but cannot endure the ways of civilized man and asks to be allowed to return to the woods. Chactas now falls into the hands of a hostile tribe and is to be burned at the stake. A beautiful dusky maiden named Atala cuts his bonds. They flee together, are madly enamored of each other. She is a Christian convert, half-white and vowed to perpetual virginity as it turns out, and she resists his advances. Fearing that she will end by yielding, she takes poison and dies in the cave of a pious missionary. All three deliver themselves of inordinately long speeches. Chactas is rather a figure from Greek drama than an Indian, and Atala straight from the Book of the Saints. Ah, but—that is where the magic comes in—the emotion portrayed is moving, and the chorus of natural phenomena is played on a mighty organ.

". . . The lightning set fire to the woods; the burning spread out like a head of hair composed of flames; columns of sparks and smoke besieged the clouds, which hurled back their thunders into the vast conflagration. . . .

". . . The cedar and the oak are covered with a white moss which droops from the branches to the earth. When at night by the light of the moon you perceive on the bare savanna an isolated live oak clothed with this drapery, you could believe it a phantom trailing its long veils after it. The scene is not less picturesque in full daylight; for a cloud of butterflies, dragonflies, hummingbirds, green parakeets and blue jays come to cling to this moss, which then produces the effect of a tapestry of white wool on which a European artist might have embroidered the insects and the glittering birds. . . ."

The Rouquette brothers were born of wealthy Creole parents, who had a house on Royal Street, New Orleans, and a country place on the Bayou Lacombe to the northeast of Marigny's plantation, Fontainebleau. When they were still young boys, the family deserted the downtown mansion for a semirural home on the Bayou St. John. There were still a few Indians living in the swamps near by, and Adrien was much attracted by them. They taught him nature lore which he never forgot. At the age of eight he began to attend the Collège d'Orléans, the leading French school in the city, of which Joseph Lakanal was then the principal.

We must digress to consider Lakanal. He had been trained for holy orders. The Revolution swept him into republicanism. As a member of the Convention when Louis XVI was sentenced to death, he is reputed to have signed the warrant. The Restoration forced him to leave France. Many in Louisiana looked at him askance as a regicide, but the story that the old families would not let him teach their children and that his term of control was the beginning of the end for the Collège d'Orléans has been somewhat exaggerated. He was an excellent teacher, nobly virtuous in his outlook. That he was unorthodox in religion goes without saying, but he was an apostle of the humanities. It may well be that conservative Creoles mistrusted him and forced his withdrawal. Adrien Rouquette never spoke against Lakanal in the years to come, but clearly owed little to the relationship. The young scholar had been more of a traditionalist than the master.

Adrien went to Transylvania University in Kentucky at fourteen, and to France for enrollment at the Collège Royale, Paris, at eighteen. He and his brother Dominique, who had also been sent abroad for his education, frequented literary circles and commenced to write verse. The prevailing theme of both was the beauty of the natural world seen through the haze of nostalgic memories of Louisiana. On a second visit to France, Adrien, who had read *Atala* meanwhile, concluded that he had a vocation for the priesthood; yet he delayed action. He published a first book of poetry, *Les Savanes,* which was praised by Sainte-Beuve, Lamartine—and Chateaubriand. Thomas Moore, the Irish bard, wrote him that he was "the Lamartine of America."

He was now spending most of his time at the Bayou Lacombe and making friends with the survivors of the Choctaw people, who lived in scattered villages. There is a tale, probably apocryphal that he loved and wished to marry a Choctaw girl named Oushola (Bird-Singer), "the daughter of a chief." Her father gave his consent, but on Adrien's return from the city, where he had gone to consult his own family, he was lastingly grief-stricken to find that Oushola had died of pneumonia.

Be that as it may, he began a serious study of theology and in 1845 was ordained a priest. Attached to the Cathedral in New Orleans, he manifested exceptional force as an orator. Crowds flocked to hear his sermons, Sunday after Sunday. Men always praised him, somehow, by comparing him with one more celebrated than himself. Now he was "the new Lacordaire." Contemporaneously, the romantic in the white habit of the Dominicans, Lacordaire, was enchanting congregations at Notre Dame de Paris with discourses which, according to Gustave Lanson, historian of French literature, were as much lyric poetry as Christian dogma and were not notably rich in ideas. This was hardly fair to Père Rouquette, who may have been less the artist, but was zealously pious.

His archbishop made no secret of the fact that he expected him to have a great career in the Church. Through the 1850's he served the Cathedral parish with distinction, though part of that time his popularity was shared with another brilliant and unforgotten priest, the Abbé du Quesnay. In 1859 he astonished his superiors with a sudden announcement. He felt that he had had a call from God to retire from public life and devote the rest of his days to missionary work among the Choctaw. Attempts to dissuade him failed. He took a minimum of baggage to the pine woods where so much of his boyhood had been spent. With his own hands he built a small wooden chapel near Bayou Lacombe, and little by little he won over the Indians to respect for his ministry. Later he established several other chapels, all tiny and very plain. He placed them in groves, usually under the branches of a live oak. It is said that occasionally he would preach from a low bough of the tree that sheltered his chapel at Chinchuba.

Much of the time he went about dressed as an Indian. The Choctaw came to love him. They gave him the name Chata-Ima, which signifies "like a Choctaw." During the War between the States his native friends hid in the swamps, fearing they might be drafted to serve in the armies. He made many trips in a rowboat across the lake, to bring them drugs, food and clothing from New Orleans. Once he was arrested by the Federals on suspicion of being a spy.

The best impression of Chata-Ima and his wilderness retreat is the one given in a letter to France by Père Pierre Alphonse

Chocarne, disciple and biographer of Lacordaire, who visited Louisiana in 1867. He writes:

"I promised you an account of my visit to the home of the Choctaw Indians, so today I redeem my word. You remember my description of the passage across Lake Pontchartrain, from New Orleans to Mandeville, which nestles near the border of the lake with the neighboring villas and charming summer residences stretching along the shore on either side. Then came the fury of a tropical storm, succeeded by a magnificent sunset in the midst of clouds of gold and fire seen beyond the giant trees. The latter, garbed in green, now illumined, as it were, by an immense Bengal flame, gave the scintillating raindrops that were still trembling on the leaves the aspect of a veritable shower of pearls and diamonds.

"This was May 17. The next day I left Mandeville for Bonfouca, accompanied by the priest, a former Italian Dominican set adrift by the troubles in his native land, and now in charge of the three or four surrounding parishes. On Sunday I preached in the church of Bonfouca and then pressed forward into the forest, into the region where the Choctaw Indians dwell.

"From Mandeville to Bonfouca requires about three hours' drive in a carriage, and as one leaves the little town by a grand avenue going straight into the woods it is easy to fancy oneself in some magnificent park. How I enjoyed the pure, perfumed air of the forest and admired the magnificence of Nature! At the end of the avenue the scene changes. Then one enters a vault of Gothic arches, formed by the tall pines whose shade gives a sense of solemn mystery to the silent solitudes. There is no undergrowth to be seen now, and no other fragrant odor than the healthful, resinous perfume which is exhaled by a silvery liquid which runs in large tears from the trunk of the tree. One has a fine view and can see far in the distance grazing herds which the neighing of a horse will send galloping away. These seem to be the sole inhabitants of the enchanting forest.

"We soon perceived that this was not the case, for a savage was approaching, his gun on his shoulder, the hunting dogs preceding him, his feet bare, his body unclothed except for a pair of short trousers, and a white band on his forehead to prevent his long hair from blowing over his face. He passed us without deigning to raise his eyes, while I almost sent mine out of their sockets in my endeavor to take in every detail of his face and figure. This was my first glimpse of a bona fide Indian. In his primitive attire, with a step firm and proud, with a wild freedom expressed in every movement, beneath the shade of the lofty pines, a place which seemed his own domain, he bore no resemblance to the Indians I had seen in the city, squatting on the pavement of the old French Market, exhibiting their wares for sale. Those wore a sad, timid, embarrassed expression, as though they felt themselves out of their sphere.

"Before noon we arrived at Bonfouca. 'And what is Bonfouca?' you may ask. 'Is it a village?' No, it is simply a church, a charming little wooden structure on the border of the bayou, and just beside the church is a tiny house for the priest, surrounded by a garden, and farther on, as a background, the great forest. Then we dined, and I had the pleasure of a little excursion up the bayou in a pirogue. It was delightful. My two oarsmen sent the little boat swiftly and silently amid the white and yellow blossoms which open at dawn and close their sleepy eyes as the sun goes down. From time to time an alligator raised his ugly head above the water, showing a double row of vicious-looking teeth, and then plunged to the bottom when he perceived our proximity.

"Along the banks of the bayou, separated from one another at a considerable distance by vast fields of cane and Indian corn, by forests of great oaks and other trees, are the dwellings of the planters. From time to time a white sail brought toward us a little fishing smack en route for the great city. We spent thus two hours in the midst of these wild and picturesque scenes. Then I landed and pushed forward alone into the interior. There was no sound of human voice, no sign of rural labors. I seemed to be in a solitary forest where man had never before penetrated. Birds of a thousand colors, every shade and hue of red, blue, brown and yellow, looked at me with an air of surprise, but with so little fear that I could almost touch them ere they stirred. . . .

"Early Monday morning I began an excursion in search of my friend, the Abbé Rouquette, the apostle to the Choctaws in Louisiana. I had made his acquaintance in New Orleans, and he was awaiting my arrival at his hermitage in order to present me to his parishioners. What an excellent man! What a noble and good heart has Adrien Rouquette! He possesses a cultivated mind, an elevated intellect, a generous soul filled with the double love of God and his country. He knew the language of the Choctaws and he went to dwell in their midst, built a church and gave his time to their instruction. The beginning was painful, for the Indian does not yield readily. To his native pride is joined a want of confidence in the white race, unfortunately well-founded in many instances. At first the savages regarded Père Rouquette as a government spy, so they watched his every movement, placed no reliance in his promises and waited proofs in actions, more persuasive than words. Later, when his entire devotedness showed how worthy he was of their affection and reverence, they themselves told him of the mysterious, hidden vigilance with which they had followed his every movement at all times.

" 'When you wandered alone in the depths of the forest,' they said, 'reading in your book of prayers, or when, retired to some hidden nook on the bayou for a bath in the deep, still waters, our eye was ever upon you, we never for an instant lost sight of you, either day or night.' Alone or in public the Indians found the Black Robe the same, the priest of God, and they gave him their veneration. And now, how he loves his Choctaw children, and how in return he is beloved by them! He knew that it was a fete for me to visit his mission, so he rejoiced almost as much as I did.

"But now, let me return to my departure from Bonfouca. The good priest there gave me his carriage, secured a guide, and I started for Bayou Lacombe, where my dear Abbé Rouquette had his dwelling. About an hour's drive through the pine forest brought me to the bayou. I then sent back the carriage and guide, and crossing the rather wide stream in a pirogue I took a beaten path that seemed to invite me to unknown solitudes. A walk of ten minutes showed me the hermitage, and before I could realize it the 'Black Robe' was almost reproaching me with his cordial welcome for having so long delayed my visit.

"Adrien Rouquette is a tall, well-made man. His long black hair falls in ringlets on his shoulders, framing a countenance sweet, gentle and noble. Large, brilliant, keen dark eyes illumine features at once fine and distinguished, responding quickly with keenest sympathy. He is one of those figures so appealing to an artist in which every emotion, every expression lives, speaks and attracts. Such is my dear Abbé Rouquette, whom I love with all my heart.

"And what shall I say of the hermitage? You would have to see it to form an idea. There is nothing borrowed, no attempt to seek the picturesque, nothing grandiose. All of its poetry is in the simplicity and poverty of the little wooden chapel surrounded by the charm of solitude, in this magnificent forest. The home of Père Rouquette, which serves also as a chapel, is a sort of chalet in wood, a square building surrounded by a gallery. The chapel occupies the main part of the first floor and the gallery serves as a sort of vestibule. The chapel is adorned with engravings, portraits of hermits and Dominican saints, among whom is Ste. Rose, for Père Rouquette is tenderly attached to the Order of St. Dominick. . . .

"But I was impatient to be off to visit the Indians, and my host enjoyed the fervor of my anticipation. After dinner he took his stick and we set out. Now there are no paths to betray the presence of the Indians' wigwams, so to me we seemed to wander aimlessly. Soon the bark of a dog announced that we were perceived, and in a few moments we reached a fence enclosing here a garden, there a pasture. Three Choctaw women were seated on the ground. They did not rise, scarcely deigned to look up, and continued their work. My presence intimidated them, and it was in vain that the Abbé tried to draw them into conversation.

The elder woman, evidently the mother, was making a scarlet garment. One of her daughters was weaving a basket, the other was parching coffee. The Mongol type is readily recognized. The Choctaw has the slightly flattened nose, the almond-shaped eye and the thick lips, while the color is a copper red.

"Père Rouquette said a few words in Choctaw regarding my presence, and they asked if I came from beyond the great lake, raising for an instant their large, timid eyes to look at me, then bending them at once upon their work. The men were away hunting, and the women were sorry not to have some game to offer their priest on the occasion of this visit of the white man. Near by was the cone-shaped wigwam made of cane reed and branches. Within were hung the arms and utensils. The guns and hunting knives were all modern. I looked in vain for bows and arrows, tomahawks and feather decorations. On the ground were mats and blankets. This was all. Near the cabin was a little fire with a kettle hung over it, and farther away a few chickens and the dog completed the inventory of this humble home.

"They envy us not, ask nothing of us but the liberty to live after their own customs, with the forest for their hunting grounds, and their independence in the solitude. The Choctaw has preserved many natural good qualities; aside from the love of drink, which he has learned from the whites, he is sober, of pure morals, hospitable and generous. He is happier in giving than in receiving. Every violation of morals is severely punished, and now rarely occurs. One of the principal punishments is to cut the hair, which is for both men and women a public dishonor and humiliation.

"When we reached home we found two young Choctaws leaning on their guns, waiting to offer a large turtle and four squirrels. The dress of these men was similar to the one seen in the forest the previous day, except that these wore a sort of white tunic. These men were short in stature, well formed, with broad shoulders and well-developed muscles. Their skin was a dark bronze. They were really splendid types of energy and savage pride.

"They received us with a smile, seemed happy to hear our exclamations of welcome. Then they received some remnants left from our dinner and departed well satisfied. As the shadows of the night began to close in around us, Père Rouquette conducted me to my cell, a tiny cabin five or six feet square, with a little couch, a mosquito bar, a table and a chair. In all my life I never spent such a happy night. I saw the shadow of the trees draw closer and closer their curtains of darkness. Then I could no longer distinguish their variety, and soon the fireflies began their dazzling dance above and all around my little dwelling. The heavens were unclouded, a light breeze freshened the atmosphere and, playing in the branches of the trees, produced a sweet and yet fantastic harmony.

"My enthusiasm is difficult to arouse, but that night I became a poet, I think, as I walked back and forth, inebriated by the enchantment of the solitude. I spoke to God in the depths of my soul. I sang in a low voice hymns of love and praise and gratitude. I prayed to the Virgin Mother and to all the saints in Paradise. I prayed for all, for France, my mother, my brother, my sister, my brothers in religion, my friends beyond the seas—for America, for the Indians, in a word for all.

"Next morning I rose early, said my Mass, and telling my good Abbé Rouquette how happy and grateful I was for his cordial hospitality, I turned my steps again toward the haunts of civilization."

For the next twenty years the Abbé Rouquette continued to live this plain life of service in the woods. His superficial eccentricities were more noticeable as he aged. He wrapped himself in the mystic's cloak, while taking on new Choctaw mannerisms. But his interior resources were ample. He was an ardent naturalist. Also, he had never ceased to write verse, apportioning his themes between the praise of God and the praise of nature. It was felicitous minor poetry. Then, shortly after his sixtieth year, Rouquette revealed the full extent of his literary preoccupation with Chateaubriand by producing a prose romance called *La Nouvelle Atala*.

The plot, conceived in the spirit of a legend, is little more than a variation of its model. The heroine, supposedly of a French colonial family and named Atala by her parents in honor of Chateaubriand's heroine, runs away into the forest where she becomes a religious devotee. Her relationship with the Indians, who know her as the "White Savage," is suggestive of Père Rouquette's own idyllic existence. Indeed, she is in many respects his feminine counterpart. This new Atala, like the old one, has foresworn the love of the flesh. On her deathbed she learns that she is actually of half-Indian parentage. The rhythmic style in which the tale is composed was praised by many nineteenth-century critics, including Lafcadio Hearn.

In 1886 Rouquette's health failed. He was removed to the Hôtel Dieu in New Orleans, where he endured a lingering illness. The following year he died and was buried in the old St. Louis Cemetery No. 1. Contemporary accounts say that the most impressive feature of his funeral was the delegation of Choctaw mourners in tribal dress. They had been waiting for days at the hospital to get the last word of Chata-Ima. Then, stony-faced, they followed the cortege to the tomb.

Dominique Rouquette, Adrien's elder brother by three years, was the finer and more original poet of the two. While living in Paris he published a volume entitled *Les Meschacébéennes* (Mississippians, from one of the original native names of the river), in 1839. Its successor, *Fleurs d'Amerique,* did not appear until 1856, long after his return to Louisiana, where he was a Bohemian figure in the salons of New Orleans. He lived until 1890. His idealization of the Indians is scarcely less romantic than that to which Chata-Ima gave himself, but the canvas is larger, the music more masculine.

Other early Creole poets were Charles O. Dugué, Urbain David, Tullius St. Ceran and Dr. Alfred Mercier. Mercier issued his first volume, *Erato,* in 1840, but he was to do his work of greatest significance after the War between the States. Up till that struggle which changed so many things there was no competition in the English language worth mentioning.

Chapter 15

The Fair North Shore

MANDEVILLE, the town on the north shore of Lake Pontchartrain to which Madame Lalaurie fled to escape the public's vengeance, had then just come into existence. It was conceived romantically by Bernard de Marigny, and it stands today as his most lasting monument. No one who writes about the region can ignore the Marignys, for in addition to their great plantation that was to become part of New Orleans they had much to do with the developing of the fair pine-wooded lands on the other side of the lake from the city. Mandeville was an outgrowth of the family estate called Fontainebleau. Frequent references have been made in these pages to Bernard and his ancestors, and yet the subject has been merely skirted. One could devote an entire book to them. As Grace King pointed out, Bernard de Marigny is the man who, more than any of his contemporaries, struck the note of fine living and generous spending which we have in mind when we say Creole aristocrat.

It will help to a better understanding of Fontainebleau and Mandeville if we revert for a moment to the riverside mansion where Louis Philippe and his brother, the colonial prefect Laussat, General Jackson, and the Marquis de Lafayette on his visit to New Orleans in 1825 were regally entertained. Laussat has left the best description. He says in his memoirs:

"The river shows itself here to the best advantage; we are situated at a point in its crescent that dominates the port. One hundred ships, some of France, some of Spain, but mostly Anglo-American, stretch out in the distance as would a forest afloat and offer a perspective worthy of the most active settlement in the world. We usually go to bed at ten, sometimes at nine, so as to

Bureau of New Orleans News

SAINT LOUIS CATHEDRAL IN NEW ORLEANS

The cathedral was built in 1794. In the right foreground is the statue of Andrew Jackson for whom the Square is named.

State Parks Commission

FONTAINEBLEAU STATE PARK ON LAKE PONTCHARTRAIN

State Parks Commission

THE BEACH AT FONTAINEBLEAU STATE PARK

Fontainebleau State Park is on the north shore of Lake Pontchartrain near Mandeville and was formerly the plantation of Bernard de Marigny.

find refuge from the attacks of mosquitoes and gnats, which at sundown take full possession of the air hereabout; they fly through the smallest apertures, swarm around all the lights, prick us to the quick with their stings. . . . Even a drawing room, in spite of the diversions usually provided there by a numerous assembly, becomes a place of torture; the passion for gambling and the toughness of one's skin, secured from long habit, alone can render these bearable. . . . We, nevertheless, appreciate the advantage of living in such a comfortable home, one charmingly situated, bathed often with cool breezes, if such are anywhere to be had, and when returning to it we always experience a new feeling of pleasure at our being once more under such a roof. The library is the greatest pleasure. I have there under my very eyes an entire collection of books, even as to my favorite ones."

Those books were assuredly the soundest proof of luxury in the New Orleans of 1803. The average colonist was notoriously indifferent to literature. But the big house buzzing with company—and mosquitoes—palled sometimes on those who lived there. That was why old Pierre Philippe de Marigny, as has been mentioned, bought the summer retreat in the forest by the lake. Erroneous tales concerning this transaction have come down. He is said to have acquired an immense tract, and although the purchase was made under the Spaniards there is a glamorous myth that it was conceded to him because of a fondness La Pompadour had had for his father, and that he named it Fontainebleau in her honor. The truth is, he never owned more than a small *pied-à-terre* near the lake.

The greater Fontainebleau was built up by Bernard, the largest parcel of land having originally been granted by Governor Gayoso de Lemos to a New Orleans merchant, Antonio Bonabel, in 1799. It is described in the deed signed by Gayoso de Lemos as "four thousand and twenty arpents of surface situated on the northeastern part of Lake Pontchartrain at a place known as Punta Verde, about one mile and a half southeast of Bayou Castine." The Marigny holdings at last expanded to 3,545.68 acres.

This was one of the loveliest spots in the country of the Choctaw. The beach was broad and clean. A short distance back from it grew magnificent live oaks draped with Spanish moss, and behind these was the murmuring pine forest traversed by narrow bayous. Magnolia trees flourished there, also. There was a wealth of flowers, including wild honeysuckle and Cherokee roses. The woods swarmed with game, and the waters of both lake and bayous with fish.

Bernard de Marigny delighted in improving his paradise during the 1820's, treating it partly as a show place, partly as a sugar plantation. It is told that when the bell for summoning his slaves to work was being cast he nonchalantly tossed one thousand Mexican silver dollars into the caldron, to give the bell a purer tone. It was rated singularly sweet. He spent more and more of his time at Fontainebleau, influenced by the double fact that his second marriage had proved unhappy and that the city house was being crowded close by his Faubourg Marigny. Then he had a new inspiration. He would build an ideal town right there on the Pontchartrain lake front.

He bought additional land immediately to the west of his estate, and he laid out streets as he had done in New Orleans, but with more zest. Personally he supervised the construction of public buildings, a church, a market hall, charming miniature bridges that crossed a stream, a hotel by the shore, and wharves. He placed lots on sale, with restrictions designed to attract the sort of people he wanted rather than to make large profits. He established a ferry service across the lake, the fare not to exceed one dollar, and as this coincided with the opening of the Pontchartrain Railroad a regular and easy contact with the city was assured. Naming it Mandeville from one of his family titles, he declared it to have been organized as a town in 1834. A mayor and council elected under a sharply restricted franchise took over its affairs.

John Davis, the noted gambler and theatrical manager, who despite his Welsh name was an *émigré* from Saint Domingue, was much interested in the town. Marigny accounted him a good friend and gave him a share in the enterprise, particularly as to the ferry line and various aspects of catering. Davis brought several accomplished chefs from Paris and they gave the restaurants of Mandeville eminence from the start. Some of them eventually opened hotels of their own, and their successors carried on the tradition of good cooking. Gambling was the master passion of Bernard de Marigny's life, so naturally he and Davis saw to it that opportunities to play were not lacking. There may have been other villages in the United States in the 1830's that equaled the gaiety of Mandeville, but there could have been none to challenge its sophistication and European air.

Two miles farther to the west was the tiny lake-shore hamlet of Louisburg, and four miles beyond that one reached the mouth of the Tchefuncte River, which was navigable for boats of shallow draft. A short distance up the river stood Madisonville, a small but important landing stage for communication with the interior. Why Madisonville had never grown was found puzzling. In 1817 the *Western Gazeteer, or Emigrant's Directory* referred to it as being "handsomely situated" and "unquestionably destined to become a great commercial city. . . . Such are the local advantages of this place that the government has fixed on the site a navy yard near the mouth of the Tchefuncte, where the keel of a light frigate was laid down in 1812, intended for the defense of the lakes. It is believed to be a more healthful location, and less infected with mosquitoes, than New Orleans." The navy yard fell idle, disappeared, and there were other discouragements. Yet five or six miles farther in a straight line, up the tortuous Tchefuncte and Bogue Falaya Rivers, Covington at the extreme head of navigation succeeded in becoming the chief town of the parish.

Covington was settled by pioneers of English stock in 1769, seven years before the American Revolution when the region was in dispute between Britain and Spain. It was first called Wharton. An attempt was made to change the name to Jefferson in 1813, but three years later the designation Covington triumphed at a political meeting at which Kentucky whisky was flowing plentifully. It seemed appropriate to honor the source of such excellent liquor (Covington, Kentucky), or so it is said. The town was made the parish seat in 1828, six years before the establishment of Mandeville. Steadily the older place has kept ahead of Bernard de Marigny's creation, but Bernard was interested neither in commerce nor in attracting a large population—not in his holiday region, at all events. He reserved such ambitions for New Orleans, where as a matter of fact he proved himself a poor businessman and little by little lost the whole of his enormous fortune.

Inland and some distance to the east of the settlements already mentioned was Lacombe on the bayou of the same name. It had only a few score inhabitants. From there westward to the Bayou Chinchuba and taking in the back reaches of Fontainebleau was the stamping ground of the main remnant of the Choctaw nation. The Rouquette family had a home at Bayou Lacombe. In 1810 the poet François Dominique Rouquette was born there. His brother Adrien Emanuel spent the better part of his life in the neighborhood, but the story behind that has already been given treatment in another chapter.

To east and west of this charming north-shore country, the water front has little to offer in the way of beauty. The two ends of Pontchartrain have attractions only for the sailor, the fisherman and the naturalist. If it were not for the expansion of New Orleans to the lake's edge, the entire southern coast would be as colorless as it is flat. Everywhere, save in the sections already described, there are long stretches of reeds half submerged in brackish water, alternating with cypress swamps and harsh beaches covered with pebbles and sea shells.

Because of the Rigolets and Chef Menteur straits, the eastern extremity is of more interest than the western. A strong tide surges daily in and out of the Rigolets, and deep-sea fish swarm inside the narrow passage, which consequently is preferred to the lake itself by knowing anglers. The crumbling walls and dry moat of Fort Pike are located on the channel, closer to Mississippi Sound than to the lake. This fortress was built after the War of

1812. It never had the opportunity to figure in a defensive action, and following the War between the States it was allowed gradually to fall into decay.

Leaving the Rigolets and turning southward, one comes to the irregular inlet called Lake St. Catherine. This is very shallow with marshy shores; there is reason to suppose that it will disappear in time by evaporation and the thickening muck created by dead vegetable matter. Just beyond Lake St. Catherine is the Chef Menteur, a passage still more restricted than the Rigolets, and which connects with Lake Borgne. It is the scene of Fort Macomb, built at about the same time as Fort Pike, and now equally in ruins.

The Pointe-aux-Herbes of the first explorers lies between the Chef Menteur and the New Orleans city line. It is an insignificant, low-lying cape densely grown with reeds. Beyond New Orleans the shore has no surprises to offer, until presently one reaches the outlet of the Bonnet Carré Spillway and the Pass Manchac which links Pontchartrain to Maurepas. The northwesterly curve from this point to the mouth of the Tangipahoa River is a desolate stretch. Then begin the glorious pine woods, the fertile loam and the white beaches that Bernard de Marigny loved and the Creole poets celebrated.

Marigny managed to keep Fontainebleau until 1852 when it was sold to satisfy his creditors. It had several subsequent owners, among them the Nort family, which bought it in 1881. Eventually about one-fifth of the plantation was organized into the Tchefuncte State Park, afterward renamed the Fontainebleau State Park, and the rest included in a conservation area. The house and outbuildings burned down years ago, but traces of the ruins are still to be seen, and one crumbling sugarhouse stands among the second-growth pines. Modern structures suited to the resort have, of course, been erected.

The story, long believed in Louisiana, that the naturalist John James Audubon was born on the Marigny property is nothing but a fable. Some writers even give the birthplace as the town of

Mandeville, an absurdity seeing that Audubon was nearing fifty when Mandeville was founded. His recent biographers, Francis Hobart Herrick and Constance Rourke, have established that he first opened his eyes in Saint Domingue, the illegitimate son of a Captain Audubon and a Frenchwoman named Rabin. He was taken to France for his education, and came to America in 1803 when he was a little under eighteen. His first visit to New Orleans was in 1820. Several of his finest bird drawings were made there, and at Oakley in the "Florida" parish of West Feliciana. There is no record of his having seen the shores of Lake Pontchartrain.

Another tale concerning Audubon is to the effect that he was none other than the Dauphin of France, son of Louis XVI and Marie Antoinette, who had been spirited out of the Temple and substituted for the just-deceased boy from Saint Domingue. That he more than once hinted at a great mystery in his past is a fact. When his own son John passed suddenly, Audubon's widow cried above the bier: "My son, my son! To think that you should have died without knowing the secret of your father's life!"

L'Athénée Louisianais, an important Creole literary society, published a poem entitled *Mandeville,* by Georges Dessommes, in the first issue of its *Comptes Rendus* under the date of July 1, 1876. This is the opening verse:

Mandeville—une plage étroite et verdoyante;
Des chênes et des pins, verts en toutes saisons,
Y dressant au soleil leur tête chatoyante,
Ombragent ses gazons.

(Mandeville—a narrow and verdant beach;
Oaks and pines that are in all seasons green,
Lifting toward the sun their changeful heads,
Shading the lawns.)

The rest of the poem, translated literally, conveys an impression on which it would be difficult to improve:

"The oaks are densely foliaged, with a grandiose aspect; their huge branches extend widely, close above the lake, which waters them incessantly with foam.

"The pines offer an inaccessible forehead to the winds; one could imagine them laughing heartily in the skies to see the passage of man, the atom, puffed up with his pride.

"These trees are covered with long gray mosses, which give the countryside a mournful air when they hang at evening without responding to the caresses of the breeze.

"Along the lake extends a shady alley, which runs beside the white houses with green blinds; my friends, they do not have the aloof grace of your smiling chalets.

"Their architecture is not distinguished; over there I should not have been able to take them seriously. But within their wooden walls, O Nature, the spirit understands thee better!

"Its tranquillity, above all, is what makes me love this countryside; always calm here, I have my immortal soul for company, and I am able to speak to God.

"The joyous talk of my brothers and sisters, as well as certain chosen friends, drives away the dream of the past that saddens and irritates me with its tears and cares.

"The noisy, curious and hypocritical world does not trouble the echo of the forest's voices. Finally, to complete the charm of this spot, but one thing is lacking:

"A chain of mountains that should mirror its summits in the depths of the silent lake, and whose altitudes would draw the poet closer to Heaven."

have been treasured up and dearly close up to the [illegible], which [illegible] has been [illegible] with them.

The [illegible] them are [illegible] [illegible] the [illegible] and [illegible] [illegible] [illegible] [illegible] [illegible] [illegible] [illegible] [illegible] [illegible] the [illegible] [illegible] with [illegible] [illegible].

[illegible] [illegible] [illegible] [illegible] [illegible] [illegible] [illegible] [illegible] [illegible] [illegible] [illegible] [illegible] [illegible] [illegible] [illegible] the [illegible] [illegible] [illegible].

[illegible] [illegible] [illegible] [illegible] [illegible] [illegible] [illegible] [illegible] [illegible] with green [illegible] [illegible] [illegible] [illegible] [illegible] [illegible] the [illegible] [illegible] [illegible] [illegible].

[illegible] [illegible] [illegible] [illegible] [illegible] [illegible] [illegible] [illegible] [illegible] [illegible] have been [illegible] [illegible] [illegible] [illegible] [illegible] [illegible] [illegible] [illegible] [illegible] [illegible] [illegible] [illegible].

[illegible] [illegible] [illegible] [illegible] [illegible] [illegible] [illegible] [illegible] always [illegible] [illegible] [illegible] [illegible] [illegible] [illegible] [illegible] [illegible] [illegible].

The [illegible] [illegible] [illegible] [illegible] and [illegible] [illegible] [illegible] [illegible] [illegible] [illegible] [illegible] [illegible] [illegible] [illegible] [illegible] [illegible] [illegible] [illegible].

The [illegible] [illegible] and [illegible] [illegible] [illegible] [illegible] [illegible] the [illegible] of the [illegible] [illegible] [illegible] to [illegible] the [illegible] of [illegible] [illegible], [illegible] [illegible] [illegible] [illegible].

[illegible] [illegible] [illegible] [illegible] [illegible] [illegible] [illegible] in the [illegible] of [illegible] [illegible], and whose [illegible] would [illegible] [illegible] [illegible] [illegible] [illegible].

Part III

THE WAR PERIOD

Chapter 16

The Pontchartrain Railroad

PASSENGERS and freight disembarked under the walls of Spanish Fort at the mouth of the Bayou St. John were, to a large extent, transferred to smaller craft that plied the bayou and the Carondelet Canal to the city. Barges and other light-draft vessels, from pirogues to schooners, were available. But what with the crowding and the dependence on sail, oars, or horsepower on the banks, this last lap of the journey was effected at a turtlelike pace. A land route also existed, though the swamps through which it passed at the Pontchartrain end made it disagreeable and unpopular. From the point at which it left the bayou, it was the identical route followed by Iberville and Bienville, by generations of colonists that came in their tracks, and by Jackson when he arrived to plan the defense of New Orleans.

This is its course on a modern map: the Grand Route St. John to Gentilly Road, then down Bayou Road to where the latter merges with Governor Nicholls Street (formerly Hospital Street) at North Claiborne Avenue, and along Governor Nicholls Street into the Vieux Carré. Despite the annoyances, a swelling traffic used either the water or land connections. Some of the movement back and forth was local, for excursionists sought the lake front, and rich families that owned homes on the far shore traveled that way.

A better means of transportation was urgently needed. In the eastern states men had begun to experiment with railroads, and as early as 1825 the Louisiana *Gazette* suggested that a line should be built from the city to Pontchartrain. No one paid much attention for the moment to so radical an idea. Three years later a lawyer named Morris Hoffman, a Marylander who had seen the beginnings of the Baltimore & Ohio Railroad, took it up and called a mass meeting. The inevitable committee to look into the matter was appointed, with disappointing results. But Hoffman brushed aside the committee and united those businessmen who had shown real interest as the New Orleans Railroad Society. This became a corporation in 1829, the Pontchartrain Railroad Company. It was authorized by the state legislature to proceed with the road, under date of January 10, 1830. Meanwhile, Hoffman had anticipated this action by making a trip east to study construction methods and engage a surveyor.

The route decided on was straight out Elysian Fields Avenue, that broad dream street which bisected the Faubourg Marigny and which had been intended to rival its namesake in Paris. Now, of all noisy and unbeautiful thoroughfares, it was to be a railroad right of way. For three and a half miles inland from the river there was a canal which appears on an American map of the city, dated 1798, as the "Saw-Mill Canal of Peter de Marigny." The railroad company bought it, along with adjoining property, for $25,000. Tracks were laid parallel to the canal, which later was filled in. Land was also purchased from the d'Estréhan family, and at the lake end, east of the Bayou St. John, a large tract for a station, shops, wharves, a hotel and bathing beach, was acquired from Alexander Milne.

Work on the road was begun on March 10 and was pushed energetically by Captain John Grant, to whom the contract had been let. The total length of the line was 4.96 miles. It was ready on April 14, 1831, and formally opened nine days later. Horses were used for motive power during the first year and a half. Then an engine was imported from England. An observer of the trial run commented that the iron horse "passed playfully up and down . . . under as complete control as a hackney coach." The era of the "steam cars" had arrived.

This midget line was the first railroad in the United States west of the Alleghenies. The further claim is made that while construction was started and trains run on several roads ahead of it, it was the first in this country to complete its trackage.

The writer has had access to the original minute book of the Pontchartrain Railroad Company.* Technical and verbose, it would be tedious if quoted entire. But the following excerpts from the first seven annual reports and one special report give a more colorful impression than any rewriting of their contents could hope to attain:

"*First Annual Report, 1830:* The whole work received a check by a considerable mortality among the hands, who could not be restrained from entering the city. . . .

"A respectable Captain of a Mobile packet is ready to receive his cargo at the lake shore, and lighter it off, the moment we are prepared even for this imperfect operation. These facts are better than volumes of speculation. The wonderful success of similar undertakings in England and in the Atlantic States loudly encourage us to proceed. If railroads are to succeed anywhere, it is on short distances near large cities. . . . It would be surprising if a short road from New Orleans (visited by so many strangers) to the lake, a place of great resort for pleasure, and on which so much business is transacted, should not afford a profitable investment.

"*Second Annual Report, 1831:* Most of the stockholders were present at the opening of the Road on the 23rd of April last. It was a signal triumph of a lofty and persevering spirit of enterprise over the fears of the prudent and the prophecies of the timid. . . .

"It was the intention of the Directors to have provided separate accommodations for the colored population, but it has been out of their power to do so. They trust this want will be remedied another season. . . .

"The receipts of the Company since the opening of the Road on the 23rd April up to the 1st December inst. amount to the sum

---

* Courtesy of the Louisville & Nashville Railroad, which bought the Pontchartrain Railroad in 1880.

of $20,414.51. This is a large sum under the circumstances. It was not until the 4th of July that there was any shelter in the shape of a house to receive visitors, or any place for bathing. . . .

"Fifty-four thousand four hundred and thirty-seven passengers have been carried on the Road without the slightest accident to any of them.

"*Special Report on a Company Circular, August 1832:* The causes which have led to the great increased expenditure of the undertaking have mainly arisen from the difficulties and loss experienced in constructing the harbours in the lake. The formation of a basin in the open sea or lake should be the work of the Nation rather than of a Company. As nothing of the kind had been constructed in our lakes it was therefore to be accomplished by dear bought experience. . . .

"On the 1st November next the road will exhibit the imposing spectacle of an engine uniting the power of 20 horses, and a train of 50 freight wagons and twelve cars and passengers. During the winter the other engine and 20 freight cars may be expected, constituting a means of transportation equal to all the tonnage on the lake.

"*Third Annual Report, 1832:* In the lake, works of great magnitude and expense have been constructed, and on its shore has been reared one of the most extensive hotels in the southern country. . . .

"The road was opened for the transportation of freight early in November last, and on the 16th of that month the Schooner *Orleans,* Captain Crocler, entered for freight. The day after the *Isabella,* Captain Vincent, arrived, and several vessels loaded with firewood; a few days after discharged and departed, while from the low stage of water at the Bayou no vessel could, during that period, either enter or depart with cargo.

"*Fourth Annual Report, 1833:* The cholera and yellow fever during the last summer have certainly reduced the receipts of the Company upwards of $20,000.

"*Fifth Annual Report, 1834:* The Directors have the satisfaction to state that since the opening of the road about 498,000 passengers have been conveyed on it, and that but one instance of injury to passengers has occurred; this instance occurred recently, and was caused to a passenger who in a state of intoxication jumped from the car when the train was at full speed.

"*Sixth Annual Report, 1835:* You will see, gentlemen, by Statement No. 1, that we have to pay in the course of the years 1836 and '37 the sum of $11,435 for the purchase of eleven slaves; the Directors thought proper to adopt this means of reducing the heavy expenses that have weighed upon the company from its origin. For when it is considered that more than $50,000 of wages have been paid since five years [presumably to eleven men] it will be seen how useful it would have been to have bought from the beginning the number required by the wants of the company.

"*Seventh Annual Report, 1836:* If the annual progression of the receipts of the Company be considered with attention and compared with those that will probably be realized in the course of the next five years, no doubt that the most partial will be forced to admit that this company should be placed in the rank occupied by the best institutions of New Orleans; for no other can be mentioned which, in the space of seven years, has more than doubled the amount of its capital paid in."

But there are details, some inspiring and some quaint, which do not appear in these reports. The officers of the company admitted that part of the time they made decisions without the advice of construction engineers. It was debated whether the coaches should rest on springs. Also whether wooden rails would not be just as good as metal ones. The rails finally adopted ran to the opposite extreme; they were of wrought iron, massive bars "somewhat in the shape of an inverted square trough with holes punched through the face of each rail to allow it to be fastened by spikes to wooden sills which were in turn bolted on cross-ties, the track being unballasted."* Let modern railroaders ponder this and shudder.

Shortly before the first locomotive was delivered from England

* Kincaid Herr, in *The Louisville & Nashville,* employees' magazine, October 1928.

there appeared in New Orleans a man named John Shields who had brought with him at great expense, by steamboat, an engine which he had invented for use on turnpikes. It had not proved satisfactory, so he changed its wheels to fit rails and was in hopes that the Pontchartrain road would adopt it. An attempt at a trial run was a dismal failure. The company bought the contraption for $1,000, however, and utilized it in its shops to supply power for the turning of a lathe and grindstone.

Then the "imposing" 20 h.p. locomotive *Creole* arrived, followed a little while afterward by the *Pontchartrain,* which boasted of 24 h.p. According to tradition, unsupported be it said by documentary evidence, these engines were equipped with sails. If the machinery broke down, up went the canvas, and—granting that the wind was from the right quarter—the train crawled on its way. Once, in 1834, the *Creole* with four passengers attached ran off the lake end of the line into shallow water. It is vaguely described as a case of spontaneous action. No persons were aboard at the time, not even the engineer.

The fare originally charged was seventy-five cents for the round trip, and the public paid it gladly on account of the novelty of the journey. Gradual reductions brought it eventually to only fifteen cents. Freight rates were correspondingly high at the start. Goods were loaded and unloaded from the cars by means of a crane, but the superintendent presently conceived the idea of freight platforms raised to a level with the floors of the cars. He built the first in America, over the opposition of his directors.

On Saturdays, Sundays and holidays, when excursions were run, an empty boxcar was always carried on an early train. It served as a jail into which pickpockets, drunks and other disturbers of the peace were thrown. At night it was hooked onto the last train, hauled to the city and its occupants were turned over to the police. This would seem to imply that, for some years at least, the railroad was the sole law-enforcement agency at its lake terminus. The founding and growth of that community, which was called Milneburg, is an important chapter in the story of the Pontchartrain line. One of New Orleans' most singular characters is inseparably involved.

We have said that the tract for the terminus was bought in 1830 from Alexander Milne. It would have been impossible to reach the lake front without doing business with him. Except for one or two sites belonging to the government, such as the fort and landing place at the mouth of the Bayou St. John, he owned the entire margin for twenty-one miles along the southern shore of Pontchartrain from a point west of New Orleans in Jefferson Parish all the way to the Rigolets. He was then eighty-six years old and had taken half a lifetime to accumulate holdings that were chiefly cypress swamps, reed marshes and sand. He had been impelled by a combination of shrewdness and eccentricity.

Milne was born at the little feudal town of Fochabers, Scotland, in 1744. The ducal house of Richmond and Gordon dominated the neighborhood, and Alexander was proud to start life as a footman at the castle. He must have made a good domestic, for he was holding the job in his early thirties, and possibly he might never have pursued larger ambitions if he had not happened to have a head of thick, flaming red hair. The duke, whose way of living had been comparatively informal in the manner of a Highland chieftain, suddenly concluded that he ought to do as other peers did. He ordered his household into livery, and this required Milne to powder his hair. The footman was small of stature and far from good-looking, but he was exaggeratedly proud of his hair. Rather than whiten it artificially, he threw up his situation and emigrated to America.

It is not known whether he tried the English colonies first. He reached New Orleans in 1776 just as the Revolution was starting and Governor Bernardo de Gálvez was preparing to aid it. The canny Milne never told where his sympathies had lain. His early years under the Spanish flag are wrapped in mystery. After a few years, however, we find him prosperously established in the hardware business. Then he bought a large number of slaves and set them to manufacturing brick. The product of his kilns was said to be the best in the city, and apparently he furnished most of the brick for reconstruction after the fires of 1788 and 1794.

Milne obtained from the Spanish Government an extensive grant of land on the Gentilly plain to the northeast of the city. This was in the late 1790's. He liked being an owner of real estate, and he became obsessed by two ideas. With genuine foresight, he formed the opinion that no matter how serious the physical obstacles might be New Orleans would someday grow out to Pontchartrain and that shore lots were a good investment. So he added steadily to his water-front property, getting much of it for little or nothing, but paying what was then a considerable price for control of the property immediately east of the Bayou St. John. In 1821 he was indemnified $2,500 for damage done to his estate by the British during the campaign of 1814-1815.

The man's second notion was extraordinary. He believed that the air of the cypress swamps was notably healthful. No one else thought so. The fevers and other maladies of the climate were all ascribed to the foul exhalations of the swamps, and the swamps were in fact unwholesome. Mosquitoes apart, the stagnant waters were breeding places of typhoid and dysentery. Alexander Milne maintained stubbornly that people would benefit by making their homes among the half-drowned cypresses. What about himself? He passed a good deal of his time in such surroundings, and was never ill. What about the Indians?*

When Louisiana became American, Milne was almost sixty, well-to-do but not the millionaire that his land schemes and the building of the Pontchartrain Railroad would eventually make him. There could not have been a trace left of the vanity that had once centered about his hair. He is described as walking the streets with his head sagging and his eyes fixed on the ground,

* Percy Viosca, Jr., New Orleans scientist, told the writer that insofar as malaria is concerned Alexander Milne's opinion was justified. The Anopheles mosquito which carries the fever does not live in dense cypress swamps, so one is safer there than in open country or cities.

seemingly lost in a brown study. His clothes were so ancient and ragged that strangers mistook him for a beggar and often offered him money. We are not told whether he accepted these gifts. It would have been typical of him to do so, less from greed than from a streak of sardonic humor he possessed. Those who did business with Milne esteemed him for his honesty, prudence and ability.

If he ever married, his wife must have died young and without issue. He lived surrounded by slaves in a freakish-looking mansion on Bayou Road, near Robertson Street, built in imitation of a Scottish castle. Real-estate transfers of the period reveal the presence in New Orleans of a brother named Andrew, who disappears leaving no other trace.

The railroad development gave Alexander the chance of which he had doubtless dreamed. Significantly, the minutes already quoted say that land was bought outright from Messrs. Marigny, Darcantel, d'Estréhan and Hopkins, but add: "The remaining proprietor was Mr. Alexander Milne who owns for a mile and a quarter from the lake upwards. With him an agreement has been made . . . for the space of land required." The aged speculator may have rented the site. Or, since there is no mention of rent paid, he may even have cannily allowed it to be used rent free for a term of years, in order to make sure that the terminus would be where he wanted it to be, and thus to benefit by the boom in land values. The railroad apparently did not get full title until after his death.

Milne plunged zestfully into the game. He created no monuments in the way of public works or buildings, but he took an interest in the laying out of the township and he saw to it that the name Milneburg was adopted. He later showed that he regarded the whole community as his memorial, and that he wanted to benefit its inhabitants. At the start, however, the main consideration was to justify his theories about the lake shore by piling up a fortune. It is said that in the course of a single week he once sold lots rated at $3,000,000. This figure is either an estimate of future values or it is an exaggeration. Milne never was worth much more than $3,000,000 all told, and no one week could have produced a turnover of the kind. That he tripled or quadrupled his wealth during the early days of Milneburg is a certainty.

He also bought and sold property in New Orleans, making a handsome profit on his deals until the financial panic of 1837 halted him. But he said that these city operations did not give him the satisfaction that he had had out of Milneburg.

In his ninety-third year Milne made his will. The rumor that he had done so spread, and there was much guessing how the erratic ancient had disposed of his property. The curious had to wait for another year. Milne died of sheer senility on October 20, 1838, aged ninety-four,* and on October 23 the *Courier* "conjectured" that he had left money for the founding of philanthropic institutions "in the hamlet that bears his name on the borders of Lake Pontchartrain." Scornfully brushing aside the old man's idea that the air of cypress swamps was healthful, the newspaper added: "It will require much improvement to render that neighborhood salubrious during all seasons of the year."

The text of the will was published a few days later. There were large bequests to relatives in Scotland. Some favorite slaves were freed and annuities provided for them. His native town of Fochabers received $100,000 for a school. The sum of $500,000 was left to establish two asylums at Milneburg, one for destitute orphan boys and one for destitute orphan girls; and also partly to endow two existing refuges of the same character in New Orleans. It was specified that the funds for the local benefactions should come from the sale of lots on Lake Pontchartrain and the Bayou St. John.

A more unfortunately worded testament it would be hard to imagine, and it led to a good deal of litigation. A typical clause read: "It is my positive will and intention that an asylum, etc., etc., and that my executors shall cause the same to be duly incorporated by the proper authorities of this State." The legislature

* Contemporary newspapers state that he had reached the age of ninety-seven, but the inscription on his tomb in St. Louis Cemetery No. 2, New Orleans, says ninety-four. Also chiseled on this conspicuous but inartistic monument is the text of the act under which the Louisiana legislature incorporated the Milne homes for destitute orphans.

acted favorably within five months, but it was another matter for the executors to get hold of the funds. At the time of Milne's death, conservative estimates valued his real estate at not less than $2,000,000. Yet the inventory filed when the will was probated totaled only $913,805.94. The appraisal of land was at nominal figures. That portion of the entire Pontchartrain water front still belonging to the estate, for instance, was held to be worth $43,500, a derisory rating. One must suppose that the intention was to defraud the charities.

Louisiana law forbade bequests to persons living in foreign countries which debarred Louisianians as heirs. Scots law said that none but citizens of the United Kingdom could inherit Scots property. So the probate court nullified the legacy to Fochabers. The Duke of Richmond and Gordon (descendant of the peer whom Milne had served as a footman) sued for a reversal and won. A school to give training for civil-service positions was opened. It is considered the most dignified and useful outcome of Alexander Milne's good intentions.

The homes for orphans came into existence after quibbling and delays. At one time it was found that a mere half-dozen children were being cared for at inordinate expense, the excuse being that a destitute orphan was *rara avis* in Milneburg. The township was finally absorbed by New Orleans and the scope of the institutions broadened. During the War between the States, the funds were mishandled by officers of the Federal army of occupation under Generals Benjamin F. Butler and Nathaniel P. Banks. The orphanages were closed in 1865, then revived after a long lapse of years. Controversies, financial and otherwise, have continued to mark their record.

One of the chief resorts built at Milneburg by the Pontchartrain Railroad, or under its auspices, was the Washington Hotel with its adjacent park and bathing beach. This was much appreciated for week ends by the citizens of New Orleans. Presently travelers arriving or leaving by boat stopped over at the Washington for a day or two, unless they were hard pressed for time. A good shell road for carriages, in addition to the railroad, soon connected the resort with the city. Its restaurant became celebrated. As early as 1832 the railroad advertised a "venison dinner every Thursday on arrival of the quarter past 3 o'clock car." It also announced that "reservations by parties may be made to view sunrise on the Lake."

Subsequently a French chef named Louis Boudro took over the restaurant and attracted the most distinguished clientele. William Makepeace Thackeray, the author of *Vanity Fair,* was a guest while visiting New Orleans to deliver a series of lectures for the Lyceum Society. Thackeray's poem on the bouillabaisse (a fish chowder) of French Mediterranean ports is a classic. In a memoir of his New Orleans trip, he paid this tribute to Boudro's creation:

"At that comfortable inn in Pontchartrain we had bouillabaisse than which a better never eaten at Marseilles, and not a headache in the morning, upon my word, on the contrary, only awoke with a sweet, refreshing thirst for claret and water."

Spanish Fort near by was the location of a similar hotel and pleasure resort started by Harvey Elkin, a well-known caterer of the day, which he called Elkinsburg. Threatened with bankruptcy he sold out to John Slidell, the lawyer-politician, and other patrons, who turned it into a social club, made him the manager and steward, and named it the Elkin in his honor. This was the first true club in New Orleans—the forerunner of many—and it was thoroughly American in character. The Creoles did not run to that type of organization. An old guidebook says that the Elkin's chef, Bertrand, was "a *cordon bleu* in gastronomy," and adds:

"Those were the days of high betting on cards and horses, the days when the fascinating game of brag [a primitive form of poker] was indulged in, to an extent almost fabulous. Several members of the Elkin Club were known to have lost large sums at the gaming table, thereby enriching some of the more fortunate fellows, and one in particular, to whose success at brag was ascribed the foundation of his subsequent large fortune. Feasting and gaming were not the only pleasures and pastimes at the Elkin. Those were also bibulous days; but to the honor and credit of that period be it said, there was no whiskey drunk in the club; in truth, that beverage was then, if not unknown, at least rejected from all social indulgencies. Madeira—and the Madeira of 1830 was famous—Madeira, sherry, clarets and Burgundies, those were the wines drunk by the Elkin Club men."

On one occasion a group of members staged a contest at which twelve bottles of various wines, to be topped by a bottle of anisette, were to be drunk by each man at the table, with a big purse as a prize. John Slidell and his brilliant old legal confrere John R. Grymes were the sole survivors and split the purse. But the contestants who had rolled under the table never tired of charging jocularly that the winners had called it a draw without attempting to down the full quota of bottles.

In 1831 the Pontchartrain Railroad Company called its station at the foot of Elysian Fields Avenue, near the levee in New Orleans, Pontchartrain Junction. The next year it was designating its terminal facilities on the lake as Port Pontchartrain. This displeased Alexander Milne, who jealously insisted that the name of the entire community was Milneburg. He had his way, for Port Pontchartrain appears only on the oldest maps, and the public never said anything but Milneburg. The name chosen by the company, however, is used in the shipping records of the 1830's. They show that the completion of the railroad had at once attracted many steamboats to the lake trade. Here are some of the arrivals at Port Pontchartrain in the fall of 1832:

The steamer *Long Branch,* from Pascagoula, with passengers, including one lady.

The steamer *Star of the West,* from Mobile via Pascagoula, with United States mail and passengers.

The steamer *William T. Barry,* from Pascagoula.

The steamer *Plough Boy,* from Pearlington, with lumber.

The steamer *Tangipahoa,* from Madisonville. This vessel made two round trips in quick succession and brought over 150,000 feet of lumber from the north shore of the lake.

The field was entered by the steamboat *Otto,* Captain B. Vincent, in October 1834, advertised to make a round trip once each week between Milneburg and Mobile. By January a sister ship, the *Watchman,* had been added, and a schedule of three departures a week from either end was maintained. "The public may rely on their punctuality," announced Thomas Toby & Brother, the New Orleans firm that controlled them. This was the first regular service on a route that was to be popular for nearly half a century.

In November 1837 the steamboat *Merchant* was advertised as being in the Gulf Coast trade. The following year the *Alabama* offered a service three days a week to Madisonville, Louisburg, Mandeville and Covington; the *Giraffe* to Bay St. Louis, Pass Christian and Pascagoula once a week; and the *William Wallace* Tuesdays and Saturdays to Mobile and intermediary points. The vessel last mentioned was described as "a fine steamboat, having superb rooms." Unfortunately, we do not know the tonnage of these craft.

Finally, the Great Mobile and New Orleans mail line was started. A poster dated 1840 read as follows:

Old Southern Route
MOBILE & NEW ORLEANS
Old and well established Mail Route from
Charleston, S. C., to Greensboro'
By Rail Road
A distance of 220 Miles—and from Greensboro' to Columbus, Geo., and Montgomery, Ala., a distance of 220 Miles, by
SPLENDID POST COACHES
And from Montgomery to Mobile and New Orleans, by
ELEGANT STEAM PACKETS
On the Alabama River and Lake Pontchartrain. This is the most certain, safe and comfortable route for travellers going South, and vice versa; running through a healthy section of country, free from the miasmatic atmosphere arising from the Florida swamps. The roads are never subject to sudden inundations so as to prevent travelling—a dangerous and uncertain sea and lake navigation is avoided; and as these lines do not pass through any part of Florida,
No Danger is to be apprehended of any Attack by Indians.
THE GREAT MOBILE & NEW ORLEANS MAIL

Chapter 17

The War between the States

LOUISIANA history during the half century from the attainment of statehood to the act of secession was marked by colorful politics and a tremendous economic boom centering in the port of New Orleans. There was close interplay between the two themes. Together they created the pattern which was so different from that of any other American commonwealth and which has persisted to this day. But attempts to trace political and economic motivation in the same summary are always unsatisfactory. They must be unbraided so to speak, viewed apart, and then rewoven if the final judgment is to be illuminating.

Villeré, the first Creole governor, successor to Claiborne, was an isolationist. He sought to limit immigration, arguing that it brought in "so many evil-disposed persons dangerous to Louisiana's well-being." What he really wanted to prevent, consciously or unconsciously, was the swamping of the French element by Anglo-Saxons. The times were far too yeasty for a Chinese Wall of any kind to be set up, and Villeré simply appeared to be a very conservative governor under whom, nonetheless, steamship traffic became important and the capital invested in sugar rose to more than $40,000,000.

He was succeeded by Thomas Bolling Robertson, a Virginian of the most courtly school. It is a curious fact that from then on few governors were of Louisiana birth. This did not happen by accident. Bernard de Marigny, who ran twice for the office, warned that the American party would permit as few real Creoles as possible to head the state. Pierre Derbigny, one of the men who defeated him, was born in France, and a bloc of American votes preferred him for that reason. Henry Schuyler Thibodaux, the fourth governor, after whom a town in the Bayou Lafourche country was named, came from Canada by way of Albany, New York. Not until 1831 was another member of an old colonial family elected. But the winner then was André Bienvenu Roman, a powerful personality who set precedents that others did not easily overturn. He was the first to go in as a Whig, a party label that meant conservatism as opposed to the wild Democrats who followed Andrew Jackson. Previous governors under the American regime had been Jeffersonians of a sort, taking small interest in national politics.

Roman was influential in electing his successor, Edward Douglass White, father of the future Chief Justice of the United States. The Creole obtained a second term from 1839 to 1843, and then stepped aside for Alexander Mouton, a descendant of the Acadians. It was a cycle of dominance, and Roman's group made the most of it. The brilliant younger men of their own race, however, were thinking of soldiering rather than statesmanship. The leadership of the parties fell into the hands of outsiders. Judah P. Benjamin, a Sephardic Jew of West Indian birth, had become by 1840 the outstanding manipulator of Whig policies. The chief Democrats were Pierre Soulé, of French birth, and the lawyer John Slidell who had come from New York at the age of twenty-seven. All three had married into prominent Creole families.

It should be understood that Louisiana's first state constitution had been designed to limit popular sovereignty as much as possible. The franchise was severely restricted by property qualifications. A queer proviso sought to give a nonpartisan aspect to the governorship. Though the names of candidates appeared on the ballot, the man receiving the largest popular vote was not necessarily elected. The legislature had the right to choose between the two men who had obtained the most suffrages. Mouton was the last governor under this archaic system. During his term a special convention rewrote and greatly liberalized the constitution.

Two pieces of sharp practice by the rival leaders, Benjamin and Slidell, undoubtedly had much to do with hastening the reforms.

In 1842 Benjamin carried New Orleans for the Whigs by paying taxes on hundreds of carriages and cabs, not all of which existed, and distributing the receipts among indigent partisans. The latter used the receipts at the polls as proof that they were property owners and entitled to vote. Slidell riposted in 1844 with a still more elaborate device. It was a presidential year, and "King John," as the Democratic boss was called, had sworn not only to swing the state's electoral vote to James K. Polk, but to deal a death blow to Whiggery. The law permitted citizens to vote at any polling place in the parish where they resided, and majorities were adjudged according to the number of precincts carried. So, on election day, Slidell took his Democrats away from New Orleans by boatloads and voted them in small precincts over a wideflung area. The Whig landslide in the city was cancelled out. Most of the offices in the state government were captured.

Slidell's party had positive objectives. First, it wanted the war with Mexico to which the Whigs were opposed. Second, it was determined to make the Democracy the ruling Southern faction and committed to eventual secession if it could not attain its ends by any other means. Benjamin, a realist not untouched with cynicism, saw which way the wind was blowing after the elections of 1844 and the constitutional convention of 1845. He trimmed his sails accordingly. Though the Whigs still had enough strength to send him to the United States Senate, he ended in the late 1850's by accepting a second term as a Democrat, with Slidell himself as colleague.

The first new-style Democrat elected governor was Isaac Johnson of West Feliciana Parish, a grandson of the Isaac Johnson who had helped set up the Republic of West Florida in 1810. He had been a boy orator, and a judge before he was forty. When his name was proposed a Whig newspaper wrote: "If we must have a locofoco [Democratic] Governor of Louisiana, we say give us the 'Boy of Feliciana' by all means. He is a worthy foe, and altogether we are sorry to see so clever a gentleman in the opposition ranks. We should be proud of him as a Whig."

Johnson reveled in the drama of the Mexican War. It was his fiery call that raised a volunteer army for General Zachary Taylor. New Orleans took to the idea of soldiering abroad with a zest that a prophet might well have found ominous. The initial chapters of a few solid military reputations were written, notably that of P. G. T. Beauregard. But hundreds of men came back drunk with adventure and eager to seek more of it wherever it offered. There ensued a period of filibustering. Two expeditions were raised to help Narciso López to liberate Cuba, and three in support of William Walker's efforts to conquer Central America. All were failures, and at least two ended in tragic massacres of Americans.

Local politics were colored by the bellicose unrest in the air. Paul Octave Hébert, the last Creole governor, won on his record as a lieutenant colonel of volunteers in Mexico. A popular reaction enabled the Know-Nothing Party, which bitterly opposed the foreign-born, to elect their candidates to the mayoralty of New Orleans three times running in the 1850's. In 1858 vigilantes fought the Know-Nothing forces in the streets for four days to insure unhampered voting. Over and above minor feuds, the conviction grew that the national crisis was fast coming to a head. Thomas Overton Moore, the sugar planter of Rapides Parish chosen governor in 1860, was an avowed secessionist.

The economic story of those last two decades before the cataclysm had been one of steadily rising prosperity. In 1837 there had been a nationwide panic which had closed many New Orleans banks and crippled business otherwise. But the city recovered swiftly. In 1840 its population was 102,193, making it the fourth largest in the United States. As a port it officially ranked next to New York, and it earnestly made the claim that it was the fourth port in the world. That year 1,573 steamboats arrived at the city by river and lake. Its exports ran far ahead of its imports, the margin finally exceeding one hundred percent. In 1846 the figures were $72,000,000 worth of exports and $35,000,000 of imports.

By 1850 the Erie Canal and the railroads connecting the Middle

West with Atlantic ports were getting much of the business that otherwise would have had to descend the Mississippi. Yet New Orleans scorned the menace. Again it had almost doubled its population and more than doubled its trade in ten years. There had been so great a rise in the shipments of cotton and sugar that the loss of other commodities passed unnoticed. Cotton alone accounted for forty-five percent of the port's commerce. New Orleans had become also the country's greatest slave market. Profits spiraled through the 1850's. On the eve of the war, the city's total trade was $324,000,000, and this by prevailing standards was something prodigious.

Far from fearing that secession would have a destructive effect, the majority of merchants as well as politicians argued that by becoming the chief seaport of an independent republic New Orleans stood to gain enormously. The mass of the South's foreign business must pass that way, while the upper Mississippi Valley would still be forced to use the river route for many products. At long last the ambition to outstrip New York would be attained.

Then the outbreak of hostilities climaxed a long series of political events too well known to the reader to call for repetition here.

The citizens of New Orleans, especially the Creoles, responded ardently to the call for enlistments. A few volunteer companies had been formed even before the state seceded. The number of these now increased at an impressive rate, the tendency being to imitate the military establishment of France. Chasseurs, dragoons and Zouaves in baggy trousers and wearing tassled fezzes shared the applause of the crowd. Recruits from the water-front section known as the Irish Channel, recent immigrants for the most part, called themselves the Louisiana Tigers. One saw many variations of guards, cadets, rifles and scouts. The cavalry arm was popular. Great pride was taken in the Washington Artillery, which had been formed by aristocratic amateurs in the 1840's before the Mexican War and had proved its worth.

The state had several outstanding military officers. The favorite with soldiers and civilians alike was Major Pierre Gustave Toutant Beauregard with his Mexican laurels and subsequent brilliant record as a United States Army engineer. Surprisingly, in view of his known secessionist opinions, he had been appointed superintendent of West Point as 1860 closed. Beauregard was a Creole of the Creoles, born and reared on a plantation in St. Bernard Parish just below the city. It is told that, as a boy, the sound of troops passing with music drew him running from his own confirmation ceremony in the Cathedral. He adored the Napoleonic tradition, had studied under two ex-captains of La Grande Armée, and carried a digest of the Corsican's campaigns as a pocket piece. His personality was curiously exciting. A taciturn man, a dream less of ambition than of glory dwelt behind his eyes like an incandescence, and he created the feeling that under his leadership nothing was impossible. He was capable of sudden bursts of eloquence. They called him "the poet in uniform."

The retired General Braxton Bragg ranked highest among the trained soldiers available. Young Alfred Mouton, son of the former governor, was the pride of the Acadian parishes. He had graduated from West Point. Much was hoped of his professional touch. The recent chief executive, Hébert, and Dick Taylor, son of Zachary and brother-in-law of Jefferson Davis, were regarded as entitled to commands, though they were primarily politicians. Unique on the roll of talent was the Right Reverend Leonidas Polk, Episcopalian Bishop of Louisiana, a West Pointer like Beauregard and Mouton, and who now stood ready to suspend his churchly functions if commissioned a general.

As soon as his state was out of the Union, Beauregard resigned his post at West Point, and reported in New Orleans. Public opinion supported him for the chieftaincy of Louisiana's forces, but Governor Moore decided to appoint Bragg. Shortly afterward Davis summoned the Creole to Montgomery, gave him his first star and assigned him to the fateful command at Charleston that culminated in the bombardment of Fort Sumter and set him on the road to Manassas. Bishop Polk received a division in Tennessee. Taylor, Mouton and Hébert began with lower ranks. Before long all of them were generals.

In the sphere of statesmanship, Senators Benjamin and Slidell were called to high office in the Confederacy. From the start the cryptic Hebrew forged ahead of the rival with whom he had so long shared the local power. Benjamin was made attorney general. He and Jefferson Davis had not been close in Washington. Once they had been on the point of fighting a duel. But the poise and shrewdness of Benjamin proved to be invaluable to the new nation's president. In a few months he was secretary of war and eventually became secretary of state. Jealous Anglo-Saxon Southerners complained that he established an occult influence over Davis. The truth was that the standard of competence in the cabinet as a whole rated somewhat less than adequate. The keenest mind in the circle inevitably shone.

John Slidell received the difficult assignment of commissioner to France, with orders to get recognition for the Confederacy. He and the commissioner to England, James Mason of Virginia, became the central figures of the *Trent* incident when a Northern warship removed them from an English steamer. Under pressure from Whitehall they were released and proceeded to their posts. Slidell was a social success in Paris. But he was unable to bring Napoleon III to the point of giving the aid and comfort so vitally needed. A discredited diplomat, he never returned to America.

Lincoln proclaimed a blockade of the Southern seaboard early in the war, and although it was not immediately effective New Orleans saw a shadow fall across the glowing picture of her dreams. By the middle of May 1861, ocean-borne traffic had subsided to a trickle. A few privateers essayed to get even with the enemy. The *Calhoun,* a steam towboat of 509 tons, was outfitted by "a company of nine gentlemen," and on her first day in the Gulf seized a Maine bark. Later, the *Calhoun* took five more prizes. The *Music* and the *Ivy,* both of smaller tonnage, got into the game with fair success. As a result the entrance of the Mississippi was sealed by the Federals, who posted two heavily armed cruisers to watch the passes.

The Lake Pontchartrain route now came into its own, and for nine months was the best means of communication between New Orleans, the middle South and Virginia. Military and official traffic to and from Richmond had gorged the only railroad, which ran through Jackson, Mississippi. Those who had the leisure used the lake boats, and connected at Mobile with the line's "elegant steam packets" on the Alabama River for Montgomery. This became, too, the city's chief link with abroad. The road across Texas to Mexico was long and hazardous. But the blockade runners made ports like Mobile easily enough, and the passengers and goods they brought reached New Orleans via Lake Pontchartrain.

That spring Raphael Semmes arrived by the lake route and took over the 500-ton passenger liner *Habana,* which was tied up at a dock at Algiers on the Mississippi opposite New Orleans. His task was to convert her into a raider. He accomplished this in two months, renamed her the *Sumter,* and on June 30 escaped to the Gulf by outguessing and outsailing the blockader *Brooklyn.* On a cruise which lasted eight months the *Sumter* captured eighteen Northern merchant vessels, of which only seven were burned. Attempts to intern some of them in neutral ports resulted in their being restored to their owners.

Early the following year the North massed a fleet under Commodore David Glasgow Farragut in Mississippi Sound. Ship Island was occupied and a military force assembled there, command of which was assumed by General Benjamin F. Butler. The objective was New Orleans. The Confederates knew that it would be impossible to prevent the passes from being forced, but they relied upon Forts Jackson and St. Philip about thirty miles up the river to prevent any expedition from passing. As a secondary defense a dam, or boom, of schooners laden with lumber and chained together had been stretched from shore to shore below the forts. A ram called the *Manassas* had been built, and work

Association of Commerce

TYPICAL SLAVE HOUSE

CITY HALL FROM LAFAYETTE SQUARE

FRENCH-STYLE HOUSE, DAUPHINE STREET

U.S.S. *NEW ORLEANS* PASSING THE CITY

was being pushed on two ironclads after the model set by the *Virginia* in Hampton Roads. The former privateers had been converted into gunboats.

The failure to realize that New Orleans was vulnerable and to make a serious effort to preserve it when danger loomed was one of the major blunders of Confederate strategy. Troops raised in Louisiana had been drawn off in excessive numbers and sent to the Virginia and Tennessee fronts. Outstanding officers, as we have seen, had all been given commands elsewhere. A state that had contributed half a dozen generals of real ability, headed by Beauregard, was left not one to counter the blow at its vital port. A third-rate general, Mansfield Lovell, with only 3,000 regulars and a few battalions of militia, had been placed in charge of the department. Even the river forts, which Beauregard himself had pronounced to be inadequate, were lightly manned and short of ammunition.

There seems to have been an honest delusion along a line that has often proved fatal in warfare: that an offensive no matter how strong must crumble against the bulwarks and weapons at the disposal of the defensive. How could warships run the gauntlet of a crossfire from both banks of the Mississippi? This notion was based upon conditions in the days of sail. Frigates tacking against the current assuredly would have been easy marks for the guns of Jackson and St. Philip. But Farragut was coming with steamers, and that made all the difference in the world.

The middle of April the Northerners pressed up to the forts. A nocturnal raiding party cut the chain dam easily enough. Exchanges of cannon fire continued for several days. Then Farragut burst past on the night of April 23-24 in a daring and brilliant operation. Confederate craft were overwhelmed, the ironclads forced to destroy themselves. The next morning New Orleans fell, its only gesture of defiance the burning of vast stores of cotton on the docks and in warehouses to prevent it from falling into the hands of the enemy. Lovell had evacuated his troops without striking a blow. The Federal army landed, and General Butler set up the most hated administration in the entire history of the city.

The nicknames given him are illuminating. He was "The Beast" and "Silver Spoon Butler." This man, who had been a Democrat in Massachusetts, had preached fraternity between North and South and had opposed the election of Lincoln, came with vengeance in his heart to scourge the people of New Orleans for the "crime" of secession. His methods were a throwback to the barbarism of Europe's religious wars in the Middle Ages. He ordered his soldiery to search houses for Confederate symbols and literature. The possession of a flag, a button, an anti-Federal newspaper article, or a private letter considered hostile was enough to cause fortunes to be sequestered and all members of the family expelled from the Union lines with nothing but the clothes on their backs and enough money to take them to the nearest "rebel" post. Furniture and *objets d'art* were looted by members of the inspection squads. There was much wanton destruction. Butler himself was credited with a passion for silverware; hence one of the sobriquets applied to him.

A proclamation required all citizens to renounce the Confederacy and "renew the oath of allegiance" to the United States. Failing this, they were to be treated as enemies and severe penalties imposed. Orleanians found it peculiarly humiliating to be ordered to go of their own volition before the courts set up for the purpose. A large majority refused to obey, and the persecution of the well-to-do element became general. It was no wonder that women devised ingenious ways of showing their hatred and scorn of the invader. They simulated illness at the mere sight of a blue uniform, stepped off the sidewalk to avoid being brushed by a soldier's sleeve, and drew shawls over their heads if forced to pass under the Stars and Stripes.

Butler cannily did not extend his rough treatment to the poor, except for the repression of crime. He had found New Orleans suffering from a serious shortage of foodstuffs. Coffee had vanished from the groceries. Flour was at twenty dollars a barrel, and common table salt at ten dollars for a small sack. A bar of soap cost a dollar. Such prices were sky-high for the period. The situation had borne heavily on the families of soldiers and soon had spread to the whole working class. The municipality had tried in vain to regulate the cost of living. It had had to establish a free market, where food was given to all comers twice a week. This charity was continued by the Federals until the opening of the river mouth and the resumption of traffic with the ports of the Atlantic seaboard created jobs for those willing to work.

Lake Pontchartrain had been isolated since the first gathering of the hostile fleet in Mississippi Sound. The boats from Mobile had ceased to run, with the exception of a few coastal luggers that occasionally slipped by. Small Confederate garrisons in Forts Pike and Macomb watched the easterly approaches. It had been thought that there might be an attempt to seize the Rigolets and send gunboats to bombard Milneburg; also, that there might be a landing at the west end of Lake Borgne in imitation of the British tactics in the War of 1812. Nothing of the kind occurred. After the capture of New Orleans, Pontchartrain became literally a backwater, for although the Federals held the south shore with its port facilities and the Pontchartrain Railroad they could make little use of them. Mobile was to remain in Southern hands until the last months of the war. The river was the great theater of naval operations, and while the armies struggled for points like Baton Rouge and Port Hudson, the interior of the "Florida parishes" of Louisiana was never the scene of important fighting.

Earlier the lake had witnessed an epoch-making experiment. A group of New Orleans men who wished to go out as privateers had constructed within the mouth of the Bayou St. John one of the first submarines ever designed. The creator was Captain Horace Lawson Hunley, who obtained backing from his brother-in-law, a planter named Ruffin R. Barrow. Two or three others soon associated themselves with the venture. The craft they produced was a crude iron hull, deep in the belly like a fish, narrowed at both ends and covered over. The length was twenty feet, the beam only four feet, the displacement four tons. It had water ballast tanks by means of which it was raised and lowered, and it was also ballasted by flat castings outside, fastened with bolts, so that in an emergency these castings could be dropped, just as later models of submarines could drop keels if necessary. The ballast tanks had sea cocks and force pumps. A shaft on each side of the boat permitted the operation of finlike plates whereby the boat could be made to sink or rise very much as a fish performs that operation, and without disturbing the water ballast. There was a mercury gauge to indicate depth.

The submarine was driven by man power. Cranks in the port side operated an ordinary propeller. The space within was so cramped that men could not pass each other forward or aft without going outside and using the hatches. The destructive equipment was a detachable lance head twenty-two feet long, at the end of which a waterproof bag containing from fifty to ninety pounds of gunpowder was hung. Inside the bag was a bottle of acid with a line attached in such a way that when the crude torpedo, or mine, had been brought into contact with an enemy hull, the bottle broke and caused a detonation as the submarine went into reverse. The technique was for the submarine to stab the quarry with the lance head, then cut the lance head loose and try to make its escape in advance of the explosion.

Hunley's strange vessel was launched in February 1862 and demonstrated with partial success in Lake Pontchartrain. It is said that on its second or third run it went to the bottom, drowning the three persons aboard, two of whom were slaves. The loss of life has been denied. It was raised, but afterward sunk to prevent its capture by Farragut. The builders removed to Mobile, where their second submarine was lost with no one aboard. Their third failed to rise on its maiden voyage, and the crew of nine drowned. This boat, named the *Hunley,* was subsequently salvaged, placed on a flatcar and sent to Charleston, where it sank a Federal warship, the *Housatonic.* The original submarine, named

Pioneer, was recovered in Pontchartrain years after the war. It is now on permanent exhibit in Jackson Square, New Orleans.

While Ben Butler was dictator a good deal of smuggling went on, back and forth across the lake, some of it with the connivance of the Federals. Trading in cotton was forbidden by the Southern authorities, even though medicines and other desperately needed supplies could be obtained that way. The Northerners made no bones about wanting the staple and would buy any amount that was slipped through the lines. Butler gave permission to many of his officers, as well as a horde of civilian hangers-on, including his own brother, A. J. Butler, to do business as speculators. There was nothing clandestine, therefore, about their cotton purchases, and only the Southerners who dealt with them could be called smugglers. But there were other and more scandalous activities.

A. J. Butler got possession of some race horses that had been confiscated from a gambler who had broken the regulations, and it is averred that he shipped them on barges to the vicinity of Mandeville and sold them to Confederate army agents. Documentary evidence of this transaction is lacking, but one finds it reported as gossip in so many memoirs that it is difficult to reject it. There is also good reason to believe that A. J. Butler imported beef cattle illicitly from Texas and sold the meat at exorbitant prices, and that certain gambling houses paid him for protection. He is credited with having made a million dollars in six months. Ben admitted under pressure that his brother had profited to some extent; even so, he was but one of scores.

In a previous chapter it has been noted that the Choctaw Indians were sufficiently affected by the war to find it prudent to take refuge in the swamps. They had been alarmed by two skirmishes which were fought in the summer of 1862 on the north shore of the lake. These were unimportant clashes between Confederate and Federal scouts, growing out of the activities of the smugglers. There was no more fighting among the pine woods of that coast until the autumn of the following year, when again two brushes are recorded. From then on the environs did not figure in the war. Confederate sovereignty prevailed in those parishes which were located back from the Mississippi.

Butler had been recalled from New Orleans the middle of December 1862, it is generally agreed because of pressure brought to bear by the French Government. Napoleon III made representations to Lincoln, through Seward, that the general's oppressive acts had caused suffering to French residents. This move had really been in behalf of the Creoles, whose houses had been looted, but who resented that less than they did Butler's notorious "Woman Order."* The new commander was Nathaniel P. Banks, a political general who had formerly been governor of Massachusetts, and who instituted a notably milder regime.

Under Banks there started a merry-go-round of civil administrations which for fifteen years wrote a chapter of Louisiana history as tumultuous and sordid as that of the most lawless Latin-American country. Governor Moore had set up his capital at Shreveport. The Unionists regarded him as having been deposed, though he controlled more than two-thirds of the state. General George F. Shepley was appointed United States executive and functioned for two years behind a hedge of bayonets. Then, when the regular date for an election came around, a so-called Free State party backed by Banks elevated Michael Hahn, while the Confederate parishes chose Henry Watkins Allen. The Bavarian-born Hahn, owner of the *True Delta,* was an opportunist who had furnished the Unionists with what they most lacked, a friendly press. The romantic figure of Allen ran to the opposite extreme. He had spent his youth adventuring quixotically, had fought under Sam Houston in Texas and under Garibaldi in Italy. He held the rank of brigadier general in the Confederate army, and

* "As the officers and soldiers of the United States have been subject to repeated insults from the women (calling themselves ladies) of New Orleans, in return for the most scrupulous noninterference and courtesy on our part, it is ordered that hereafter when any female shall, by word, gesture or movement, insult or show contempt for any officer or soldier of the United States, she shall be regarded and held liable to be treated as a woman of the town plying her avocation.

"By command of Major General Butler."

had been wounded desperately at the battles of Shiloh and Baton Rouge.

Both Allen and Hahn had legislatures that observed the forms of the Louisiana constitution. The Confederate served until the last gun had been fired and then left for Mexico, an "irreconcilable." Hahn did not finish his term and was succeeded by various nondescript personages until, in 1868, with Reconstruction in full swing, young Henry Clay Warmoth was elected by the Republicans. He was only twenty-six years old, had been a provost court judge under Banks at twenty-two, a lieutenant colonel in the Union army at twenty. The new order which he represented had disfranchised most whites and given the vote to the ex-slaves. A black house painter had gone in as lieutenant governor, and the legislature was composed of carpetbaggers, scalawags and a large minority of Negroes.

The rampant corruption of Warmoth's regime almost passes belief. Taxes rose 450 percent and the public funds were wasted and stolen shamelessly. Yet there was something about the man, a certain largeness in his banditry and color in his swashbuckling, which Louisianians understood. Warmoth adroitly knifed to death a newspaper executive who assaulted him on Canal Street. He used his gubernatorial powers to favor his friends, to get other individuals out of trouble simply because he liked them. He acquired great plantations below the city and entertained lavishly. The time came, years afterward, when many of his old opponents hobnobbed with him.

The black lieutenant governor elected with Warmoth died in office and a free man of color named Pinckney Benton Stewart Pinchback was chosen president pro tem of the Senate, with the right of succession. This Pinchback was a scarcely less remarkable adventurer than Warmoth. He had been a gambler on Mississippi steamboats, learning the business from George Devol himself and practicing the master's tricks among the Negro deck passengers. But he had an excellent mind and powers of leadership that were far from negligible. Warmoth has described him as a restless, ambitious man, and one "to be reckoned with at all times." Only the prejudices that naturally sprang from the circumstances of Reconstruction have deterred Louisiana historians from admitting that Pinchback was the ablest colored politician of the crisis and an interesting personality in his own right. He was acting governor for thirty-three days while impeachment charges against Warmoth were being heard. Shortly after he was elected to the United States Senate, but at the end of three years of debate the seat was refused him.

The evils of Warmoth's term became fouler during the utterly shameless administration of the carpetbagger, William Pitt Kellogg. The Democratic candidate, John McEnery, who actually had the support of a disgusted Warmoth, was counted out by the Republican returning board. Kellogg and his entourage imposed their will by force, despite the fact that they took one serious beating in the streets of New Orleans. Infuriated citizens and members of the White League routed the Metropolitan Police in what is known as the "September 14 Battle," 1874, with casualties on both sides running to thirty-two killed and seventy wounded. President Grant's orders to the Federal garrison maintained Kellogg in power to the finish.

In 1876 Francis T. Nicholls, a Confederate general who had lost an arm, a foot and an eye in action, swept the state for the Democrats. Again there was a steal in favor of the Republican, Stephen B. Packard. The carpetbagger entrenched himself in the St. Louis Hotel, the temporary Statehouse, and stood a siege of several weeks, while Nicholls installed his government in another building. Both issued proclamations. Both vowed to make civil war of it within the commonwealth rather than quit. But that was the year of the disputed national election between Hayes and Tilden. The vote of Louisiana in the electoral college was needed to seat Hayes. A compromise gave the presidency to the Republicans and allowed Democratic governors to take office throughout the South. Federal troops were withdrawn from New Orleans. As Nicholls thrust Packard aside, the horrors of Reconstruction ended at last. Hayes consoled the loser by appointing him consul general at Liverpool.

The accounts of unbiased observers are unanimous in admitting the degeneration that overtook the region during this epoch. Politics apart, a unique society that had developed in southern Louisiana under three regimes—the French, fifty years; the Spanish, forty years; the first American, fifty years—was irremediably damaged. Despite the jealousy between Creoles and Anglo-Saxons, a solidarity had come to pass. Witness the ardor with which they had rallied to wage the war for an independent South, aristocrats and commoners, a Beauregard joining hands with a radical like John T. Monroe who had been elected mayor of New Orleans on the Know-Nothing ticket. In the chaos from 1861 to 1876 the Creole element suffered the more heavily. Their fortunes were simply wrecked, and they were never able as a class to recover from the blow. But the ante-bellum Americans were in the same box with them and were almost as hard hit.

The commerce of New Orleans began to revive in 1862 as soon as Farragut captured the lower river and cleared the way for shipping to and from the ports of the North. Shallow commentators have observed that whereas veterans returning to Richmond, Charleston, Atlanta and Vicksburg had to start afresh in the midst of ruins, the men of New Orleans found their city doing business at the same old stand. Yes, but to whose advantage? The docks, warehouses, banks and office buildings were uninjured. But the original proprietors were faced with the fact that the advance guard of carpetbaggers had taken over in their absence. This condition became worse through the ten years of Reconstruction.

Warmoth admits in his memoirs that when he assumed the governorship there was no money in the treasury. The city was dirty and impoverished, with a "bloodthirsty gang" in control. Violence was rampant. "The people were almost without hope." And these miseries were intensified by the financial panic that swept the whole country in 1873.

The fruits of misgovernment showed in the arrested progress

of the port during the terrible decade, as compared with the rising curve that had prevailed from 1820 to 1860. Gradually Southerners regained control of business in the Crescent City after 1876, but the majority of those who reached the top were not descendants of the romantic builders.

Chapter 18

Postwar Railroads and Lake Boats

The first railroad line connecting Louisiana with other states had been extended into Mississippi before the war. It was the New Orleans, Jackson and Great Northern, later absorbed into the Illinois Central Railroad's system. The route skirted the western end of Lake Pontchartrain, passed between that lake and Maurepas, and struck due north. Its importance to the military operations of the Confederacy has been mentioned. Traffic on the great inland sheet of water was not affected by it, for since the closing of the Manchac passage by Andrew Jackson all incoming ships were from the east along the Gulf Coast. Immediately after the war, however, plans for other railroads were pushed. This was about the only large-scale activity that the stricken South attempted without delay, for it was felt that there could be no recovery without an improved network of communications.

As early as November 1866, the New Orleans, Mobile and Chattanooga Railroad Company was chartered in Louisiana and elsewhere. Its chief project was to build a line of road from Mobile to New Orleans. This was to be extended by means of two great trunks to Chattanooga, Tennessee, and to Houston, Texas. The original company never achieved its ambitions, but by engaging in high finance of a somewhat frenzied nature it raised the funds to construct the Mobile-New Orleans link. This is the road which concerns the present narrative, because it dealt a deathblow to the steamship route from the Gulf ports to Milneburg. The year 1869 is usually given as the date of the opening of the railroad, but it would appear that a through service was not established until October 1870. A few months later the company was reorganized and changed its name to the New Orleans, Mobile and Texas Railroad. The Chattanooga branch had been abandoned, or rather had been taken over by other interests.

Great engineering difficulties attended the building of the 141 miles of track between Mobile and New Orleans. Also, for the first time in American railroading the problem of the teredo, or shipworm, was encountered. This can best be described by a technical expert. The Louisville & Nashville Railroad, which in 1880 absorbed both the Mobile-New Orleans link and the little Pontchartrain Railroad, recently published a survey of the company's annals in its employees' magazine. The following is quoted from it:

"Although the property was in good shape when acquired, the *status quo* was difficult to retain, due to the insidious underwater activities of a pest known as *teredo navalis*. The latter is a worm native to salt waters, whose principal item of diet is untreated timber.

"The construction of the railroad from Mobile to New Orleans had been manna from heaven to this marine nuisance. It was known when the line was built that creosoted timbers would withstand the ravages of the teredo, and a plant was constructed in 1869 for such treatment, but the work, at first, was imperfectly done. As a consequence a goodly part of the piling which supported the roadbed for long distances between Mobile and New Orleans, and which had been driven into position in 1869 and 1870, was destroyed in nine months' time by the teredo, whose potentialities for damage are all out of proportion to his size, which is about that of a lead pencil, or somewhat larger, when fully grown. He, or she, works in much the same manner as the termite, honeycombing the structure attacked and terminating its usefulness in short order.

"The activities of the teredo were obviously of an expensive nature and further aggravated a situation which was badly frayed around the edges and wearing thin in the middle. In some places, in order to prepare a roadbed for the original line, a canal had been dredged through the marshes and watery wastelands encountered and the displaced material, with some admixture of foreign soil, was piled on the south side of the canal, forming an embankment for the roadbed. This latter had a tendency to slip back into the canal, so much expensive piling had to be driven as a protective check against such slides.

"The old New Orleans, Mobile and Texas also had the distinction of being one of the few railroads, if not the only one, in the United States to have an anchored roadbed. Because of its proximity to the Gulf of Mexico, as well as because of the fact that in a good many places the roadbed was not very much above sea-level, high tides frequently washed over the tracks, sometimes returning to 'home base' with booty in the shape of segments of the roadbed aforesaid. To prevent such disasters posts were driven down at intervals between the rails and were then bolted to adjacent cross-ties, thus securely anchoring the track and discouraging any seagoing tendency.

"After its first disastrous experience with the teredo, the management of the New Orleans, Mobile and Texas went into the matter of creosoting timber a little more closely and eventually emerged with a process of forcing the creosote oil into the timber under pressure—an importation from England. This proved to be quite successful, so much so that the Louisville & Nashville soon after its acquisition of the line extended such treatment to all timbers used along its lines in trestles, etc., in order to balk decay.

"The operation of trains on the New Orleans, Mobile and Texas was somewhat haphazard. Freight trains took about twelve hours to make the 141-mile trip between Mobile and New Orleans, and storms blowing in from the Gulf Coast played hob with the schedule. However, a gay speedster known as the Barrett Lightning Matinee Train, on February 3, 1874, ran from New Orleans to Mobile in two hours and forty-seven minutes, returning in three hours and eleven minutes."*

---

* Courtesy of *The Louisville & Nashville,* employees' magazine.

No matter how primitive and subject to interruptions the railroad might be, the margin in its favor over ships that had to ease their way through the narrow Rigolets and traverse the lake was enormous. Indeed, the trains at their best could make the run in one-tenth the time. Few passengers bound for New Orleans from distant points or from Mobile itself cared to bother with the old means of transportation. The steamship line continued to carry a diminishing quota of freight to Milneburg, but its doom was forecast and in a few years' time it ceased to operate. The heyday of Milneburg as a back door to the city was ended, and the value of the Pontchartrain Railroad as its commercial feeder declined. Both port and shuttle, however, retained a place in the scheme of things, for the reason that the interior traffic of the lake was growing. The south shore had several pleasure resorts, of which Milneburg was the center, and mounting numbers of Orleanians wished to enjoy the pleasant retreats among the pine woods on the far side.

The fifty-odd years ahead of the Pontchartrain Railroad after it became a branch of the Louisville & Nashville may be called its plebeian period. More and more, its excursion trains were the chief reason for its existence. It ran seven or eight every Sunday, and as many as a dozen on special holidays. The cars were jammed to suffocation with *hoi polloi,* who liked to picnic at the camps along a wharf and on piers running out into the lake, where shacks of one or two rooms could be rented by the day. So many anglers used the line that the cars had a distinctly fishy odor. A locomotive that came into use shortly after the war and lasted until the road was abolished was known as "Smoky Mary," because it burned soft coal and trailed a dense plume behind it. This name caught on to such an extent that people applied it to the road itself. "Let's run out to Milneburg on Smoky Mary," they said. There was an alternate engine, of course, and the meticulous distinguished it as "Puffing Billy." But the latter cognomen never gained popularity. Smoky Mary was on the lips of everyone, and although she begrimed the clothes of passengers and blew cinders into their eyes, she was regarded as a good old friend.

Well-to-do patrons of the Milneburg hotels and the newer resorts at West End near the Jefferson Parish line now seldom used the railroad. They preferred to go in their carriages over the several good driving roads that had been built since the early days. The guidebooks of the 1870's and 1880's point out that there was a great difference in the prices charged at the lake for food. A mere "eating house" would serve the tripper a meal at from twenty-five to sixty cents. But at a pretentious place, "the excursionist can hardly get a good fish dinner under $2.50 to $5, without wines." As to the bill of fare, the following is enough to make one's mouth water:

"*Soups:* Oyster, terrapin, turtle, crab, crawfish, chowder, bouillabaisse.

"*Boiled:* Hard-shell crabs, lake and river shrimps, red snapper, blackfish, redfish, codfish, sheepshead, stingaree.

"*Stewed:* Shrimps, eels, perch, redfish, red snapper, sheepshead, grouper.

"*Baked:* Terrapin, hard-shell crabs, fresh and saltwater trout, flounder, and all the other leading classes of fish.

"*Fried:* Softshell crabs, croakers, trout, and the other principal varieties.

"*Salad:* Cold fish with cold sauces. The lake shrimp is in the foremost rank for a salad.

"*Broiled:* Spanish mackerel, bluefish and pompano. The other varieties are also broiled, but beside these three they pale their ineffectual fires.

"During the war a poor fellow, born and raised in New Orleans, when trying one cold, rainy day just as he was out of hospital to eat some tough 'blue beef,' suddenly startled his comrades by exclaiming in a semi-tragic, semi-comic tone: 'Oh, if I could get back home just for a day, boys, and could go down to the Lake and eat a dinner of soft-shell crabs and pompano once more, I'd be willing to eat blue beef all the rest of my life.' "

The boats that plied across and around Pontchartrain were of two types. There were many small craft, ranging from steam barges to sailing luggers, which voyaged more or less as tramps picking up freight wherever they could find it. Some of these traded on Lake Maurepas, where no towns existed, but where landing stages served the requirements of a scattered population. It is impossible to estimate their number; an idea may be gained from the fact that some forty wrecks and other serious accidents to small craft on the two lakes were reported between the years 1879 and 1921. The second type of ship was a fairly large paddle-wheeler which maintained a regular schedule for travelers from the New Orleans lake front to Mandeville and other points on the north shore of Pontchartrain. There appear to have been six of these in the latter half of the nineteenth century and the first two decades of the twentieth, though at no time were there more than three running simultaneously, and for long spans of time only one.

Most famous of the paddle-wheelers was the *Camelia,* "old" and "new," whose metamorphoses were curious. She was launched in 1847 as the *Zepphyr,* was seized by General Butler after he captured New Orleans and used as a dispatch boat. Shortly after hostilities ceased she was christened the *Camelia* and put into service from Milneburg to Mandeville and ports of call on the Tchefuncte River. Several years later she was rebuilt from the same hull and given the name of *New Camelia.* Tens of thousands of Orleanians remember her in this her final incarnation. Under the command of Captain William Hanover, she chugged back and forth across the lake, a joy to excursionists, an institution treasured by the community. Now and then she met a mishap, such as stranding on a bar, or breaking a shaft.

André Lafargue, the Creole littérateur, told the writer that on a Fourth of July in the early 1890's—research has failed to establish the year—a considerable quantity of firecrackers left over from the celebration at Mandeville exploded in a cabin on the *New Camelia* as she was returning to Milneburg. It was late in the evening and dark. The firecrackers made a tremendous noise. The woodwork of the cabin ignited and smoke poured forth. An effect far more sinister than the facts justified was produced. The passengers could not be blamed for thinking that the ship was blowing up, or was being bombarded by a mysterious enemy. Panic spread along the crowded decks. At least one person jumped overboard. Lafargue recalls an incident which makes him chuckle almost as heartily as he did when it occurred.

A friend, also a Creole, was standing by the rail leaning on a walking stick which he had had for years and valued greatly. Suddenly this man addressed the elements in tones that might have been employed by a tragedian at the Théâtre Français. "I sacrifice my beloved cane to you," he cried, and hurled the walking stick into the lake, as though he believed that the act would purchase the safety of everyone. In fifteen minutes or so the fire was got under control. But on reaching Milneburg the ship had to lay up for repairs and missed several voyages.

The *New Camelia* at last became unseaworthy, and at the time of World War I she was anchored in the Tchefuncte River and took summer boarders. By 1920 she was just too weak to float. She went to the bottom quietly in January of that year.

Other paddle-wheelers on Lake Pontchartrain were the *Cape Charles* and the *Susquehanna*. The first had been built for a route in Hampton Roads and Chesapeake Bay, hence her name. Both she and the *Susquehanna* operated from West End instead of Milneburg. They never attained the reputation or the popularity of the *New Camelia*. Improved railroad service, as well as busses and the vastly increased use of the private automobile, finally caused the lake passenger steamers to become unprofitable, and there are none running today.

The Pontchartrain Railroad outlived the paddle-wheel steamers. Smoky Mary made her last trip on March 15, 1932, when the Louisville & Nashville closed the line. The tracks were torn up two or three years later.

There was achieved in the 1870's an engineering work of the most far-reaching consequence, which solved once and for all the problem of keeping open the mouth of the Mississippi River. It assured the future of New Orleans as a great port. Negatively it affected the destiny of Lake Pontchartrain, because it put an end to all dreams of widening the Rigolets and dredging a channel that would enable the city's backway entry to recapture some of its commercial importance. These were not practicable plans, anyhow. The lake was incurably shallow. But the victory over the river was a thing that had been envisaged from the time of the French, and always it had failed until genius in the person of Captain James Buchanan Eads came along. What he accomplished was begun during the blackest days of Reconstruction. It was backed by the Federal Government, though skeptically, and paid for by the nation. Louisiana was fortunate in receiving this boon at a time when she was being politically oppressed.

As has already been remarked, the entire delta region has been built up through the centuries by silt brought down from the interior by the Mississippi. The amount of material that shifts yearly is estimated at 406,500,000 tons, a figure so huge that the mind can scarcely grasp it. The river disposes of some of this on the mud flats for miles above its mouth and dumps the rest into the Gulf. There has never been only one exit of the Mississippi. At the tip of the delta the stream separates into three main passes, as they are called, and several smaller ones. Their form has been notably changed within the 245 years since the coming of Iberville and Bienville. Solid land has been created southward. The French used the flat, swampy island within the Southwest Pass, which they named the Balize, as their first and last port of call. By 1850 the Balize was no longer an island, and debarkation facilities had to be moved up to Pilot Town.

Cutting its way through the passes, the Mississippi had from time immemorial deposited ridges of sediment just beyond each exit. These were the notorious bars, foundation bases for a further extension of the land. Though the river poured out 175,000 cubic feet of water each second, its force was diffused the moment it hit the open sea. The bars crept up on it, and when they came close to the surface there was no telling in which direction the current would turn to bore a new channel and create a new bar. Ships had infinite difficulty in clearing these obstructions. True, it was possible to enter or leave safely by keeping to the exact center of the current of the moment. None but the most expert pilots could do it, resident pilots who studied the vagaries of the river's mouth from day to day. One of the evils of the situation was the exorbitant charges made by these pilots. If a ship's master tried to cross the bar unaided and went aground, the local towboats, which were in league with the pilots, would refuse to haul him off at any price. An ever-increasing number of accidents had occurred each year.

During Bienville's governorship, iron harrows had been dragged back and forth over each bar to deepen the channels. It had been effective in an extremely limited way. New sediment quickly replaced the old. Attempts were made, off and on, through the Spanish and American regimes to scoop up the mud in buckets and unload it ashore. This decidedly was a losing game. Just after the war Federal engineers used a steam-propelled dredge which they kept almost continuously in service for three years, but that did not do much good either. Then Captain Eads arrived on the scene.

This remarkable man had never had any formal education in engineering. Even the little mathematics he knew had been self-taught. From early youth, however, he had been impassioned over the river and its mysteries. He founded a business for salvaging wrecks, invented his own diving bell and explored the environs of every sunken craft he hoped to raise. He also built the first glass-works west of the Mississippi. Before he was forty he was able to retire, a rich man.

Eads was a Hoosier, and when the war broke out he got back into action—to the sorrow of the Confederacy. Ironclad gunboats designed by him and built with amazing speed had much to do with giving the North control of the inland waterways. Later he constructed the bridge across the river at St. Louis which remains his most spectacular monument. Experts had declared it could not be done according to the specifications laid down by Congress. Eads, the amateur, calmly went ahead and created a span that not only met all practical requirements, but has been admired ever since for its beauty and durability. He went to the mouth of the Mississippi in 1873, and after studying the problem he announced that he could guarantee a clear channel, twenty-eight feet deep, through Southwest Pass and beyond the bar to the Gulf. Jetties would be his device. A jetty is in effect an artificial bank which narrows a stream and compels it to flow with accelerated force. In the case of the Mississippi, this would churn up the mud and carry it out to sea. By projecting the jetties over the bar into deep water, it stood to reason that no fresh obstacle could be built up for a very long time by the falling sediment.

The theory was plain horse sense. Doubtless for that reason, a perverse humanity refused to accept it. Wild objections were raised. New Orleans business interests argued that the jetties would cause the Mississippi to back up and drown the city. Army engineers declared that the necessary pilings would be washed away in storms. Eads thereupon offered to build the system as a gamble. His price would be $10,000,000, to be paid in installments over a period of years by the United States Government—only if his jetties performed as he promised, and continued to do so. A Congressional committee insisted on a stingy, unscientific compromise. The experiment must be made at South Pass, because it was shorter than Southwest Pass, and the total payment would be $7,250,000 in the event of success. Eads pointed out that the heaviest volume of water flowed through Southwest Pass, which made it the proper one to harness. Congress would not be budged. So Eads agreed to South Pass.

He commenced operations on June 12, 1875. Soon it became clear that he was meeting with success, and a few vessels began to use his uncompleted channel the following year. Yellow fever hampered him during the epidemic of 1878. On July 8, 1879, the government board of inspection reported that the task had been brought to a conclusion. There existed at the mouth of the Mississippi not the trough twenty-eight feet deep which he had guaranteed, but one of thirty feet. The doubting Thomases wondered whether it could be maintained indefinitely. Eads said that it *would,* and it has been to this day. Indeed, the average depth now is thirty-five feet.

A few years afterward Congress authorized the army engineers to proceed with a similar work at Southwest Pass, and by following the methods of Eads a channel was dug there, too. Both have afforded safe entry and egress for the largest ships, and without interruption except during the raging of major tempests.

The landing stage at the seaward end of South Pass is called Port Eads, and the open space at the river end of Canal Street, the central thoroughfare of New Orleans, is Eads Plaza. The little Hoosier engineer was entertained at a banquet at the St. Charles Hotel in December 1882. State and city rightly honored this former military foe as one of their greatest benefactors.

Chapter 19

Cotton Exposition Days

RELATIVELY calm days followed the restoration of popular government. Anywhere else in the United States, to be sure, New Orleans with its poverty and crime, its blatant gambling and harlotry, would not have rated as a quiet city. But in comparison with what it had just gone through, the surcease spelled tranquillity to a pleasure-loving populace. Indeed, there were graceful aspects, and a phase of intellectual development, and not a little glamour. These were the days of the Cotton Exposition, of the Louisiana Lottery at its gaudiest, of a revival of sports culminating in the first heavyweight championship match with gloves when John L. Sullivan lost his title to James J. Corbett. They were the days also of the last and finest effort in French by Creole writers, of the rise of George W. Cable and the strange literary pilgrimage of Lafcadio Hearn. The most singular genius in the history of chess, Paul Morphy, lived out his short term. The opera flourished under the directorship of Placide Canonge. Antoine's, one of the world's noteworthy restaurants, set a standard of excellence. Such matters will be touched upon in this chapter, not necessarily in chronological order.

The World's Industrial and Cotton Centennial Exposition, to give it its full name, was the most important event of the period. It was promoted for the purpose of stimulating Southern industry, which sadly needed encouragement after the war. As far as New Orleans was concerned, the advertising of the port was the prime objective, the Eads system of jetties having lately been completed. The idea of an exposition originated at the annual meeting of the National Cotton Planters' Association in 1882. It was recalled that the first cotton exported had been in 1784 when six bags (about one bale) had been shipped from Charleston to England. The sale to foreign countries had increased to 4,000,000 bales per year, out of a total production of 7,000,000 bales. A celebration seemed in order. After a while the project was expanded into a general world's fair, but the public always knew it as the Cotton Exposition.

Congress passed an act of incorporation, and voted $1,300,000. After New Orleans had been chosen as the location, the city appropriated $100,000 and the state of Louisiana $100,000. The balance of the funds needed was raised by popular subscription and sums voted by other states and by foreign countries. The site was the old Foucher plantation and a part of the De Boré plantation where cane sugar had first been granulated on a commercial scale in Louisiana. It was a tract of 247 acres which had lately been acquired by the city as a park, and which some years after the exposition was renamed Audubon Park.

The main building was the largest of its kind that had been erected to date. It covered thirty-three acres of ground, or about 1,650,000 square feet. The Crystal Palace, London, was 1,400,000 square feet, the main building at the Centennial Exposition in Philadelphia 872,320 and that at the Paris Exposition of 1855 only 545,000. There were several other huge buildings at the New Orleans fair, including the famous Horticultural Hall, where tropical fruits and flowers were grown in hothouses, and a display of the rarest fruits imported on ice was constantly maintained. This last was regarded as a prodigious novelty. It had been inspired, at least in part, by the fact that Minor C. Keith had been pioneering in the banana business in Costa Rica and had shipped his first full cargo to New Orleans in 1881. A taste for the tropical luxury, as it then was, had been developing. Now, with the help of the exposition, New Orleans rapidly became the chief banana port in the United States.

Much admired at the horticultural display were water hyacinths from Venezuela, then seen locally for the first time. Garden lovers bought plants as a curiosity and set them out in pools and ponds.

The hyacinths spread into near-by streams, multiplied with great rapidity, and in a few years became a scourge. Waterways in the South are choked with them. It takes a constant effort to keep channels open for navigation.

The Cotton Exposition placed much emphasis on machinery, a field in which the improvements have been so vast that the exhibits of 1884 seem infantile today. There is still a thrill in the circumstance that the city got its first view of electricity on a large scale at this fair. The whole grounds were lighted by it. The public went mad over it. The announcement of the management that the battery consisted of "4,000 incandescent and 1,100 standard arc lamps, which require 1,600 horse-power of engines" sounded prodigal, and the result was hailed as magic from the Thousand and One Nights.

As with all the earlier fairs in America, a secondary and useful outcome was the interest taken in the local scene by visitors whose concern was other than commercial. New Orleans received advertising that made it better and more sympathetically known to intellectual circles elsewhere. The press of the world sent reporters to cover the exposition, and the editors of New York and Boston magazines came down. Discriminating articles were published; because of the contacts made with the visiting correspondents, local writers began to be given a hearing in the profitable literary market of the North.

Inevitably, there was also a tremendous influx of adventurers, gamblers and crooks. The underworld flocked about expositions in the riotous latter decades of the nineteenth century. Those who came to New Orleans were no worse than the average. They reveled in the "good-time town" between river and lake: its horse racing, its dog fights and cockfights, casinos where money could be risked on every conceivable game, dance halls and vaudeville in the utmost variety, a wide-open red-light district—and saloons unhampered by a closing law on Sundays or any other time. One of the attractions, undoubtedly, was the celebrated lottery.

Charles T. Howard and six associates obtained a state lottery monopoly from the carpetbag legislature in 1868. Admittedly the votes to put it through were bought for cash, as much as $300,000 according to reliable evidence. Governor Warmoth signed the bill, though he had received a good many protests against it. The charter was to run for twenty-five years, and it granted exemption from taxation with the proviso that the lottery company pay $40,000 yearly to the New Orleans Charity Hospital. Howard and his silent partner John Morris, a New Yorker, were the dominant figures in the enterprise. They commenced business with a capital stock of $1,000,000. Modestly they issued tickets for twenty-five cents, and offered a capital prize of $3,750. Soon this was raised to a fifty-cent ticket and a $7,500 prize. Further increases provided for one-dollar tickets which could win as much as $15,000, $20 tickets with a top reward of $300,000, and semiannually, a $40 ticket with a capital prize of $600,000. Of course, there were buys to be had at every intermediate price. Fractions of tickets were sold, the more expensive ones usually being subdivided among several purchasers.

The venture moved slowly at the beginning. The details of selling chances and dramatizing the results appear to have been clumsily handled. In the early 1870's Dr. Maximilian A. Dauphin was appointed manager, and business immediately looked up. This shrewd individual decided that it was of prime importance to convince the public that the drawings were absolutely honest. It has never been claimed that the lottery company cheated. There was no reason for it do so, because the percentages had been so calculated that it was sure to make around fifty percent. But Dauphin knew the value of theatrical methods. He induced General P. G. T. Beauregard and General Jubal A. Early to preside over the public drawings at salaries of $30,000 a year each. The Confederate heroes were required only to sit on the platform, though naturally they had access to any records they wished to examine. The actual drawing of numbers from the lottery wheel was done by blindfolded children.

Sales of tickets doubled and tripled every year until 1879 when the legislature suddenly repealed the charter. Howard and Morris hurried to Baton Rouge and reversed the decision. They offered the state an annual payment of $1,250,000 divided among various good works, including a fund for building and repairing levees on the Mississippi. An extension of the charter until January 1, 1895, was written into the new constitution to be submitted to the voters. As it was a question of getting rid of the constitution imposed during Reconstruction, the issue was scarcely in doubt.

Fifteen years of grace were accorded the lottery. It used them to branch out in extravagant fashion, while laying plans to obtain another renewal in 1895. Offices were opened throughout the country and in some foreign cities, and these produced an enormous revenue. The business presently grossed $30,000,000 a year, and lottery stock rose from $35 a share to $1,200 a share. A slice of the juicy profits was used to buy good will locally. The company met the deficits of the French Opera House and contributed lavishly to the support of Carnival. It provided sinecures on its payroll for hundreds of persons—relatives or friends of the influential. The semimonthly distribution of winnings attracted throngs of sight-seers, and the two semiannual drawings were turned into gala affairs. A New Orleans barber once won $300,000 on a whole $20 ticket. He was in the audience when his number was called, and the prize was immediately paid him.

The Louisiana Lottery was condemned in the bitterest terms by moralists, churchmen and reformers generally. One cannot see, however, that it was any worse fundamentally than the sweepstake schemes licensed by some governments today. It was an evil because of the involvement with politics, because venal lawmakers encouraged it to bribe them. Intelligent regulation was not even attempted. At that, it furnished an outlet for the gambling lust which has always gripped the people of New Orleans. Probably, though figures are unavailable, it reduced the indulgence in backroom games which offered the players even less chance of getting something for the money they risked.

But there was a wave of antilottery sentiment in the United

States. A Federal law was passed forbidding the mailing of lottery tickets or advertising. Other restrictive measures piled up. Francis T. Nicholls came from retirement to win a second term as governor of Louisiana on a platform that vowed undying enmity to "the octopus," as it was called. The legislature voted a renewal, but Nicholls vetoed it, and a two-thirds majority to override the veto could not be obtained. A referendum was taken to the people. The lottery lost. It transferred its seat of operations to the Republic of Honduras in 1895 where, unable to cope with postal and other difficulties, it soon went out of business.

In 1887 Lafcadio Hearn, then a feature writer on the New Orleans *Times-Democrat,* wrote to a friend in New York that the paper had secretly changed hands. He had heard that the Louisiana Lottery Company had bought a controlling interest, and he feared there would be a radical shake-up of the staff. The rumor proved well founded. It was one of the factors that decided Hearn to leave the city where his unique talent had been ripening for the past ten years. New Orleans should count that against the lottery. No doubt other influences would shortly have caused Hearn to move on, but the longer he stayed the better it would have been for local culture.

There had never been so discerning a study of the scene as he brought to it. Rivals in English were not his equals, a judgment which does not exclude the reputation of George W. Cable.

Before he left Cincinnati in 1877, the shy little myopic man—half-Irish, half-Greek—had been impressed by one of Cable's short stories in *Scribner's* and had looked him up a little while after he got to New Orleans. The two became friends, briefly, and exchanged literary raw material. They shared one conviction: that the Negro was not being given a square deal. Otherwise, the difference between them was immense.

Cable had been born and brought up on the American side of town, his mother a New Englander who seems to have been the chief influence in shaping his character. He enlisted in the Confederate army and fought through the war. Hostilities were barely over when he took the stand that the Lost Cause had best be forgotten, that the Union and most of its works were good, and the Negro should be treated as a brother. Few would have condemned him for privately holding these defensible views, but it was indiscreet of him to advance them so early in his native city. Cable was puritan-pious. He landed a job on the *Picayune,* but resigned when told to edit the theatrical column. He considered the stage wicked. Years later, while on a lecture tour with Mark Twain, nothing could induce him to travel on Sunday.

Before the event, it would have been difficult to imagine Cable choosing Creole life as his specialty. Yet he made his success with a long series of tales on this theme. His descriptions of places are marvelous: no one has better caught the atmosphere of the Vieux Carré houses with their dim arches, their courtyards and balconies, or the French farmhouse style of romantic cottages. His characterizations have much merit within a limited scope, for only the virtues are really portrayed, evil being dismissed with platitudes. His plots are little more than sentimental situations, some of which he uses over and over in slightly different forms. The favorite presents a beautiful octoroon girl with whom a white man falls in love, and after considerable heartbreak because he cannot marry her—of course, you've guessed it—she turns out to be white after all.

There was, however, another element in Cable's writing. He subtly ridiculed the Creoles, ascribing to them shiftlessness, vanity, bombast and other mirth-provoking defects. Doubtless there was plenty of that sort of thing to be found among them. Every race has its foibles and absurdities. Cable rubbed it in by means of a very amusing rendering of the garbled English spoken by Creoles at that time. They did not like the picture he painted of them. They particularly resented his using material drawn from family histories. So the anomaly existed of a New Orleans writer hailed by the rest of the country as a genius following the publication of his stories in magazines and his novel, *The Grandissimes* (1880), but denounced by his fellow citizens. The Creoles never forgave him. Eventually he declared that the North was his spiritual home and moved there.

Lafcadio Hearn had little sympathy with Confederate ideas. He was disinterested in politics, anyway. But his Mediterranean temperament was charmed by New Orleans, its sights and sounds, and especially by the customs of the Creoles and their dependents, the former slaves. Puritanism was anathema to Hearn. He went to the opposite extreme from Cable, for he practiced a cult of sensuality, had openly had a colored mistress in Cincinnati, and formed attachments for various girls in the bordellos of New Orleans. He was hypersensitive about his appearance. One eye was blind and covered with a white film, and the other was protuberant. This has been cited to explain the sort of company he kept, but it is hard to believe that he would have been less of a Bohemian if he had had no physical defects.

After a period of semistarvation he joined the staff of the *Item,* a co-operative newspaper recently started by eleven journeymen printers out of jobs. In its columns for about three years and in those of the *Times-Democrat* for about six, he charmed his readers with a brilliant, highly personalized journalism that set a new standard of taste, and coincidentally interpreted New Orleans to itself. He was essayist, columnist and literary critic at one and the same time. His translations of contemporary French works introduced such writers as Flaubert, Maupassant, the Goncourt brothers and Zola to a Latinized public that received them avidly. His local material was a superb gallery of impressions of the city's life. He was particularly devoted to folklore and the Gombo patois which Creoles picked up from the colored people and used when it suited them to do so.

Before he went to the French West Indies and finally Japan, Hearn was contributing to New York magazines. He published *Chita,* a stylistic masterpiece based on the destruction of Last Island on the Gulf Coast of Louisiana by a tidal wave in 1856.

It is curious that English letters in New Orleans should have owed so much to the exotic Hearn who had no roots there, and to Cable, the fish out of water, the puritan in a city that was no place for puritans. They were followed by a line of emulators, predominantly women, none of whom had their power. The best was Grace King, author of *The Pleasant Ways of St. Medard,* etc. Only in the generation after that did the awakening produce a solid school of writers, some native-born and some naturalized.

The literature of the Creoles was an entirely different matter. In the 1870's and '80's the outstanding figure was the aging historian, Charles Gayarré, direct descendant of an official who had come to New Orleans with the Spanish governor Ulloa. He had started out in politics, had been a judge and Louisiana's secretary of state in the 1840's, had been elected to the United States Senate, but had had to resign his seat on account of illness. Thereafter he devoted himself to history. Gayarré wrote in both French and English, but French was the language that came naturally to him, and his English editions convey the feeling of translations made by himself. His *History of Louisiana* (1885) is a standard work. His researches in the Paris archives had laid the foundation for all books that touch on the colonizing of the region, including this one.

Gayarré had ardently supported the Confederacy, had invested his private fortune in its bonds, and had been ruined financially. He found it difficult to make ends meet in his later days, for his scholarly articles were hard to sell and brought low prices. He managed, however, to build a cottage in the woods of Tangipahoa Parish, north of the west end of Lake Pontchartrain and of Lake Maurepas. It was named Roncal. He spent his summers there. Grace King has left an evocative description of the retreat in her *Memoirs of a Southern Woman of Letters.* The dignified old man did almost no visiting and rarely attended public gatherings. On the other hand, his modest home in New Orleans was a salon to which the discriminating flocked. Here, led by Gayarré himself, was heard the most mordant of the criticisms leveled at George W. Cable.

A group of younger Creole intellectuals felt it urgent to organize for the preservation of their language and traditions. Most Creoles had suffered terrible material reverses during the war and Reconstruction. Their prosperity had been anchored in the old order of things, and as a people they lacked the business acumen, the energy—the modernity, perhaps—to adapt themselves and rebuild as the Americans were doing. The danger of their complete submergence was very real. If that happened their literature and press, already threatened by the pressure from all sides of the English language, would certainly go out of existence.

The group in question was composed largely of professional men, who wrote as an avocation. Its leading spirit was Dr. Alfred Mercier, to whom reference has already been made. He and his friends founded in 1876, before Reconstruction ended, a society called L'Athénée Louisianais with three professed objectives:

1. To perpetuate the French language in Louisiana.
2. To concern itself with scientific, literary and artistic efforts, and to protect them.
3. To organize itself into a mutual-assistance association.

Founding members included Dr. Alfred Mercier and his brother Dr. Armand Mercier, four other physicians, a judge, several lawyers and General P. G. T. Beauregard. Armand Mercier was elected president, Beauregard vice-president, and Alfred Mercier secretary-treasurer. Additional doctors soon joined. As a result the proceedings of the first few years and the early articles printed in the society's organ, *Comptes Rendus,* are heavily weighted with medical lore. But literature was the *raison d'être.* Frankly L'Athénée Louisianais modeled itself upon the Institut de France. It held yearly contests for the best essays on a specified theme. The winner was crowned laureate and medals were presented. In addition, good verse, short fiction and belles-lettres that Creoles were writing usually received their first hearings in the *Comptes Rendus.* Lafcadio Hearn wrote in the *Item,* in 1880:

"We must remark that there are few magazines printed in English in this country which contain articles as interesting and as unique as this French periodical."

Ambitious work was stimulated. Dr. Alfred Mercier would no doubt have written his fine novels, *L'Habitation Saint-Ybars* and *La Fille du Prêtre,* even if he had not founded L'Athénée, but the society enlarged the public for them, as it did for Père Rouquette's *La Nouvelle Atala.* Other authors owed a direct debt to the activities of the new cultural circle. Several novels by lesser authors and a number of volumes of poetry were issued under a New Orleans imprint. This French renaissance had run its course by the end of the century. Edward Larocque Tinker, the critic, has pointed out that the year 1900 was like a curtain falling at the close of a play. Up till then books of some importance were frequently published in the old tongue, but since 1900 not one has appeared. The French daily and periodical press has slowly gone out of existence—with a sole exception.

"On the day when we stop speaking French in Louisiana, if ever that day should come—which we by no means believe—there will no longer be any Creoles," said Dr. Alfred Mercier. "The original and forceful group which they constituted in the great national family of the United States will have disappeared as wine does, both its taste and its color, if one pours it into a passing river."

There was no danger of the language dying in the Acadian parishes. In New Orleans, however, its salvation as a cultural medium owes much to L'Athénée. The group's second president was General Beauregard, and its third Professor Alcée Fortier, the acknowledged successor of Gayarré as a historian. It is as active as ever today under the presidency of André Lafargue. Other societies with similar ideals are functioning. But only L'Athénée publishes an organ. The *Comptes Rendus* has reached its seventieth year.

Placide Canonge, director of the Opera, was also an essayist and critic. He contributed regularly to the old New Orleans daily newspaper, *L'Abeille.*

A Creole writer of the second half of the nineteenth century who did all his work abroad must be briefly mentioned. Albert Delpit, son of a rich New Orleans tobacconist, went to France in

LOCK GATES IN INDUSTRIAL CANAL

Association of Commerce

NEW ORLEANS LAKEFRONT HIGHWAY

The Highway extends along the southern shore of Lake Pontchartrain which once was swamp and marsh. The building in the left foreground is the Southern Yacht Club, established in 1849.

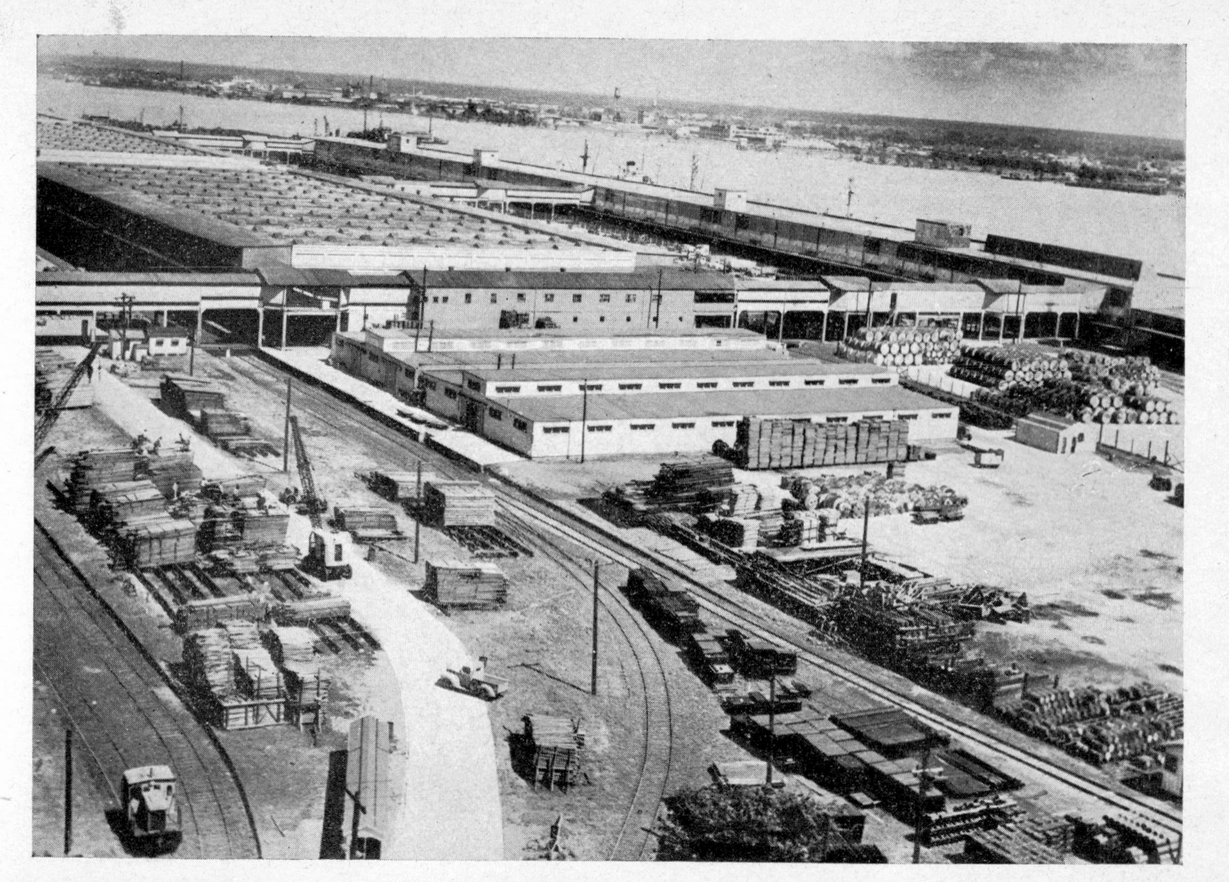

PUBLIC COTTON WAREHOUSE

1868 to seek his fortune, at the age of nineteen, against his father's wishes. He worked on papers sponsored by Dumas *Père*. He won an open contest at a literary matinee at the Gaiété, for the best poem in praise of Lamartine. This launched the young Delpit, who by the middle 1870's had novels and a volume of verse to his credit, and had had a play produced. The Académie Française crowned two of his poems. A drama was accepted for the Comédie Française, where it had a long run. Through the years he poured out works that were both distinguished and successful. His remarkable career has been undeservedly forgotten in his native land.

The chess prodigy, Paul Morphy of New Orleans, was inexplicable by ordinary standards of appraisal. In the last days of his life he obviously was not quite sane. But his precocious brilliance is remembered with a kind of awe. He passed examinations in philosophy, mathematics, law and a dozen other subjects with such ease that he was graduated from college and admitted to the bar before he was twenty. Meanwhile, from the age of twelve on, he had been routing all comers at chess, playing that most difficult of games as if by intuition, playing it blindfold or under any other limitations his opponents cared to suggest, and almost invariably winning. He was a Creole of the Creoles, his father of Spanish ancestry and his mother of French from Saint Domingue. The idea of becoming a professional chess master would not have entered his head. It would have smacked of commercialism.

But when he was twenty-one his admirers persuaded him to accept an invitation to take part in tournaments in Europe. Morphy won every one of his matches. He overturned every champion who consented to meet him, and laughed indifferently at those who refused in a panic to risk their titles against him. The Prussian, Anderssen, was then the acknowledged champion of the world. Morphy defeated him by seven games to two. He started back to New Orleans in May 1859, and his journey from New York south was a continuous ovation. On reaching his home he issued, without response, a challenge offering to yield the odds of pawn and move to any player in the world. Then, in his twenty-third year, he renounced chess, declaring that his proposed career as a lawyer made it inexpedient for him to play in public again.

To this illogical decision he rigidly adhered. For a few years he contested games with friends now and then, showing undiminished power. On revisiting Paris in 1867, he refused even to attend a session of the international chess tournament which was in progress. However, in 1872 he published his important commentary, *Games of Chess.* Thereafter, he never played.

He had failed utterly at the practice of law. How that could happen to the prematurely developed, glittering Morphy baffled his admirers. They tried to explain it away by arguing that conditions in New Orleans just after the war were unfavorable to any young attorney. Actually, this supernormal mind could not adapt itself to realistic human problems. He became more and more eccentric. He would wildly misinterpret commonplace remarks addressed to him, and particularly if they had to do with chess. The mere mention of the game threw him into a frenzy, as though chess were a temptation that haunted him at Satan's instigation. He grew devout and was often to be seen at the Cathedral, where he prayed dramatically and indulged in queer miming before the sacred images.

Morphy did not marry. He lived at his parents' house on Royal Street until July 1884, when he died suddenly in a cold bath taken while he was overheated from walking. He was only forty-seven.

Those middle 1880's and early 1890's had a savor which is gone forever from the life of New Orleans. Unique characters were always doing something to astonish a public that loved sensations. It might be a Myra Clark Gaines finally winning at the age of eighty the chief points in the incredible lawsuit which she had waged against the city for a little longer than fifty years. It might be "Gentleman Jim," the bank clerk from San Francisco, participating in the three days' boxing carnival held by the Olympic Athletic Club and knocking out the great Sullivan. The fight is too well known to bear repetition. But a line or two about the Gaines case may not be amiss.

Myra was twenty-seven and married when she learned that she was the daughter by a secret marriage of Daniel Clark, the politician and rich merchant who had dueled with Governor Claiborne. Furthermore, two witnesses assured her that Clark had read to them a will in which she was made his sole heir. That will had never been found. One written two years earlier was probated, and part of the estate was bought and resold by the City of New Orleans. Myra sued to have the will favoring her substituted on oral testimony that it had existed. Nothing like that had ever been heard before in an American court of justice. The legal struggle that ensued, marked by reversals of judgment from one decade to another, remains unparalleled. The case was tried in Louisiana thirty times and went to the United States Supreme Court seventeen times. Myra had barely obtained a decision that she was legally Clark's daughter and entitled to about half a million dollars when she died, in 1885, and was borne to a tomb in St. Louis Cemetery No. 1. This has since been shown to sight-seers as the last resting place of a champion.

There are old-timers who will tell you that their most nostalgic memory of the period is not the Cotton Exposition, but Faranta's Show. The latter was set up under canvas, in 1884, on what was then the vacant lot at the corner of Bourbon and Orleans Streets, where the famous Théâtre d'Orléans had once stood. It was run by an Italian impresario as a combined circus, vaudeville show, and outdoors theater which sometimes gave operas, comedies and even the works of Shakespeare. The great charm of the place, apparently, was its atmosphere of a Creole amusement park in the heart of the Vieux Carré. The acrobats, the bareback riders and the minstrels—the actors on the elevated stage with its pull curtain—these contributed but half of the fun. The rest was to be found in the environs of the tent.

A carnival society, the Olympians, recently made Faranta's

Show the subject of tableaux in a Mardi Gras pageant. It would be hard to find a better evocation of the scene than the following from the program distributed to guests:

"As one approached the entrance to the show, numerous vendors and peddlers could be seen moving nonchalantly amid the throng, which was pushing and shoving in a frantic rush to reach the ticket booth; others, apart from the crowd, were seated on boxes or folding stools along the curbstone. Yes, all the characters so intimately associated with the times and the customs of the old city were there: the Negro woman *pain-patate* vendor, with her characteristic *tignon à la chinoise* offering her confection made of sweet potatoes, *sucre brut* (brown sugar), an overdose of *poivre noir* (black pepper), some *écorce de canelle* (cinnamon bark) baked and made more appetizing by a luscious rich brown crust; the *bierre douce* vendor offering his cold ale, brewed by the dispenser and made of fresh *ananas* (pineapples), sugar, apples, a handful of grain corn to accelerate fermentation, and ginger and sassafras root to give added zest and aromatic stimulation; the toy windmill and the balloon vendors with their multicolored displays whirling and moving agitatedly with every whiff of air; the *maïs tactac* vendor carrying a wicker basket on his arm with a generous supply of popcorn dipped in candied cane syrup and shaped in golden balls; and the *marron* vendor peddling his roasted chestnuts in the conventional paper bags, each offering his or her particular confection in inimitable fashion and with characteristic cry.

"It was: *'Pain-patate, Madame!'—'Bierre douce, cinq sous le ver'!'* (Ale, five cents a glass)—*'Maïs tactac avec siro cane pou piti garçon!'* (Popcorn rolled in candied cane syrup for the little boy.) Then somewhat apart from the surging crowd, seated on a box with her basket resting on her knees, and holding a large black percale parasol over her left shoulder, Liza, the slave-born, jovial-faced colored woman, offering her rich brown *estomac milatte* (ginger cake) and *baton zamande* (almond-flavored cookies), both freshly baked and oftentimes still warm. She would greet her clientele with an affable, *'Bonjou, Musieu et Dame, estoma' milatte et baton zamande pou zenfants!'* (Good morning, Sir and Madam, ginger cakes and almond cookies for the children) while amid the turmoil and the rush, above the din of the two-wheeled dumpcarts and heavily laden drays rolling over the cobble-stoned streets, and the jubilant and enthusiastic outbursts of the children, the strident cry of the balloon man and the raucous voice of the windmill vendor rose in discordant tones: 'Bah-loons! Bah-loons for the bay-bi!'—'Windmills for the boys and girls!'"

A ditty composed to celebrate the popularity of the place had this refrain:

"My beau's a dago.
Who told you so?
He sells bananas
'Round Faranta's Show!"

Chapter 20

The Filibuster and the Lake

New Orleans has sent out its share of filibusters, from the "Gray-Eyed Man of Destiny," William Walker, who did change the course of history in Central America, down to many a cheap and rapacious Anglo-Saxon bandit masquerading under the title. Reference to some of them has been made in a previous chapter. But there has been only one filibuster who hailed from the "Florida parishes," whose youth was largely spent on the lakes, and who has on his record an exploit performed in part on Pontchartrain. He was Leon Winfield Christmas, commonly known as Lee Christmas. Despite his personal crudity and the total absence of grandeur from his conceptions or his deeds, he in a sense ranks next to Walker. The latter had able contemporaries whom he overshadowed. But that generation had passed away when Christmas arrived on the stage. A new note was struck by this Christmas individual, and his emulators never succeeded in taking the spotlight from him. He rode high just previous to and during the "Dollar Diplomacy" era of Washington's dealing with Latin America. By the time the "Good Neighbor" policy rendered filibustering unthinkable, he was dead—his legend already firmly crystallized.

He was the son of a man who had fought in the Mexican War and had then settled down to cotton planting on the banks of the Amite River, in Livingston Parish, nineteen miles below Baton Rouge. The year of Lee's birth was 1863, and according to his own story the Yankees came along about that time, seized all the cotton they could lay hands on and devastated the homestead. The elder Christmas appears never to have been much more than a "poor white." His health broken, he moved to the sawmill township of Springfield, deep in cypress swamps where two streams met and flowed into Lake Maurepas. There Lee grew up with a smattering of education. His father died when he was sixteen, but the loss could have made little difference to Lee economically. At the age of twelve he had gone to work as a cook on the schooner *Celeste,* which was commanded by a Captain Bob Caldwell, and the following year was promoted to able seaman. The *Celeste* was of such light draft that she could mount the Tickafaw and Natalbany, so-called rivers, to Springfield. At fifteen we find Lee skipper of another schooner of the same type, the *Surprise,* and a short time later skipper of the schooner *Lillie Simms.*

All these boats plied between Springfield and the New Basin, New Orleans, carrying lumber and miscellaneous freight. Their route was the ancient one through Maurepas, the Manchac Pass and Pontchartrain. The future filibuster gained his experience under canvas and in a type of trading that had not altered since Louisiana was a French colony.

Tiring of the water under conditions so unpromising for a man who wanted money and excitement, Lee went to McComb, Mississippi, where he worked for a few months as a waiter and then became a railroad brakeman on a New Orleans run. Soon he was a locomotive fireman, "learning the trick in the days when wood was burned," as he expressed it afterward. At twenty-two they let him graduate as an engineer, and one can only assume that the Brotherhood was not very discriminating at that period, for Lee's technical knowledge had been picked up here and there. He was quarrelsome, fond of the bottle, and almost illiterate.

He made New Orleans his headquarters. Running freight engines was his vocation, but he played ward politics as a side line. One day in 1891 he had gone on an election carouse immediately after coming in from a run. He was located hours later by a messenger with orders that he move a trainload of bananas. Pushed into his cab by friends, he presently fell asleep at the throttle and the train crashed into another one. He was badly shaken up, scalded, and received an injury to an eye. The railroad fired him. As an engineer he was black-listed in the United States.

Lee Christmas knocked around as a tramp, and a particularly drunken, worthless one, for the next three years. He had a wife and children for whom he did nothing. In 1894 he tried to straighten up. Hoping to get back with his former employers, he took an examination which revealed that he was color-blind. Doubtless he had always been so. The vision test was something new, but there could be no appeal from it. He had heard that American railroad men were being sought for work in Honduras, so on an impulse he bought a steamship ticket and went there. The Honduras National Railroad was glad to see him and asked no inconvenient questions about color blindness. He was given a train that made three round trips a week between Puerto Cortés and San Pedro Sula in the interior.

Where would it have been possible to find a less likely candidate for power than this broken-down engineer who could not get a job in his own country! His background and personality were much against him in Honduras. He spoke no Spanish and behaved as if he scorned all "yellow bellies"—the males of the species in any event. Low bars and brothels were his places of amusement. He was foul-mouthed, ill-humored, and in the eyes of Latins he seemed downright stupid. Three years passed without his doing a thing to improve anyone's opinion of him.

Then in 1897, when he was not quite thirty-four years old, opportunity wearing a grotesque mask was tossed his way. A small body of Honduran revolutionists slipped over from Guatemala, where they had received backing, and took possession of Puerto Cortés. When Christmas reached the environs with his train from upcountry the next day, he was ambushed and captured. The revolutionists told him that if he did not agree to pilot his engine in their behalf he would be shot instantly. He concluded that the answer to that was to throw in his lot with them.

He mounted a Hotchkiss quick-firer on a flatcar protected with sandbags, and placed this moving fort ahead of the engine. He took command of the sharpshooters posted about the gun. When the Federals attacked, he conducted himself with reckless bravery and developed qualities of initiative that were a large factor in winning the skirmish for his side. To him it was "a new game," one that he liked. He used those words in after years to describe his sensations. It did not matter that his first revolution proved abortive. His reputation as a daredevil grew, and when his companions were forced to flee back over the mountain into Guatemala he went with them. The dictator of that country gave him a post in the secret service.

Lee Christmas bungled his next assignment, which involved actual filibustering. He was sent to New Orleans to make an illicit deal for the purchase of arms and ammunition. Just what happened is not clear, but his Guatemalan employers dropped him. He waited around until an amnesty was declared by Honduras in connection with the recent revolt, went back to Puerto Cortés and started running his train once more. But he was now admired and feared. He reveled in this, and although he played the bully it was with a swagger that men preferred to his former sullen manner. The very government against which he had taken the field used him in some capacity, probably as a secret agent. For he quit the railroad and lorded it over the district, with plenty of money in his pocket though he had no visible source of income.

The president of Honduras was Terencio Sierra, one of three leaders who had overthrown a previous administration. The others were Dr. Policarpo Bonilla and General Manuel Bonilla, who although they bore the same family name were not related. Policarpo Bonilla had served a full term and handed on the office peacefully to Sierra. The agreement from the beginning of the triple partnership had been that Manuel Bonilla should succeed Sierra. But Sierra yielded to the temptation to perpetrate a double cross. In the usual Central American way, he started to build a military machine and to corrupt the officials around him. Finally he took a step that was sensational even in Honduras. He called

Lee Christmas to Tegucigalpa, the capital, and in May 1902 appointed him chief of police with the rank of colonel.

There have been many stories about American adventurers swashbuckling their way into positions of command in Latin America. The majority contain a large element of fiction. This is one of the few authentic cases. It enraged the local press and offended the political elements not on the president's side. Sierra paid no attention. He needed a ruthless fighter to head his bodyguard, which was what the 185 gendarmes in Tegucigalpa amounted to, and he thought he had found the right man in Lee. Ordinarily it would have been a good bet. The thing that spoiled it for Sierra could not possibly have been foreseen by him.

Manuel Bonilla, the prospective candidate for the presidency, was serving as minister of war. Lee was thrown into contact with him for the first time and they became fast personal friends. The basis for their mutual regard is inexplicable. There does not seem much in common between the Louisiana roustabout who never read a book and had barely learned to express himself in garbled Spanish, and the rather scholarly half-Indian Bonilla. They liked each other without knowing or caring why. It has been said that in his whole life Lee was unswervingly loyal to only two comrades, one of whom was the Honduran. But they concealed their friendship at the start in Tegucigalpa.

Sierra found it advisable to hold the election, which he planned to rig. In addition to the expected opposition candidate, he encouraged a third man to run. Bonilla polled the most votes, but did not get a clear majority. On these grounds, which were novel in Honduras, Sierra annulled the election and arranged to have himself petitioned by the legislature to retain the power. One night, at the last moment of the crisis, Bonilla and his friends left the capital. Along with them went Colonel Lee Christmas and his 185 policemen.

The details of the civil war that followed would be superfluous in this narrative. Lee showed instinctive talent not only as an animator of guerrillas, but as a tactician in the field. When

Bonilla returned to Tegucigalpa with victorious eagles, the American was beside him, a formally commissioned brigadier general now and confirmed in the office of chief of police. To the end of his days, the former tramp railroader gloried in the military title. He sent to Paris for a dress sword and a uniform heavy with gold braid. A white horse was indicated to go with such splendor, so he acquired one. He really did. It was wonderful to be General Lee Christmas.

For three years he rode high. Then the inevitable counter-revolution was launched, and although Lee played his part courageously and shrewdly Bonilla was overthrown. The president escaped to British Honduras, where he bought a plantation and let it be understood that he was out of politics. The American took refuge in Guatemala, alternating between the secret service and railroading. He met with better success in that country than he had the first time, yet always felt dissatisfied. Honduras was in his blood.

Men like Manuel Bonilla never retire voluntarily, and the Lee Christmases of this world stick to dull occupations no longer than they must. We find Don Manuel and Lee corresponding through late 1909 and early 1910 about the possibilities of a new coup. In the summer of 1910 they attempted one, but it fizzled. Among their volunteers was an interesting young fellow, Guy Molony of New Orleans, who at seventeen had fought in the British army against the Boers and later had seen service under the American flag in the Philippines. He was better educated and more of a man of the world than Lee, but just as much of a hothead. Both the chief conspirators came to like and trust Molony, and they made an appointment to meet him in New Orleans.

Bonilla had found an American backer who still remains anonymous, though in certain circles his identity is not regarded as a mystery. This man had agreed to contribute a twenty-year-old yacht that had been partly armored for naval use in the Spanish-American War, and also a limited supply of ammunition.

The ship was what Bonilla valued, because he wished to launch his next attack by sea. He had plenty of rifles and machine guns cached in Guatemala.

The *insurrecto* boss and Christmas reached New Orleans in December. They were placed under observation by the United States secret service. This was no more than they had expected, but it irked them to discover that their boat, too, had attracted unfavorable attention. She needed refitting, and the only way to do it without getting her seized was to bluff brazenly. Lee took charge at the shipyard. He had her old name, *Alicia,* painted out and rechristened her the *Hornet.* The alterations that were being made, he announced, were to equip her as a collier. He told this to several men whom he was dead sure he had spotted as government agents. They probably thought he was lying, yet when the time came to load the vessel it indubitably was coal that was placed aboard.

Every evening Lee, Bonilla, Molony and a Honduran called Dávadi forgathered openly. They dined together. Sometimes they went to see a show, but more often they made the round in "Storyville," the restricted red-light district that was then a gaudy, undissembled feature of New Orleans night life. This was the sort of amusement that Lee had always preferred. The young fellows, Molony and Dávadi, might be expected to follow his lead. Don Manuel Bonilla, oldish, foreign, seemed an odd boon companion for them. Therein lay the crux of the deception, however. Bonilla played the part of a nitwit spender, squandering money for champagne in one "parlor house" after another and showering the girls with tips. It appeared that the other three men were making a sucker of him, and that such a foolish person could not be engaged in a serious filibustering plot.

The *Hornet* got her clearance papers, after officials had satisfied themselves that she had no contraband aboard. On December 20 she steamed down the Mississippi. Suspicious United States inspectors accompanied her to Pilot Town and saw her off into the Gulf, ostensibly bound for a South American port. Lee pretended that after he had seen her loaded he had no further interest in her. He diverted himself with his friends as usual that evening, and the following night the four of them staged a big party at the establishment of a madam on Basin Street who called herself the Countess Willie V. Piazza.

Detectives were still on their trail. Lee had noticed two of them on the street corner across the way, and a third entered the parlor of the bordello to keep them under close surveillance. The schemers behaved as if they did not have a care in the world. Don Manuel bought the wine with more abandon than ever. It is said that he drank very little himself, but he laughed and jested, danced as often as his years would permit, and sang Latin-American ballads.

It was almost three o'clock in the morning when the secret service man gave them up as a harmless lot of roisterers and left the place. He was observed joining and exchanging notes with the other sleuths on the corner. Presently they all took their departure.

The members of the Honduran revolutionary group at once dropped their masks. They hurried to a rendezvous near by, where an automobile was waiting for them. At the top speed that could be got out of a car in 1910, they drove to the mouth of the Bayou St. John. A cabin cruiser was awaiting them there, a short distance from the ruins of old Spanish Fort. She belonged to the backer from whom the *Hornet* had been obtained, and she had on board a consignment of rifles. Bonilla and his friends went below deck until the powerboat cast off and raced into the darkness out of sight of land. Then they reappeared on deck and shook hands all around, laughing exultantly.

If Lee had any sense of romance, which is doubtful, it must have given him a special thrill to return thus to Pontchartrain, the scene of his boyhood hazards. It was the first time he had sailed the lake since he had been skipper of the *Lillie Simms*.

At dawn they were chugging over the shallow waters eastward and approaching the Rigolets. The other craft they sighted did not suspect them of a nefarious errand. The cabin cruiser had often been seen on the fishing grounds thereabouts. When, later that day, the not-so-secret agents in New Orleans wondered where the dissipated old Honduran, the rowdy Lee and the rest had gone, it did not occur to them to check Pontchartrain as a means of exit. They had forgotten the little history they might once have known, forgotten that the backdoor route employed by the French and Spanish colonizers was still good.

The small craft carrying Lee and his friends passed unobtrusively through the Rigolets and continued down Mississippi Sound until she was opposite Biloxi in the late afternoon. Then she stood off for Ship Island, where Ben Butler had massed his forces for the capture of New Orleans in the War between the States. This was the rendezvous, and it was hoped that the signal lights of the *Hornet* would be picked up that night. Nothing happened. The filibusterers were more seriously worried than they had been at any moment since their departure from the Bayou St. John. They had no information whether or not the *Hornet* had actually been permitted to get any farther than Pilot Town. The following day was nerve-racking, for in order to seem innocent they thought it wise to cruise along the coast, pretend to fish, and even to call at one of the mainland resorts. There was a strong possibility that the Coast Guard had been notified to look out for them.

At dusk they started back to Ship Island, rounded its western tip and at once noted, at some distance to sea, the arrangement of colored lights which had been agreed upon. They joyously put on a burst of speed and ran out to the *Hornet*. The rifles were quickly transferred. Lee and Bonilla thanked the sportsman who had brought them that far. Along with Molony and Dávadi, they climbed aboard the converted yacht, which immediately headed south.

The revolution started in this piratical manner turned out to be an exciting affair. Christmas improved his military standing and Guy Molony put himself on the map as a soldier of fortune. Roatán, one of the Bay Islands, was the first point seized. Then the Bonilla forces descended on the north coast of Honduras and fought several engagements, winning them all. Within a few weeks the *Hornet* was confiscated by the U.S.S. *Tacoma* and taken back to New Orleans, but by that time she was no longer of vital importance to the campaign. Washington favored the government in power, was even then negotiating a "dollar diplomacy" treaty with it. The Honduran Congress, alarmed at the victories of Bonilla and at popular approval of his denunciations of the deal it was making, executed a rightabout-face and voted down the pact. The commander of the American naval unit in those waters then proposed a peace conference, to which both sides agreed. It was held on the *Tacoma.* Hostilities ended, the president of the Republic resigned, and elections were called.

While this was going on, while an American admiral was treating with Bonilla and incidentally recognizing Lee as a bona fide general, all the persons connected with the *Hornet* episode were indicted in the United States District Court, New Orleans, for filibustering. The proceedings had a comic aspect. Only two of those named, the skipper of the yacht and the nominal owner, could be brought into court. There was a mistrial the first time, and when the case was heard again they were acquitted. The indictments pending against the others were then nolle prossed.

Manuel Bonilla won overwhelmingly at the polls. He was inaugurated on February 1, 1912, and one of his first acts was to appoint Lee commander in chief of the army. Next to the presidency, that office was the best plum that could fall to a man in Honduras. It meant almost unlimited power, if he knew how to use it. The perquisites were endless chances to enrich himself. Lee tried to improve his opportunities, but he had a poor head for business. He acquired a great coconut plantation. He bought the old Louisiana Lottery Building in Puerto Cortés and converted it into a hotel. Both these ventures were only moderately successful. Spending money, however, filled Lee's pockets from many illicit sources. He had what he most valued, and this was the prestige that enabled him to strut about the country, entertaining lavishly and being entertained.

It did not last long. Fourteen months after he had assumed office, Manuel Bonilla died. His successor allowed Lee to remain commander in chief for a while, and then eased him out. The rest of his career was anticlimax. He adventured in Guatemala. He tried to float various enterprises, including petroleum wells, copra and the catching of sharks in quantity for their skins and oil. When World War I broke out, he tried for a commission in the United States Army and was turned down, officially on account of his age, which was fifty-four, but quite probably for other less flattering reasons. He died of a complication of tropical diseases in New Orleans when he was sixty.

The record would be incomplete without this footnote: young Guy Molony got the chance to serve in Europe that had been denied Lee. Later he rose to a colonelcy and in the early 1920's he was appointed superintendent of police of the City of New Orleans by a reform administration.

Part IV

THE LAKE IN OUR TIMES

Chapter 21

Hell and High Water

IN NEW ORLEANS prior to 1900 the water in the ground was almost level with the surface of the earth. This startling assertion originates with Dr. Isaac Monroe Cline, who for over fifty years was an official of the United States Weather Service, and who at eighty-five is by all odds the most famous meteorologist of the Gulf Coast region. Dr. Cline explains that waste water used to flow through open drains on each side of the streets of New Orleans, and in many places very sluggishly. After a storm or flood the water flowed off as best it could, without the aid of man. Sewage that was not thrown into the street was piped into wells, one or more to each residence plot, walled up and sealed over so that it had no escape but to soak slowly into the soil and become part of the general moisture. Subsurface drainage was commenced in 1900, and three years later sanitary sewers were built. An immediate result was to lower the permanent water level to from six to eight feet below the top of the ground. The new drainage system relieved pressure when there was a deluge by discharging rapidly into Lake Pontchartrain.*

The gruesome picture evoked explains many of the drawbacks of living in New Orleans under the old conditions. There had been some improvement since 1878. But no wonder the yellow-fever and malaria mosquitoes still swarmed. If those open gutters had not been already closed, the task of immunizing the city in 1905 would have been much more difficult. No wonder the burial of the dead had had to take place aboveground in vaults and "ovens." But the object in this chapter is simply to show the re-

* Isaac Monroe Cline, *Storms, Floods and Sunshine* (New Orleans: Pelican Publishing Co., 1945).

cent part played by the lake in disasters and the prevention of disasters.

Levees to control the Mississippi had been built higher and higher. Yet crevasses went on occurring in bad years, with resultant floods and threats to the safety of New Orleans. As in the past, the worst blows were struck at the Carrollton bend, creating the peril that the city would be swept from west to east. Only the fact that the rear territory was lower saved the important riverfront districts on several occasions. There was no guarantee that it would always be possible to get rid of the excess water into Pontchartrain before irreparable damage had been done.

Warnings of the approach of high water in the river were properly regarded as an essential service, because this would give time to repair levees and top them with sandbags. But until Dr. Cline was appointed chief of the weather bureau in New Orleans, in 1901, the forecasts were indefinite and of no great value. The previous year he had been stationed at Galveston, Texas, and had proved the hero of the calamitous hurricane that decimated the city. By driving up and down the beach before the wind struck and personally warning the residents to move to the higher parts of town he is credited with having saved thousands of lives. His own wife was drowned, and he managed with the utmost difficulty to save his three young daughters.

The doctor got his first chance with the Mississippi when the river started to rise abnormally in February 1903. He points out that the custom had been to make vague official statements, such as: "The impending flood will prove very destructive," or, "Additional warning is given to residents of threatened districts to remove from the region of danger." After closely scrutinizing the situation he made up his mind that a record height of twenty-one feet at New Orleans was indicated. If unchecked, it would probably destroy the city. Therefore, the second week in March, he issued bulletins containing the specific warning. His chief in Washington told him to withdraw them until it was certain that twenty-one feet would be reached. Cline felt that to wait for a certainty would be to wait too long. That had been the trouble in the past. A scientific prediction was needed. He ignored orders, let his warning stand and repeated it. The Levee Board raised bulwarks. A crevasse above the city relieved some of the pressure. Even so, twenty and a half feet was touched at New Orleans, March 26, which was itself a record.

The justification of success saved Cline's job for him. He became an institution, and in the future he had his way about forecasts. In April 1912 he concluded that a greater flood than that of 1903 was approaching. Before it came within striking distance of the city it broke westward through several crevasses. Warnings enabled the population over a large area to leave in time and save much property.

Cline's experience at Galveston had given him a special interest in tropical hurricanes. While they did not hit Louisiana as often as the Mississippi floods, the peril was always there. He preached the necessity of establishing listening posts in the Caribbean. The Weather Bureau and the United Fruit Company decided to cooperate in this work, and in the spring of 1913 Cline had the satisfaction of personally setting up observing stations on Swan Island off the Honduras coast, and on Cape San Antonio at the western tip of Cuba. Two years later their value was dramatically shown.

On September 22, 1915, word was first received that a hurricane had appeared in the eastern Caribbean. It passed through the Yucatan Channel during the night of the twenty-seventh, bearing directly on the middle Gulf Coast. Cline measured the storm tides every few hours. He found that they were centering at the mouth of the Mississippi, and that the rotating wind would unquestionably pass over New Orleans. The blow fell as predicted on the twenty-ninth. Nearly every building in the city was damaged more or less by a wind that attained a maximum speed of 110 miles per hour, and a torrential downpour of 8.36 inches of rain within a few hours. Extraordinary phenomena occurred in Lake Pontchartrain. A tide thirteen feet high was whipped up at the west end of the lake. This wall of water hurled itself against the trees, while behind it the bottom of the shallow depression was visible for thousands of yards, and in many spots was laid bare. As the tide receded, a tremendous backwash from Pontchartrain lapped over into New Orleans along the entire lake front.

Dr. Cline states that the knowledge acquired in the study of storm tides enabled his office to foresee all the conditions. "We issued extraordinary warnings with definite advice to the people in the threatened area, indicating where the storm tide and hurricane winds would be dangerous to life and property. People in certain sections were warned that their lives were in great danger. The telegraph and telephone were used to the fullest extent; and localities which could not be reached in this way were reached by special messenger at government expense. Motor boats, automobiles and every means of conveyance, even to the horse cart, were used.

"Schools were advised early on the morning of the 29th to close for the day and to send the children home to their parents. Merchants were told to close and barricade their stores, and send their employees home. The police and fire departments were instructed to warn people to stay off the streets to avoid being killed or injured by wreckage which would be driven through the streets by high winds like missiles shot from a cannon. The railroads were told to stop their trains at Slidell—that trains endeavoring to cross the bridge to New Orleans in the afternoon would be blown off the bridge into Lake Pontchartrain by the hurricane winds. All ocean shipping was advised to remain in port. Our instructions were heeded and the loss of life, when the extent of the area covered and the fury of the storm is considered, was very small.

"There was only one notable instance where the warnings were not heeded. A man named Manuel and his wife were keepers of a club at the Rigolets. Some twenty-five people lived near the clubhouse. Manuel was called about nine A.M. on September 29 over the long distance telephone by the Weather Bureau Office, warned of his danger and told to have everybody come to New Orleans on the next train—their last opportunity to escape with their lives.

"Manuel said, 'That train will not stop on a flag signal for us.' He was told to put a cross-tie on the track and put up a danger signal. Manuel replied, 'They will put us in jail.' He was told, 'You would be better off in jail than where you are now, and for God's sake stop that train at all hazards and come to New Orleans.'

"Manuel stopped the train, but the people were not there to get aboard the train. The rising storm tide was jeopardizing the lives of the passengers on the train and it could not wait for Manuel to go and collect the people from their homes. Manuel returned to his companions, and when the storm had passed and the tide had receded the sun beamed down on the lifeless bodies of Manuel and twenty-five of his friends scattered over the marshes."

An adjoining fishing camp, which could not be reached with a warning, was wiped out, the casualties running to about thirty. Comparatively speaking, more destruction was wrought and more people were killed in the thinly settled Rigolets district than anywhere else. This illustrates the freakishness of hurricanes. The eastern rim of the circular tempest seemed to dip down upon the Rigolets and scour everything bare. The western rim was not quite so malignant. Mandeville, almost at the center of the storm's pathway, escaped with little damage. But on the south side of the lake, opposite Mandeville, the settlement of Bucktown where Jefferson Parish adjoins West End was flattened. First the onrushing wind and then the receding tide of the lake passed over Bucktown—drowning just one old man, as against the half-hundred deaths at the Rigolets.

There was then no railroad bridge over the Mississippi at New Orleans. The transfer ferry *Mastodon* had just been loaded with the cars of a train from the west when overtaken on the morning of September 29. The gigantic ferry was spun around and driven onto a mud bar, where it was isolated for twenty-seven hours. Hundreds of passengers cowered under the screaming gale and the lashing waters, yet none was injured. Down near the mouth of the river, two seamen were blown from the deck of the passenger liner *Creole* and never heard of again.

The New Orleans *Item* summed up the visitation by remarking:

"About twenty years ago a West Indian hurricane, far lighter in force and stress than the recent storm, struck the Gulf Coast. Over 2,000 lives were lost and many millions in property. Ten days ago another West Indian hurricane came with tremendously increased intensity. But the loss of life in all the vast stretch of marsh and bayou and sealine is only 275. The property damage is infinitely less.

"There is one specific reason for this difference in results: Increased efficiency in the Weather Bureau and an increased and extended service rendered possible by enlarged personnel and extended range of observations."

The harnessing or deflecting of a cyclone would be a task beyond the capacities of man. One can but study the monster, chart its course in advance, and warn probable victims to get to a safe place. It has been another story with floods. Science is at last justified in hoping that it has established a reasonably tight control over the Mississippi. Dr. Cline has had a share in this victory.

In the spring of 1927 conditions indicated that exceptionally high water was a certainty, and that it might prove to be the greatest of all recorded Mississippi floods. The Weather Bureau gave out full details, but at first the merchants of New Orleans shortsightedly persuaded the newspapers to withhold publication, on the grounds that there might be a panic which would harm business. Dr. Cline put a stop to that. He announced that he would use the mails, the telegraph, the telephone and the radio to circulate his warnings. The merchants and the press then fell into line. The alarming news caused thousands to leave the city every day, but there was no general panic.

Forecasts showed that while central Louisiana and the state of Mississippi would suffer heavily, New Orleans would probably be saved by their misfortunes. The levee up the river would give way and the waters spread over a wide territory. This was what occurred. Nevertheless, as an extra precaution, it was thought wise to dynamite the levee at Poydras, below New Orleans, and create a spillway. Enormous damage was done, but relatively little of it in the region that comes within the scope of this book. The flood horrified the whole nation. It moved the Federal Government and Congress to take action. Herbert Hoover, as Secretary of Commerce, hastened to the scene and made an exhaustive study of conditions. Army engineers moved in afterward. They carried out a diversion plan of the sort that experts had been advocating for a hundred years, but which till then had been believed too complex and expensive ever to be translated into reality.

Cutoffs straightened some of the river's loops. In addition to improving the channel for navigation, this insured a more easily controlled flow when there was high water. An outlet into the Atchafalaya Basin was constructed. Most important of all, the huge Bonnet Carré Spillway was built a short distance above New Orleans for the purpose of discharging flood waters from the Mississippi into Lake Pontchartrain. Its maximum capacity was 250,000 cubic feet of water a second.

Bonnet Carré had always been a point of pressure. Crevasses had frequently occurred there, with resultant floods that had traveled toward the lake and dissipated themselves in its basin. The engineers took advantage of this natural drift, but placed it under a faultless mechanical restraint. The spillway was completed in 1931. Until it could be put to a test, gloomy critics objected that it might do harm as well as good.

For instance, the views of Charles Ellet, Jr., a civil engineer of the preceding century, were resurrected. In 1853 Ellet had advocated a spillway at Bonnet Carré, though his plan was merely to cut two trenches from river to lake, use the displaced earth to form two parallel levees 4,000 to 5,000 feet apart, and then remove a section of the Mississippi River levee. This would have meant a continuous flow of water whenever a given level was reached, and as the permanent levee on the river was low in his day the pouring of water into the lake would have occurred practically every year. Ellet said that the outlet he proposed would protect the country from the mouth of the Red River to the sea. He added that silt deposited by the Mississippi ultimately would convert Pontchartrain into a swamp, but offered figures to show that it would take at least 500 years of annual overflows to do it.

He also believed that navigation on the lake would be impaired and finally destroyed, and that in the course of only one century there might be more than a hundred islands and shoals scattered over the lake. The height and sometimes the position of these would be variable, and in consequence the channels would be shallow and uncertain. Ellet's theories disturbed the people who lived on the shores of Pontchartrain seventy-five years later. But the liveliest apprehension among laymen was that use of the new contrivance would shift the flood peril from the lands adjoining the river to those adjoining the lake.

The first trial came in 1937, when there was high water almost as serious as that of ten years before. By degrees 285 of the Bonnet Carré's 350 bays were opened, and enough water passed through them to cover 1,250,000 acres to a depth of ten feet. The operation was maintained for forty-seven days. No other floodway in Louisiana was opened. It sufficed. For more than a hundred miles the river stages were lowered to the point of safety and kept lowered. New Orleans was relieved of all danger. Soundings taken after the spillway had been closed established that even at the west end of Pontchartrain, where silting action would naturally be most pronounced, there was hardly a measurable raising of the lake bottom. It is impossible to guess how many years would be required to make a real difference. Water drawn from the crest of a flood is less charged with sediment than are the undercurrents of Ol' Man River as he eternally goes rolling along.

Chapter 22

Sport on the Lake

Lake Pontchartrain is a marine preserve in more senses than one. As a conservation measure, the state does not allow large-scale commercial fishing, crabbing or shrimping there. No seines, trawls or traps may be employed. The individual, however, may go out and do all the angling with hook and line that he wishes, and it is permissible for him to sell catches made in that way. Limited operations of the kind do not spoil the paradise for amateur fishermen which the 600 square miles of inland waters constitute.

The lake is also an extraordinarily favored spot from the standpoint of the aquatic life which it nurtures. Its salt-water fish are not subject to the diseases that affect them in the ocean. All fish and crustaceans grow faster and to larger sizes in Pontchartrain than elsewhere. The reason for this phenomenon is to be found in the physical characteristics of the lake, which, as has been explained farther back, has many of the attributes of an estuary of the sea. It is usually somewhat brackish. The great amount of fresh water which pours into it from rains, streams and bayous—and contrariwise the ebb and flow of salt water through the Rigolets and Chef Menteur—has the effect of flushing it out periodically. Percy Viosca, Jr., former consulting biologist of the Louisiana State Department of Conservation and probably the leading authority on Lake Pontchartrain, says that it is the equivalent of a millionaire's private fishpond.

Nowhere else does one discover such a commingling of fresh-water and salt-water fish. They are distributed, of course, according to the saline content of given localities, more ocean species being found at all times at the east end than at the west. But there is the widest variation of currents. A stream of fresh water may have flowed through the middle of an area predominantly brackish, and in consequence one will encounter almost side by side such definitely marine fish as tarpon, croaker, flounder and kingfish, along with bass of several varieties and gars which elsewhere are confined to rivers. The remora, the little parasite fish which attaches itself to sharks, has been seen near the entrance of the Manchac Pass, a remarkable circumstance since the remora's haunts are the salt deeps where it may expect to run across sharks.

We must bear in mind that the ocean species in Pontchartrain, and this includes the shrimps and some other crustaceans, are transients. They retreat from the lake at certain seasons and are at times driven to leave it by an excess of fresh water. But they never fail to come back. The Rigolets is deep though narrow, and the tide runs strongly there. It is a roadway which may be compared to the air lanes traced by migratory birds.

Most of the material concerning the fauna of Lake Pontchartrain was furnished to the writer by Viosca, who is a rare combination of scientist, sportsman and practical man of affairs. He has even originated an artistic use for the scales of the giant alligator garfish. After noting resemblances that the scales bear to leaves, petals, arrowheads and other objects, he devised methods of coloring and polishing them for the manufacture of artificial jewelry. Conservationists hold that this craft serves a valuable purpose in their own field, for it provides a commercial stimulus to the campaign against the gar, a prime destroyer of weaker varieties and of nets.

The following are the principal species which sport fishermen catch in the lake: Tarpon, redfish, croaker, drumfish, flounder, jackfish, kingfish, speckled sea trout, white sea trout, all of them ocean dwellers; rockfish, several kinds of bass and gars, which emerge from fresh water into the lake; perch, pickerel, bowfin and bass, which can be had only by mounting the Tchefuncte and other streams, or penetrating bayous and near-by swamps. Unlimited numbers of crabs and shrimp are to be found in Pontchartrain, crayfish and bullfrogs in the marshes.

The general public has heard enough about tarpon fishing to idealize it as the aquatic sport *par excellence.* Many an ardent fisherman would agree. A dash across the blue with a silver king at the end of one's line has been compared to a cavalry charge. The pitting of strength and ingenuity against the quarry is literally a wrestling match in which it is not always the man who wins. Tarpon ordinarily is deep-sea game. An annual so-called rodeo is held off Grande Isle on the Gulf Coast of Louisiana in August, and it is one of the sporting events of the year.

But tarpon regularly penetrate to Lake Pontchartrain. They are thickest in the Rigolets and at the eastern end of the lake. They are frequently caught off New Orleans within the city limits—a silver king weighing 145 pounds is the record in this locality—as well as directly opposite at the mouth of the Tchefuncte. Sometimes they reach as far west as Manchac Pass. The usual size caught is from five to six feet in length, with a weight of 75 to 150 pounds, but specimens seven feet long and weighing 200 pounds have been landed.

The tarpon is a migratory fish. It appears on the Louisiana coast in late spring, and there is a steady increase in numbers until late August or early September. The first cold snap in the autumn drives it south. It preys on mullet and other small fish, particularly a kind known locally as the silver eel. A heavy running tide appears to exhilarate it, and large schools of tarpon may be seen playing, leaping and pursuing bait fish amid the foaming tide streaks. Yet the silver king also likes Pontchartrain where choppy water takes the place of tides.

Tarpon are usually taken with a trolling spoon or dead bait dragged slowly about one hundred feet behind a motorboat. Occasionally live fish are successfully used as bait without trolling. The standard tournament rod is six feet long and nine ounces in weight. A Number 24 line is the maximum allowed in tournament fishing, though an 18 to 21 line is preferred by the majority.

Sportsmen consider the jackfish second only to the tarpon as a provider of thrills. True, it is smaller, but its habits are similar. Jackfish schools come from deep tropic waters to Louisiana in June. Many individuals are to be seen at the east end of Pontchartrain early in July, and through August and September they are to be found all over the lake. The standard bait for tarpon will attract them. When hooked, jackfish never leap from the water, and so are less spectacular than the silver king. They make up for this with so violent a rush to escape that they are credited with breaking more tackle than all other big-game fish combined. No one lands a jack without a long chase and a memorable tussle for supremacy.

There are three members of the drum family which live permanently in Louisiana waters, travel freely between the ocean and Pontchartrain, and provide limitless sport. They are the black drum, the redfish or channel bass, and the croaker. The first-named commonly reaches a weight of between 100 and 150 pounds, the second is often caught at 50 pounds, and the third is a relatively small but lively customer. All these drums are bottom feeders, preying on oysters, clams and crabs, which they take whole into their mouths and then crush between the hard, toothed plates in their throats while in the act of swallowing. A considerable number of the giant black drum are caught. Their flesh is coarse, however, and they are not much valued for food unless taken young and small.

It is a different matter with the redfish, which may be termed the prize of which the everyday angler dreams. Not too big to be handled at the end of a stout line and hauled into a rowboat, it is big enough to be impressive. The average length of a redfish at the age of five years is three feet, while it often attains four feet. Viosca says that more than any other species to be caught in Lake Pontchartrain the redfish is a bad-weather rover; it will bite vigorously when the water is so disturbed that practically all other fish stop biting. Young or adult, its flesh is delicious. A baked redfish served whole is indeed one of those dishes celebrated in song and story as being fit to set before a king.

That lesser drum, the croaker, is without doubt the species taken in the largest numbers by Louisiana salt-water and lake fishermen. It swarms wherever there is a bottom covered with the small shellfish on which it feeds. Pugnacity is a marked trait of the breed, and consequently it provides good sport. When pulled out of the water it utters a queer persistent croak; hence its name. Anglers are agreed that croakers caught in brackish Pontchartrain are more finely flavored than those from sea water. Just why, nobody knows.

The rockfish or Atlantic striped bass is the largest game fish encountered in the fresh waters of Louisiana. It is an ocean dweller, but spawns in the shallow waters of bays and estuaries, if it cannot find rivers to ascend for this purpose. Curiously, in the region of New Orleans it will enter only Pontchartrain, and while occasionally met along the northern shore it seeks the Tchefuncte, the Tangipahoa and other streams flowing into the lake. One also runs across it in the Manchac Pass, Lake Maurepas and the latter's tributaries.

Most bass weigh from less than a pound to five or six pounds, depending on the variety. But the huge rockfish has been known to reach a weight of 125 pounds, and in the ocean specimens of around 70 pounds are hooked from time to time. None of these exceptional sizes have ever been caught in Louisiana waters. They have been seen at 30 pounds in the Tchefuncte River. The rockfish is very wary. The best way to catch one of these great bass is to anchor in the middle of the stream and wait patiently until the quarry is observed striking at small fish near by. Then, and only then, a cast may be made with a floating plug resembling live bait. If it is done expertly the rockfish will be fooled into biting. The number-one spot for getting rockfish is held to be on the Bogue Falaya, a branch of the Tchefuncte, a short distance outside the town limits of Covington.

Flounder and sheepshead are popular with anglers. They are caught at all points in Lake Pontchartrain, even from the New Orleans city water front. The sheepshead is noted for its singular teeth, which are shaped and arranged very much as in the mouth of a human being, and are adapted to crushing the shellfish on which it feeds. Five or six pounds is the average weight of a sheepshead. The bowfin, locally called *choupique,* is plentiful in the swampy bayous and sloughs near the lake. Le Page du Pratz noted this fish in 1718 as a favorite food of the Indians living on the Bayou Choupic, the native name of the Bayou St. John. The word, as applied to waterway or fish, means "muddy" or "mud creature." The bowfin today is regarded as the game fish of the Negroes, logical inheritors of the sport which primitive tribesmen pursued two centuries ago. It strikes large artificial lures violently and puts up a stiff battle.

When the Bonnet Carré Spillway was opened in 1937, the river water pouring in at the rate of 131,000 cubic feet a second turned the world of Lake Pontchartrain upside down. It took two weeks for the silt-laden fresh water to reach the east end of the lake. Marine fish were driven before it and were caught in far larger numbers than usual in pockets along the northeast shore. But they never wholly deserted the area, and a few months later when the saline balance began to be restored migrations from the ocean quickly returned to normal. Meanwhile incalculable quantities of river shrimp and other creatures which constitute the diet of game fish had been washed in. The effect was to restock both Lake Pontchartrain and Maurepas. The damage that had been done at the beginning was more than offset by this gain. The same phenomena occurred on a smaller scale when the spillway came into service once more in 1944.

The environs of the lake are a rich preserve for hunters. A dozen varieties of ducks, one or two of geese, as well as coots, rails and snipe are found in abundance. Most duck hunting is done from blinds set up near some lagoon in the swamps, or by shooting from a boat masked by vegetation. The chief kind of duck that

Courtesy of J. A. Bascle, Jr.

POWER BOATS RACING ON TCHEFUNCTE RIVER

Bureau of New Orleans News

REGATTA ON LAKE PONTCHARTRAIN

AIR VIEW OF PONTCHARTRAIN BEACH

may be shot on the lake itself is the lesser scaup, known locally as the *dos gris* (grayback). This bird feeds partly on clams, diving to the shallow bottom to get them. Inland from the north shore there is an abundance of small game, principally cottontails, water hares and fox squirrels, with white-tailed deer not uncommon, and black bear now and then.

Outside the realm of sport it should be mentioned that muskrats, Louisiana's huge and profitable stand-by in the fur business, are trapped in great numbers each season in the marshes at the east end of Pontchartrain's north shore, as well as back of the southern and western reaches of Borgne.

Sailing and boat racing add up to one of the greatest joys that Orleanians derive from Pontchartrain. The Southern Yacht Club, located on the lake at West End, was established in 1849 and is the second oldest yacht club in America. It has always occupied its present location. A building put up in 1878, on piles and over the water, still forms part of the present fine headquarters. The clubhouse occupies made land and has its own extensive basin. Leslie P. Beard, active in yachting since 1912 and twice commodore of the club, has remarked with a touch of humor that the 1878 structure had been thought luxurious and costly at $12,000. Further improvements that are planned will run to many times that sum.

The pleasure craft go cruising in every month of the year, for the climate of New Orleans is semitropical, and occasional storms are the only drawbacks. The regular racing season runs from April to October. It starts off with an annual regatta for all classes of boats, and thereafter a weekly schedule for different classifications is maintained. There is a "race around the lake," with a course of about 55 miles. At New Year's a special regatta is held in connection with the Sugar Bowl football game. Forty or more craft often participate in the Pontchartrain contests. The long-distance races to Mobile, Biloxi, Pensacola and other points along the Gulf Coast will attract as many as sixty. Schooners, sloops and several other standard types of craft are entered on the club's lists. Fishing yachts are well represented; events for them occur throughout the season. An annual fish-class championship is contested, the trophy being a cup given by the late Sir Thomas Lipton. The story behind that is interesting.

When Lipton was a young man and knocking around the world in search of a way to fortune, he found himself in New Orleans. Broke, he took a job as conductor on a mule-drawn Girod Street car. He remained for only a few months, and then drifted on to wider fields and eventual millions in the tea business. New Orleans had made a deep impression on him. In 1916, after he had become internationally famous as a result of his several attempts to win the America Cup with his yachts named *Shamrock*, he paid a visit to the Crescent City. He was entertained as a guest of honor at the Southern Yacht Club. This moved him to donate the trophy for speedy fishing boats. The event was first held in 1920, and has never been interrupted by war or other alarms. The twenty-seventh occurred as the present volume went to press.

Leslie P. Beard holds that Lake Pontchartrain is an excellent body of water for cruising and racing. Racing has been going on for practically a century and, he believes, has proved itself. He does not consider the shallowness of the lake a drawback. Yachts are not deep-draft commercial craft, and on Pontchartrain they have all the water they need. He pooh-poohs the idea that the weather is unpredictable, to the point of causing a dangerously rough surface before a boat can get to shelter. Beard says that he does not subscribe to the theory of "sudden squalls." No one ever saw a squall leap out of the void. The barometer, the forms assumed by the clouds, and other warnings enable a skipper with a knowledge of seamanship to judge twenty or thirty minutes in advance what he may expect. The sport on Pontchartrain is really enhanced by the fact that a skipper has to meet challenges by keen observation and quick thinking.

Commodore J. A. Bascle, Jr., of the New Orleans Power Boat Association, shares this opinion in a general way. But he admits that small motor craft which lie very low in the water sometimes have trouble on account of the ground swell and choppy waves when Pontchartrain is temperamental. An international regatta arranged in 1923, with Gar Wood and other headliners taking part, had to be modified and certain events postponed because of unusual storms. Yet powerboat races are now conducted with great success year after year, every second Sunday, or an average of twelve contests a season. Bascle declares that in order to attract both participants and the public, a sport must provide some semblance of danger, and that this applies notably to boating. It is certain that the speed and maneuverability, not to mention the thunderous noise, of the motor-driven craft appeal to the gallery far more emphatically than the graceful but slow technique of sail.

Racing by all types of boats is held, when conditions are favorable, on the Tchefuncte River which runs into the lake from the north. On account of its remoteness and the lack of townships around its shores, Maurepas has never been a scene of the sport.

Rowing clubs existed in New Orleans long before there was yachting of any description. In the 1830's organizations called the Wave, the Lady of Lyons and the Algerine were active. Sometimes the members fought it out on the river, but more often on the lake. In August 1839 a regatta took place at Madisonville on the Tchefuncte. The tradition is carried on today by the New Orleans Rowing Club.

Fishermen, hunters, yachtsmen and other enthusiasts of the outdoors have told the writer that a description of the sunsets to be enjoyed on the lake should positively be included in any book about Pontchartrain. Asked for leads, they hemmed and hawed, shrugged, and lamely mentioned mountainous clouds of all colors in the rainbow. That's the trouble with sunsets. The better they are the less they can be described. A sunset over Pontchartrain refuses to be described at all.

Chapter 23

The Industrial Canal

WAR, the public-works program of a dictator, and then war again were the chief factors in the past thirty years that led to the enhancement of Pontchartrain's role as a waterway, and that brought about vast improvements along the lake shore at New Orleans. Railroads and shipping companies helped, of course. Business interests of all kinds had long been clamoring for the things that were finally done. Routine politics had tended to put a brake upon progress. It took exceptional dynamism to give results. Louisiana had had a long succession of administrations which had promised much and accomplished little, though since 1900 an energetic dock board had, in the face of difficulties, bettered the port of New Orleans. Without the stimulus afforded by World War I, however, it is most improbable that the Inner Harbor Navigation Canal, commonly called the Industrial Canal, would have been started at the time that it was.

The advantages of a ship canal all the way from river to lake had been understood from the city's earliest days. It will be recalled that Governor Carondelet had linked the Bayou St. John with a basin dug just beyond Rampart Street. The Marigny Canal had run from the Mississippi to the swamps just below the future Milneburg. Between 1832 and 1835 an old drainage ditch was enlarged into a navigable canal from West End to what was known as the New Basin in the middle of the city. The Carondelet and Marigny cuts were eventually filled in, as was part of the third canal. Their value had been limited, because their builders had not dared to make complete links of them. The fear that held them back was well founded.

Except during a season of abnormal drought, the level of the

Mississippi is at all times higher than that of Lake Pontchartrain. At flood stage in the spring the difference is often as much as twenty feet and occasionally an inch or two more. Manifestly a wide-open canal would become a spillway and put the entire area of the city under water. A lock system was needed, and locks were a device with which the older engineers were not familiar. Men knew what they must do long before the work was actually undertaken, but they lacked official backing and funds.

In 1917 the national demand for a "bridge of ships" with which to overcome the German submarine menace brought matters to a head in New Orleans. Old plans for a waterway that would merely float barges and other shallow-draft vessels were abandoned. It was decided to have one through which fairly large ocean-going freighters could pass, and also to make provision for docks and possible shipbuilding yards along the banks of the canal. Work commenced in 1918. The war emergency ended that year, fortunately without halting or diminishing the scope of the enterprise.

The canal dug was five and one-half miles long, twenty-four blocks to the east of the route the Pontchartrain Railroad had followed. Its depth was 30 feet and its bottom width 150 feet, but allowances were made for further widening of the bottom to from 500 to 600 feet. A lock, designed by General George W. Goethals, builder of the Panama Canal, was located 2,000 feet from the river, its length being 640 feet, with a width of 75 feet by inside measurement, and a depth of 31.5 feet. The lock was provided with five sets of gates, each driven by a 57-h.p. motor. Vessels could be passed through either way in about twenty minutes. Four bascule bridges crossed the canal, three with a clear span of 100 feet each, and one at the south end of the lock with a span of 75 feet.

The project was completed in 1923 and opened for general use the year after. The total cost of construction, including lock and bridges and the purchase price of the land was $19,200,000. But there was additional work to be done. Promptly after the canal was finished steps were taken to develop it as an inner harbor. Some five squares above the lock, a wharf six squares long, built parallel with the western bank of the waterway, was rushed through in 1924 at a cost of approximately $1,800,000. It had a total area of 638,310 square feet, 476,000 of which were covered over with sheds. This is called the Galvez Street Wharf. It stretches to the canal's turning basin. Beyond the basin, the smaller Florida Avenue Wharf, 81,624 square feet in area, was constructed in 1942.

From the beginning a large unit for the handling of freight had been planned by the Dock Board for just north of Florida Avenue. It was to consist of four slips at right angles to the canal, with piers that would provide berthing space for twenty vessels. Warehouses were to be built at the far ends of the piers. When the present war broke out the dredging of the four slips was all that had been accomplished. Even this was something to go on. By running up emergency wharves, the United States Navy was able to use two of the slips throughout the conflict, and the Delta Shipbuilding Company the other two.

The canal early proved its value and became more and more important with each passing year. A total of 3,251 vessels with a tonnage of 262,308 traversed it in 1924. In 1943 these figures had risen to 27,165 vessels and 9,632,802 tons. A great deal of the traffic was in connection with industries located on the inner harbor, at the Galvez Street and Florida Avenue Wharves, and at other points along the banks. Perhaps twenty-five percent was destined for the lake, or had originated there. The comeback for the old Pontchartrain route constituted one of the chief gains, but it was temporary.

Furthermore, the Industrial Canal has a role in the Intracoastal Waterway maintained by the Federal Government from Boston to the mouth of the Rio Grande River. Intracoastal is a system of almost completely protected water routes, more than 3,000 miles in length. It connects with the Industrial Canal at a point below the turning basin, follows down to the river and cuts westward through the Harvey Canal and Bayou Barataria. The Louisiana section of Intracoastal was first used in August 1934, when a barge tow transported 1,400 tons of steel from New Orleans to Houston, Texas.

What captures the imagination is the growth of a new port at the very heart of the city, a port which belongs to the lake no less than to the river. It has been apparent to all students of the subject that some day wharf building would have to turn from the Mississippi to some other location. The necessity for employing end-to-end *quai*-type docks along the river would soon exhaust the available sites. To extend the wharves north and south beyond the city limits would not be economical. The system had to be enlarged and geographically compressed at one and the same time. Pontchartrain was so shallow that lake-front piers would be impracticable. The canal was the obvious answer, but even its warmest advocates did not dream that it would boom so rapidly during and after World War II. The following is an official statement in the *Port Handbook of New Orleans:*

"The port commission [dock board] own all lands bordering the canal. Industries may lease from the commission these waterfront lands for periods of 99 years or less. They may build their own wharves and may operate them for their own raw materials and finished products without paying any charge to the port commission except land rental. They are exempt from taxation under certain conditions.

"Under very favorable terms deep-water laterals may be built connecting privately owned land with the canal. Industries may buy outright waterfront lands on such laterals and may build their own wharves for their own industries. If the wharves of any industry located on the canal or its laterals are used for other cargo than its own raw or finished materials, the vessels handling that cargo shall pay the same charges as though the vessels had handled that portion of the cargo not belonging to the industry at a public wharf. Privately owned wharves on laterals will be held in all respects on a parity with private wharves on the leased lands on the canal.

"Public wharves on the canal are open to commerce on exactly the same terms and conditions as are the public wharves on the river front. The canal and lock are free to all vessels visiting either industrial or public wharves on its banks. A small toll is charged vessels navigating the canal merely as a thoroughfare between the river and lake."

Development is reflected in rentals of sites. These increased from approximately $30,000 per annum in 1935 to $200,000 in 1945. The total does not seem enormous, but it must be borne in mind that the rate per acre has been kept very low as a matter of policy. Conversion of war plants on the canal to peacetime production came quickly after the ending of the war in the Pacific.

The Industrial Canal had not been long in operation when another and even more ambitious project began to be discussed. This envisaged a tidewater channel to connect the canal with the Gulf of Mexico by way of Lake Borgne. From New Orleans eastward, Pontchartrain is separated from Borgne by a peninsula that narrows as it approaches the Rigolets. The idea was to cut a ditch, forty feet deep, through the peninsula, following the route of the Federal Intracoastal Waterway for the first twenty miles and then inclining to the right. The egress would be opposite Grand Isle and, if the channel were to be used by large vessels, a trough would have to be dredged in the shallow bottoms of Lake Borgne and the Mississippi Sound as far as Chandeleur Light.

Such a tidewater channel would fulfill the ancient dream of freeing part of New Orleans' commerce from the vicissitudes of the river. Direct access to the inner harbor would be possible without employing the lock and without ships having to pass through the Rigolets. But another advantage was seen: a limitless enlargement of the inner harbor itself. Both banks of the channel, starting at the point where it entered the canal at right angles, could be developed in the same way that the canal had been. Parallel docks could be built, or slips created for piers. The easily reclaimable marshland beyond would provide sites for warehouses and factories.

The plan has had enthusiastic advocates for the past fifteen years. It has recently been revived, with the backing of the Dock Board and an association composed of private citizens. If accomplished, it would reduce Pontchartrain once more to comparative unimportance as a link with New Orleans for shipping from the outside world.

Chapter 24

The Works of Huey P. Long

NO UNDERSTANDING of modern Louisiana or any phase of its story, political or economic, is possible without a true view of the dictatorship established by Huey Pierce Long. The man was a portent, a genius in all the arts of politics—blackguardism not excepted—an egocentric, self-anointed voice of the people. His regime dispensed great material improvements, but at the price of a tyranny never equaled in an American state, and some of his successors in power were cheap thieves. The times had been ripe for a change. The leaders in the post-Reconstruction years had owed their prestige to their Confederate records. Then had come a period, as in most Southern states, when predominantly drab figures had served as governors and other high officials, accepting backward social conditions as an incurable ill because of the region's poverty. Here and there a radical like Tom Watson of Georgia, or a progressive like John M. Parker of Louisiana, would make a brief stir. Experts predicted that an extreme type of demagoguery would be sure to attract a following among the disheartened. But to rate Huey P. Long as a mere product of this state of affairs would be an error. He was *sui generis,* as he once arrogantly said of himself. Though his rise was speeded by conditions, he probably would have slashed his way to power in any epoch.

He was born the eighth of nine children in Winn Parish, one of the poorest farming sections of north-central Louisiana. There was not a trace of Creole influence to be found there, and very little Confederate sentiment. The majority of Winn people were opposed to the War between the States. Huey's father, whose ancestors had come from Pennsylvania via Ohio, Indiana and

Mississippi, was forcibly conscripted into the Confederate army and never had a good word to say about it. He and his wife were narrow fundamentalist Baptists. Each day a chapter of the Bible was read aloud in the family circle, a custom of inestimable value in forming their son's oratorical style. By the time he was growing up they were in fairly comfortable circumstances, yet could not afford to send him to college. He is reputed to have been "bright" in high school, but not startlingly precocious. He completed his own education by reading incessantly and forgetting nothing he had ever seen on a printed page. It is noteworthy that his knowledge of history was almost wholly gained from a stilted, old-fashioned work which catalogued the deeds of conquerors and the rise and fall of dynasties, Ridpath's *History of the World*.

At the age of sixteen Huey became a traveling salesman, a calling for which he was fitted by his extrovert personality, his tireless energy and gift of gab. He sold cottolene, a vegetable shortening, to housewives, which was an easy assignment for him; if resistance offered he'd push his way into the kitchen, clap on an apron and bake a cake with cottolene. The housewife loved it. He also sold books through a countryside where few opened any volume except the Bible, and he made a success of it. The story goes that he decided if he could sell books in north-central Louisiana he could sell anything—including himself as a political boss. He appears to have regarded the job of commercial drummer with a sort of hilarity, as a tryout of his talents, but no career for a man who intended to get to the top of the world. One firm discharged him for being careless about his expense accounts.

Huey enrolled at the Oklahoma State University law school when he was eighteen and passed a disordered year, attending classes when he could and selling produce on the side. He married at twenty, and shortly afterward borrowed $400 from a brother and moved to New Orleans really to master the law. It is at this point that his legend starts to become astounding. He entered Tulane University where the three-years' course was regarded as difficult. Working overtime, losing weight seriously as he deprived himself of food in order to economize, he went through the course in eight months. The state bar examinations were to be held six weeks later. The young dynamo could not wait. For one thing he was broke and needed to earn money at his new profession. He went to the Chief Justice of the Louisiana Supreme Court and feverishly petitioned for a private examination. This was granted, and he passed it with distinction, three and a half months before his twenty-second birthday. If it seems hard to believe that such a result could have been obtained without favoritism, remember that two United States Supreme Court Justices afterward called him one of the outstanding attorneys to have appeared before them.

The tin shingle that he hung out in his native Winnfield had cost fifty cents. The clients who came to him were dirt poor, but he easily won cases for them and began to prosper. His eye was on politics. As he said about his bar examination, "I came out of that courtroom running for office." Louisiana's constitution specified the age of thirty as the minimum for nearly all elective posts, and thirty-five for some. Through an oversight, no limitation had been set for the Railroad Commission, so at twenty-four Long entered the race for a vacancy, barnstormed the district and was victorious. The duties of the job were shortly transferred to a new Public Service Commission, on which the youth not only retained his seat but maneuvered himself into the chairmanship.

He behaved like a hornet, pursuing the oil, electric, telephone and other public-utilities corporations, exposing their abuses and forcing them to reduce rates. Often when the companies filed suits, he baffled the participants and impressed the public by volunteering as his own commission's attorney. On such occasions he would speak for hours without referring to his notes, citing previous cases, quoting columns of figures—and never making a single factual error.

Many were convinced that he was a Sir Galahad of reform. His physical appearance was not unattractive, though already one could observe signs of the coarseness to come. He had a broad, heavy face with a cleft chin, a tip-tilted nose, and a wide mouth. The usually laughing brown eyes could become hard as agates. His hair was a dark red.

The day he was thirty and just eligible—less than forty-eight hours before the nominations closed—he filed in the primary for governor. At once he issued the list of promises that afterward became so familiar. He would cover Louisiana with a network of hard-surfaced roads in place of the wretched system then prevailing. He would build toll-free bridges wherever needed, build schools and colleges, and provide the students with textbooks gratis. For an upstart challenging old and entrenched leaders, he did well, coming in a strong third, and with only 11,000 votes separating him from the winner. Before the year ended he was re-elected to the Public Service Commission by a plurality of eight to one. This was the revelatory straw in the wind, if his opponents had been able to realize it. They had issued a poster against him in the gubernatorial race, reading: "It Won't Be LONG Now!" The emphasis should have been on the *now*.

Four years passed and the next election for governor came up. The Huey P. Long that campaigned this time was a political thug, terribly effective among the "poor whites" who constituted a majority. He repeated his pledges: good roads, free bridges, better schools, free textbooks. In addition, he attacked all vested interests with a savagery, a Rabelaisian humor, a flouting of the laws against libel, that delighted the mob. He called his enemies "thieves, bugs and lice," excoriated "the rattin' old gang, shovin' to get back at the trough," vowed that he would "bite a chunk out of the corporations' fat." High officials were accused, without proof, of sexual immorality or of having Negro blood. A delivery of machine-gun sharpness and rapidity added force to his invective. But at moments he would interrupt the bitter flow with poetical passages that derived from the King James version.

There was never much question how the election would go. Huey P. Long, who would not have been allowed to live a week if the code duello had still been in force, had made the conservatives ridiculous with his unavenged insults. He ran first by a wide margin, and although the combined vote of his two opponents exceeded his the runner-up did not care to enter a second primary. The young hell-raiser from the scrub-pine lands would be tame enough in office, like most radicals, it was thought. Besides, he had only a small minority of followers in the legislature. Where could he get with his mad slogans of "Share the Wealth" and "Every Man a King"?

Before he had even taken office, the governor-elect demanded that the incumbent start free ferries at the east end of Lake Pontchartrain to break the monopoly enjoyed by a privately owned vehicular bridge that had lately been completed there. This Watson-Williams Bridge, as it was called, had got its franchise through shady political deals and had been financed by dubious means. It charged exorbitant tolls; a round trip for an automobile with five passengers was eight dollars and forty cents. Huey, when Public Service Commissioner, had inveighed against it and promised that someday he would build a non-toll span.

He did not persuade his predecessor to put on the ferries, but he was no sooner inaugurated than he bullied the legislature into authorizing a new bridge at a short distance from the other. The work was rushed. The following summer he dedicated his free span, turning the occasion into a circus of self-advertising. A banner featured his name in letters three feet tall. The shareholders of the Watson-Williams Bridge were, of course, hard hit. Tolls had to be reduced to a point where the enterprise ceased to show a profit. Some years later it was purchased by the state, renamed the Robert S. Maestri Bridge, and made toll-free.

Huey drove hard for the accomplishment of the rest of his program—the material phase of it, at all events. The matter of royal dignities for Louisianians could wait. He built other bridges, roads, schoolhouses, and gave out the scores of thousands of textbooks he had promised. They were paid for by enormously increased taxes, mostly assessed against industry, and by a $30,-000,000 bond issue. It must not be thought that he had his way without opposition. At first the legislature balked at everything he proposed. He had been governor for a year when an attempt was made to impeach him. But he always won, and by the middle of the term he was practically an undisputed despot. The most astonishing thing about this man was his attainment of such power without the backing of a machine created in advance. The voters who had elected him were not Fascist legionnaires. Yet he was able to give the impression that they were behind him so solidly that he could plunge the state into bloody revolution if he were thwarted by lawmakers or judges.

At its opening session the lower house received a flood of bills, some implementing the administration's program, but the majority private measures such as were introduced each year in the hope that a few would pass. A Long member proposed casually that the entire calendar be adopted without debate. This was taken to mean that in return for giving the governor what he wanted, the grinding of all the little personal axes would be allowed. The legislators did as suggested, but Huey calmly signed his own bills and vetoed the others, with one or two exceptions in favor of men he believed he could attach to himself. The disgruntled members raged and struggled to block his next moves. They found that they had established a precedent which could be used against them. If they had voted for his first list of laws, why not the rest? Huey appealed over their heads to the voters, and the public opinion he whipped up terrorized the legislators into submission.

A state senator threw a book in Huey's face at a committee meeting, crying, "Maybe you've heard of this book. It's the Constitution of the state of Louisiana."

The governor tossed it aside with a sneer. "I'm the Constitution around here now," he answered. On another occasion he bragged that he had "dealt" the legislators "like a pack of cards." Of a member he had won over to his side he scoffed, "We got that guy so cheap, we thought we stole him." A similar purchase had been had "like a sack of potatoes."

All this was but the dress rehearsal for an autocracy marked by brutality as well as clowning, which grew ever harsher and more expensive to the taxpayers, but which the little people applauded gleefully, convinced that they were the gainers. It is no exaggeration to say that Huey turned the state police into a *gestapo*. He promoted the right officers for his purpose and soon had an instrument that carried out his wishes ruthlessly, from smashing the cameras of annoying newsmen to putting the fear of God into political antagonists. Kidnapings at his orders took place. He perverted the National Guard into an additional police force, using it to conduct raids without a declaration of martial law. Appalling thugs, some half-dozen of them, were hired as his bodyguards.

In 1930, midway of his term as governor, Huey announced his candidacy for the United States Senate. With the greatest ease he routed quiet old Senator Joseph Ransdell, whom he had nicknamed "Trashy Mouth." But his lieutenant governor, Dr. Paul Cyr, was not of his faction and he resolved to leave the seat in Washington vacant until he had manipulated the succession at home to his satisfaction. Scenes of incredible buffoonery resulted. Cyr had the bad judgment to take the oath of office as governor before a notary public, declaring that the election had created a vacancy. This was manifestly incorrect, for no one is a United States Senator until he has resigned any previous posts he may have held and has been sworn in. Huey turned around and proclaimed that Cyr's act had nullified his status as lieutenant governor. It was an equally absurd contention, but Huey knew how to make his dictum stick.

He set his *gestapo* on Cyr. The latter was shadowed, and motorized troops surrounded the office of the secretary of state to prevent him even from filing the document recording his oath. The secretary of state, incidentally, was Alice Lee Grosjean, comely and about twenty-five years of age, Huey's private secretary whom the dictator had appointed to succeed the deceased incumbent. In a spirit of hilarity and to vex his enemies, Huey once absented himself in circumstances that made Alice acting governor for a day or two.

Dr. Cyr abandoned the fight at last. The president pro tempore of the state senate, A. O. King, was recognized as heir to the governorship for the few remaining months of the term, and Huey assumed the toga. In the elections held that year he put in as governor a subservient, commonplace man from Winn Parish, Oscar K. Allen, who had lent him $500 when he was running for railroad commissioner in his first campaign. He proposed to go on being chief executive of Louisiana, in fact if not in name. There commenced the last phase, during which Huey commuted between Washington and Baton Rouge.

His national career need not be recited in these pages. There is a school of thought which holds that, if he had lived, he could scarcely have been prevented from reaching the White House. Without doubt, he had both major parties worried. But his conduct at home was now of so scandalous a character that one finds it hard to believe it would not have arisen to damn him if he had ever been nominated for President. He was young, of course, and he might have built up in time a nationwide organization of ignorant fanatics after the Fascist pattern. We shall never know. One of his most mordant quips was addressed to a Washington newspaper correspondent who asked him whether he thought Fascism would ever prevail in America. "Certainly it will, my boy—under the name of anti-Fascism," he replied.

On his visits to Baton Rouge he bossed the legislature as it had never been bossed before, even by him. He prepared the texts of the bills he wanted passed, strode onto the floor with them and required that they be adopted unread. Voting was by a mechanical system. If any member seemed to hesitate, Huey would rush over and furiously push the "Aye" button under the man's nose. He treated his hand-picked governor, "O.K." Allen, as something less than an office boy, as an automaton he needed to transmit his less important orders and to sign papers. In New Orleans Huey maintained a suite at the Roosevelt Hotel where he forced bankers, politicians and concession seekers of one kind and another to grovel for his favor. Often he would lie around half-naked at these interviews and interrupt the proceedings with obscenities. His bodyguards stood ready to slug the recalcitrant.

He waged a ferocious feud with Mayor T. Semmes Walmsley of New Orleans, whose organization, the "Old Regulars," was the only one in the state that still opposed him. On the pretext of being shocked at protected gambling and vice, he conducted incessant raids with his soldiery, and it is said that cash found on the premises of the sinful went into Huey's war chest. He cut off legitimate revenue needed by the city to pay its employees. In the end Walmsley was rendered impotent.

Throughout his seven years as despot, ruffian and sinister mountebank, Huey had been steadily changing Louisiana State University, at Baton Rouge, from its old run-down condition into one of the South's important seats of learning. It was his pet. He spent millions on it, declaring that he wanted the youth of his state to have the educational advantages that had been denied him. His sincerity in this was but another of the paradoxes that marked his character.

The night of September 8, 1935, Senator Long was in the new skyscraper capitol he had built at Baton Rouge. He came out of a committee room and, with members of his bodyguard preceding him and following him, he started for Governor Allen's office. He met several of his henchmen in the corridor and paused to talk with them. At that moment a slight young man dressed in white, Dr. Carl A. Weiss, of Baton Rouge, stepped from behind a pillar, thrust a gun in Huey's direction and fired once. The dictator staggered aside, clutching at the wound and exclaiming that he had been shot. The bodyguards got into action instantly. Like maniacs—for it would have been obviously better to take the assassin alive and endeavor to learn whether or not he had acted as a lone wolf—they poured bullets from their tommy-guns into Weiss's body. Later it was found that he had been pierced by sixty-one balls.

Huey was rushed to a hospital. He had been shot through the intestines and a kidney. An emergency operation was decided on, but he was beyond saving. Two days afterward he died at the age of forty-two. They buried him on the grounds of his capitol, in the presence of a crowd of mourners from all over the state that was estimated at 150,000.

Dr. Weiss, it transpired, was the son-in-law of a judge whom Long had been about to legislate out of office. No other motive for the deed was put forward officially. But it is widely believed in Louisiana that Weiss, who had studied in Vienna and New York and was known to detest autocracy, was a member of a secret society formed for the purpose of doing away with the tyrant. According to this theory, he drew the shortest straw and carried out his bargain. It is quite credible, in view of Louisiana's temperament of a Caribbean country.

Like most "strong men," Huey had not trained a successor of his own type. One may fall back on *sui generis* and argue that it would have been impossible to find one. He could at least have designated a person capable of understanding, as he did, that if you take everything into your own hands you must give the people material benefits in return. Caring much more for power than for money, he had spent prodigious sums on his improvements. These were so many monuments to his egotism and made him feel like a god.

On his death some of his more greedy and venal followers partially took over the machine he had created. They had to complete some of his unfinished works and to extend others. But their general policy was to grab as much as they could. They invented new taxes and pocketed the proceeds. They voted huge benefits for themselves, and not content with this they stole public property and engineered low frauds such as selling furnishings twice over to state institutions. One may imagine that even if they had been so disposed it would have been difficult for them to file income tax returns; those they did file were grotesquely false.

The machine had enough momentum to keep running for five

years, though with increasing discord and ineptitude toward the end. The Federal Government moved against it, and convicted and jailed on income tax and other charges a dozen of the gang, headed by the new governor, Richard W. Leche. A reform administration was elected in 1940. The winning candidate had differentiated between Huey P. Long and his successors, had said that the larger services given Louisiana by the dictator were good and must be maintained.

A community pays through the nose for such services. It is worth pondering that whereas in 1921 only four kinds of tax were imposed in Louisiana, by 1944-1945 the number of separate levies had jumped to thirty-five, twenty-eight of them of major importance. The dictatorship was not responsible for all of them. A few originated with the reformers, who caught the fever and launched public-works and social-security schemes of their own.

Aside from the general school and road-building program inaugurated by Long, the Lake Pontchartrain region benefited by the toll-free spans at its eastern end, already mentioned, and by the following works:

A seven-mile sea wall along the New Orleans lake front. This reclaimed many acres of swamp and enlarged the city's area; Milneburg and Spanish Fort are now some distance inland. The sea wall also served as a dike to protect the city from the backing up of the lake during floods and storms. It was the first step toward the creation of Lake Shore Park, which was afterward developed by W.P.A.

New Orleans Airport, formerly called Shushan Airport. Huey designed it to be the largest and most modern in the world at that time. It was built at an approximate cost of $3,000,000 on filled-in land and completed in 1935. A platform with a ramp projected into the water and made the port available for sea as well as land planes. The president of the Levee Board, Abe L. Shushan, supervised the erection of the building, which the ring decided to name after him. He put the word "Shushan," or the letter "S," in every available spot, repeating it literally scores of times in metal and stone. Once he boasted that it would cost not less than $50,000 to remove his trademark. When Abe joined the ranks of the convicted, the airport was rechristened and his signature eliminated with much trouble and expense.

The Huey P. Long Bridge, which spans the Mississippi three and a half miles above New Orleans. This imposing and invaluable work was not conceived by Huey, but without his backing the idea would probably have languished for many more years. A bridge for the Southern Pacific Railroad was planned in 1892. It could not be financed at that juncture, and trains continued to be shifted across the river on ferries. The Public Belt Railroad Commission, an agency of the city of New Orleans, kept the project alive. It received a permit from the War Department to go ahead in 1926, but found it necessary to revise its design the following year and again in 1930. Huey was then governor. He tossed $7,000,000 into the pot, and it became possible to start the work. It was finished in 1935 at a cost of $13,000,000, just as he was assassinated. The state administration, comprehensibly enough, attached his name to it.

The bridge is of the cantilever type with eight spans and is a combination railroad and highway structure. The center span is 790 feet long. Its total length, including approaches, is 4.4 miles. The roadways attain a height of 135 feet above the flood level of the Mississippi, while the midstream pier, standing where the river is 80 feet deep, rests on a solid stratum of sand 90 feet below the river's bottom. It had been feared that no bridge could ever span the Mississippi so far south in the delta, because the comparatively new and shifting soil could not give a foundation. The problem was solved by the discovery of underlying sand packed to the firmness of rock.

The sole direct highway to the west from New Orleans, the Old Spanish Trail (US 90), now crosses the Huey P. Long Bridge.

Chapter 25

Present and Future

We are too close to World War II to attempt an inside story of the work done on or near Lake Pontchartrain to forward the national effort. Some of the information has not yet been released, and some is still buried too deeply in general reports to be disentangled. Three large firms played their part: Higgins Industries, the Delta Shipbuilding Company and the Pendleton Shipyards Company. All these built vessels on the Industrial Canal at the heart of the city, manufactured various accessories, and repaired damaged craft. Because of the vivid personality and sensational methods of its founder, Higgins Industries is undoubtedly the best known to the country at large.

Andrew Jackson Higgins had been engaged for some years in the pleasure-boat business in New Orleans. When the war broke out he started two plants, one on the Bayou St. John for wooden craft, and one on the canal for steel craft. He invented the landing barge called by his name, and perfected a type of motor torpedo boat. Both proved well suited to the new naval operations, especially in the Pacific. He also designed seagoing cargo ships, 185 feet in length and carrying 1,200 tons and more of merchandise. By applying the principle of the moving production line for the first time to shipbuilding, he was able to complete on each assembly line an average of one vessel every other day. The record for a single month was 750.

A total of roughly 30,000 craft of all models was turned out by Higgins Industries. It is claimed that the secrecy of records required during the war makes it impossible to break down this figure. But the ubiquitous landing barges are stated unofficially to account for 21,000 units. The Navy said it needed 80,000. The balance—whether the full quota was obtained the writer does not know—were manufactured by other companies, using the Higgins patents with royalties waived.

Every vessel finished by Higgins on the Bayou St. John and the Industrial Canal was tried out on Lake Pontchartrain. It was considered ideal for this purpose, precisely because its shallowness caused ground swells and subjected it to violent commotion when even a light gale blew. It was felt that bucking such temperamental water and maneuvering against the sloping shores guarded in many spots by masked sand bars approximated the difficulties that would be met with among coral atolls. Another Higgins contribution was to facilitate the training of 30,000 men of the armed forces in handling small boats.

The Delta Shipbuilding Company launched 155 Liberty ships during the war. The Pendleton Shipyards Company built nine seagoing tugs, besides doing a great deal of repair work and outfitting vessels that had been constructed elsewhere.

Lake Pontchartrain, as the facts brought out in this book demonstrate, has no future as a waterway for heavy shipping. Even the light-draft commercial vessels which now use it are likely to decrease in the face of competition by railroads, trucks and other land vehicles. Should the proposed tidewater channel ever be dug from the inner harbor of New Orleans to the head of Lake Borgne, outside sea-borne traffic will have no temptation to come or go through the Rigolets. But Pontchartrain will be more than a yachtsmen's and fishermen's Eden. The dream of the pioneers concerning the north shore will almost certainly come true. How soon depends upon two prospects, both as yet in the speculative stage. Will a proposed causeway be built across the lake from New Orleans to Mandeville, or Madisonville? With or without the causeway, will oil be discovered beneath the waters of Pontchartrain?

The hopes concerning oil date back to the 1930's when the plunderbund that had inherited the state from Huey P. Long disposed of some 470,000 acres in the various lakes to an operator who assigned the lease to a corporation. No immediate attempts to exploit were made. Some years afterward a reform administration moved to recover the lease. The suit was compromised by the company accepting a reduction to 45,000 acres. Actual drilling did not take place until 1946, when tests to 12,000 feet were begun at three locations, two of them close to the New Orleans water front, and the third two miles out in the lake from the mouth of Bayou Lacombe on the north side. Such work is costly, and unless the oil engineers believed that there was an excellent chance of the black gold gushing they would not undertake it. Petroleum wells are now paying off in several lagoons along the south coast of Louisiana, and even in the Gulf of Mexico a couple of miles offshore. So why not in Pontchartrain?

Success would mean certain obvious advantages: wealth for a few individuals, jobs for hundreds, perhaps thousands. Also, it is possible that an oil city would spring up somewhere in the region. There would be disadvantages, however. The water could not escape pollution, and fishing, sailing and bathing would suffer. The shore of Fontainebleau State Park and the pleasure beaches of New Orleans might be seriously affected. Commercial crabbers and fishermen fear that their business would be destroyed, because of the poisoning of marine life. It is at least a debatable question whether a state so rich in undeveloped oil resources elsewhere should risk the befouling of queenly Pontchartrain at this time. The wonderful marine preserve described in the preceding chapter is a heritage worth guarding.

The causeway project has been agitated for the past two years, but is not new. It was first proposed twenty years ago and allowed to lapse because there seemed no way of raising the $13,000,000 which engineers said it would cost. Curiously, the idea was not taken up by Huey P. Long. The need for such a road is manifest. At present the only means of getting from New Orleans to the central and most desirable section of the north shore is by making a long, roundabout trip, either across one of the bridges at the narrow eastern end of the lake and circling back, or by going about the same distance to the west and cutting between Pontchartrain and Maurepas. The direct route would be a little under twenty-four miles, a saving of more than half.

What the backers have in mind, though no actual plans have been submitted, is a stone structure with several traffic lanes, for the use of pedestrians and vehicles of every description. Unless a drawbridge were provided at some point, the lake would be cut in two so far as navigation is concerned. That is a detail to be settled later. Even if it should prove necessary to divide the lake, the price would not be too high a one to pay. The expanses of water on either side would remain ample for pleasure boating and fishing. A brisk suburban development could be expected on the north shore. It is not unlikely that Mandeville or Madisonville, or both of them, would soon become populous. The men who did business there in the last century envisaged a city and were astonished that one did not grow. They failed to realize that there was no mercantile reason for a large community, that there could never be one until there was a closer link with New Orleans than the steam ferries of old. The causeway now being discussed would be the ideal link.

The powerful Association of Commerce, New Orleans, has taken the lead in sponsoring this project, and has found many supporters among legislators, business firms and the public. An assignment of state funds is being asked to begin the work. Several million dollars might then be raised by selling bonds, the interest to be met and the principal eventually redeemed out of tolls to be charged for a period of years. It has been pointed out that the original estimate of $13,000,000 would probably be greatly exceeded today in view of the mounting costs of material and labor. But the enthusiasts refuse to be discouraged.

Still another improvement hoped for is the building of a protective levee along the south shore of Pontchartrain, from the western limits of New Orleans to the Bonnet Carré Spillway.

This is held to be necessary to cope with the raising of the level of the lake in flood years. It would be a Federal responsibility, with the state contributing about twenty-five percent of the cost.

Pontchartrain is probably due to be shackled a bit, involved more narrowly in the utilitarian schemes of man. Such is the pattern of civilization. But nothing can ever detract from the beauty of the lake, except incidentally, or destroy the phenomena which have led naturalists and philosophers to call it the most interesting in America.

A few geographers, thinking of the eastern passages where the salt tides surge in, call Pontchartrain an arm of the Gulf. To those who know it, it is not part of anything but an individual in its own right—a lake.

The final test is that of the emotion which springs from visual impressions. Afloat on Okwá-ta—the Wide Water of the Choctaw—or roving its shores, one has an overwhelming sense of its individuality. The contrast of breathless calms and sudden turmoil of whitecaps is different from anything to be encountered at sea. The converging of rivers and bayous gives one a feeling of a receptive body that is more or less circular and quite complete. Its birds and its fish move in a round which suggests that—at least for the time being—they know of no other habitation. Pontchartrain is not an offshoot or pendant, but a strange entity, and that is what made the telling of its story an irresistible temptation.

APPENDICES, ACKNOWLEDGMENTS AND BIBLIOGRAPHICAL NOTE

APPENDIX A

THE HOUSE OF PONTCHARTRAIN

THE Phélypeaux family, under its titles of Pontchartrain and Maurepas, had a prominent part for five generations in the government of France. We hear first of Paul de Phélypeaux, who was styled the Sieur de Pontchartrain. In 1596 he became secretary to Henry IV, and four years later headed the establishment of the consort, Marie de Médicis. He was appointed a secretary of state in 1610, stood out as one of the most distinguished ministers of the reign, and left an important volume of memoirs covering the period from 1610 to 1620.

A son of Paul de Phélypeaux carried on the tradition, though less impressively, as chief of various departments. But his son Louis rose to the highest honors under Louis XIV as Comte de Pontchartrain. He became controller-general of finances in 1687, secretary of state for marine affairs in 1690, and finally chancellor of France in 1700. This was the man who commissioned the Sieur d'Iberville to explore and settle Louisiana, and after whom Lake Pontchartrain was named. Ironically enough, his management of the department of the marine, which at that time had charge of the colonies and in connection with which he is best remembered, was not brilliant. However, he was a competent finance minister, and he shone in the chancellorship as an elder statesman. The intimate friend of Boileau, he did much for men of letters and scientists. He retired voluntarily just before the death of the *Roi Soleil*.

Meanwhile, he had been succeeded at the marine office in 1699 by his son Jérôme, the Comte de Maurepas, who later succeeded to the title of Comte de Pontchartrain. Jérôme struggled none too effectively with the problems posed by Louisiana and other budding colonies. His enemies said that his administration was deplorable. Saint-Simon criticized him in his *Mémoires* as frankly as he had praised his father. Though Jérôme had his ardent admirers, he was forced out of office during the regency of the Duc d'Orléans.

The fifth Pontchartrain was Jean Frédéric de Phélypeaux, son of the preceding. He chose to be known in history as the Comte de Maurepas.

He, too, was secretary of state for marine affairs, serving in the post for many years. He made an excellent minister. French historians credit him with a subtle and penetrating intelligence. They usually add that his surface manner was frivolous, and that he owed a great deal to his wit and his expert handling of court intrigues. In 1749 he overreached himself and was dismissed for an epigram directed at La Pompadour. Louis XVI recalled him toward the end of his life, appointing him to the department of finance where, briefly, he made a good record.

APPENDIX B

GENERAL VICTOR'S PROCLAMATION

THIS document has a place among the curiosa of historical records. It has been reprinted only once or twice, and never in English so far as the author knows. When Louisiana was returned to France by Spain under the Treaty of San Ildefonso, Napoleon Bonaparte appointed General Claude Victor captain general of the colony. As told in Chapter 7, the prefect Pierre de Laussat came to Louisiana to represent the French Government in 1803, but Victor never came. He forwarded the following proclamation, which, however, was held in reserve:

PROCLAMATION. In the Name of the French Republic

Virtue Fatherland

The General of Division Victor, Captain-General of Louisiana,

To the Louisianians

Dear Louisianians:

By a treaty made between the French Government and His Majesty the King of Spain, Louisiana has become once more a territory of the French Republic. I come, in the name of its First Magistrate, the immortal Bonaparte, to take possession of your interesting colony, and to associate its lot with the brilliant destinies of the French people.

Up till the present, dear Louisianians, despite your wise conduct and all your efforts toward the aggrandizement of your colony, you have been able only to make a small impression with the activities which you pursue within the narrow circle of your ancient properties; you have not been able to profit by all the resources for agriculture which a vast and fertile territory offers you; you have not been able to turn all the riches of your fortunate soil to account in the enlargement of commerce.

I come in the name of your Government to offer you the means of multiplying your rewards; I bring you the laws that have created the glory of the French nation, even as they have assured her tranquillity and happiness. Supported by honest and intelligent magistrates, we shall be in rivalry with your own to establish incorruptible justice among you. A wise and foreseeing administration will give movement and life to agriculture, as well as to all the branches of industry and commence. I bring you finally new brothers who, like me, know you well enough in advance to esteem and cherish you.

Henceforth, all of us delightfully mingled, we shall constitute a single family, all of whose members will work for the happiness of each one and for the prosperity of all. I have become your father, and I shall have the full tenderness of a father; ceaselessly I shall stimulate the solicitude of the mother country so that she may supply whatever may be lacking in the colony.

Dear Louisianians: Fear nothing from the imposing mass of soldiers that surrounds me. The glory that they have won in combat makes them already worthy of your esteem; the virtues which characterize them will cause you to love them. They will respect and will make respected your rights and your belongings, should anyone seek to attack you, and I swear that you will have reason only to praise their conduct.

As to me, dear Louisianians, I shall have done enough for my own happiness, if I am able to guarantee yours by my watchfulness and my care.

VICTOR.

ACKNOWLEDGMENTS

THE author gratefully acknowledges the facilities placed at his disposal by the Louisiana State Museum Library, the Howard-Tilton Memorial Library, and the Athénée Louisianais, New Orleans. He thanks André Lafargue, Sidney Louis Villeré, Mme. Laure Castellanos May, Percy Viosca, Jr., James Nelson Gowanloch, George Raffalovich, Stanley Clisby Arthur, Miss Catherine Dillon, Leslie P. Beard and J. A. Bascle, Jr., all of New Orleans, for information furnished and friendly assistance rendered.

His grateful appreciation is expressed to the Louisiana Historical Society for its permission to quote from the *Louisiana Historical Quarterly;* to Dr. Isaac Monroe Cline for his permission to quote from his book, *Storms, Floods and Sunshine;* and to the Louisville and Nashville Railroad Company for their permission to quote from their early records and from their employees' magazine.

BIBLIOGRAPHICAL NOTE

THE story of the discovery and colonization of Louisiana is richly documented in the archives of Paris, which fortunately escaped destruction during the French Revolution. Reports and letters by Iberville, Bienville, St. Denis, D'Artaguette and many other pioneers are represented. The mass of this material was made available to American students by the researches of Charles Étienne Arthur Gayarré, the Creole historian, who went to France in the second quarter of the last century and sifted out the important records. A considerable part was used in his *Histoire de la Louisiane,* published in French in New Orleans in the late 1840's. This was afterward expanded, translated into English and issued in various editions: New York, 1854; New Orleans, 1885; New Orleans, 1903. Documents not employed by Gayarré were catalogued under his direction and can be consulted in the Archives Nationales, under the heading of "Colonies." Manuscript copies of a large number of items have been made for the reference libraries of Louisiana.

Supplementing the work of Gayarré, though not exclusively concerned with Louisiana, are the extensive compilations by Pierre Margry: *Découvertes et Etablissements des Français,* Paris, 1876-1886; and *Mémoires et Documents pour Servir à l'Histoire des Origines Françaises de Pays d'Outre-Mer,* Paris, 1879-1888. These priceless volumes can, as yet, be read in full only in the French. Emile Lauvrière rests heavily upon them in his *Histoire de la Louisiane Française,* reissued in the original by the press of the Louisiana State University, Baton Rouge, in 1940.

The first historian of the province was Antoine S. le Page du Pratz, who wrote from his personal experience and the testimony of companions. His *Histoire de la Louisiane* appeared in Paris in 1758. It is extremely valuable for its sincerity and the attention paid to the habits of the Indians, agriculture, and flora and fauna. But Le Page du Pratz did not have the perspective needed for a definitive chronicle of his times. The second historian was Judge François Xavier Martin. He published his *The History of Louisiana from the Earliest Period,* New Orleans, 1827-1829. Lacking the material soon to be organized by Gayarré, Martin's work falls short of adequacy, though he furnishes important surveys of political events during the regimes under which he lived.

Following Gayarré and worthy to be regarded as his successor was Alcée Fortier, whose *History of Louisiana* was published in New York in 1904. Laville Bremer was a writer of promise, whose researches corrected some of the unwitting errors of his predecessors. He planned an exhaustive history of the old province, but due to ill health and other causes he was able to complete only disjointed sections, some of which never got beyond serial publication in periodicals. His *Amichel: A Narrative History of the Gulf Coast,* admittedly a fragment, issued by himself under a New Orleans imprint in 1940, merits close attention. *Louisiana: A Record of Expansion,* by Albert Phelps, Boston and New York, 1905; and *The Story of Louisiana,* by William Oscar Scroggs, Indianapolis and New York, 1924, should be consulted for general interest, though the author found little in them that had a bearing on Lake Pontchartrain.

There is only one sound chronological account of events in the city of New Orleans, considered apart from the province or state: John S. Kendall's *History of New Orleans,* Chicago, 1922. It suffers from prolixity, but remains a mine of information without which it would be hard to trace the city's political story.

The Commerce of Louisiana during the French Regime, 1699-1763, by Nancy M. Miller Surrey, New York, 1916, is an erudite work of which we have too few rivals in connection with the region under discussion. Drawn directly from the Archives Nationales of France, it gives all the available facts implied by its title. This is a book intended as source material for historians and economists, and in no wise aimed at those who read for light entertainment.

Writers who produced historical studies but did not confine themselves to history, who came after Gayarré and owed much to his creative scholarship, include Grace King, George W. Cable and Lyle Saxon. Miss King, who served for some years as Gayarré's secretary, repeats the master's findings in many pages of her *New Orleans, the Place and the People,* New York, 1895; and *Creole Families of New Orleans,* New York, 1921; while adding her own observations. Her original research, however, in her biography of the founder, *Sieur de Bienville,* New York, 1892, is a notable contribution. She sums up her life interestingly in her *Memoirs of a Southern Woman of Letters,* New York, 1932.

Cable's short historical sketch of the French civilization, *The Creoles of Louisiana,* New York, 1884, is of more lasting significance than the fiction on which his reputation with the general public rests. Lyle Saxon has a flair for colorful and bizarre happenings which graver annalists ignore. This gift shows at its best in his beautifully written *Fabulous New Orleans,* New York, 1928. It permeates his *Old Louisiana,* New York, 1929; and is but a little less apparent in his topical story of man's struggle with the river, *Father Mississippi,* New York, 1927.

Apologists generally are tiresome and unrewarding on the printed page. Yet two books of this sort must be mentioned. James Parton, satellite and admirer of Ben Butler, published a defense of his hero before the War between the States was over: *General Butler in New Orleans,* New York, 1864. Henry Clay Warmoth, the precocious scamp who became the first carpetbag governor of Louisiana at the age of twenty-six, waited for sixty years to issue his *War, Politics and Reconstruction,* New York, 1930. Parton's special pleading is better organized and consequently more irritating than that of the casual Warmoth. Both make admissions in spite of themselves, which throw light upon the periods of misgovernment they discuss.

Good biographers are comparatively few. John Walton Caughey's *Bernardo de Gálvez in Louisiana, 1776-1783,* Berkeley, Calif., 1934, is about the only life of an important official of the Spanish regime. Hamilton Basso's *Beauregard, the Great Creole,* New York, 1933, is easily the best modern treatment of the general. *Lafitte the Pirate,* by Lyle Saxon, New York, 1930, paints a vigorous if somewhat romanticized picture of the swashbuckler who did his bit in helping Jackson to defeat the British in 1815. Constance Rourke's *Audubon,* New York, 1936, is the biography of the naturalist which most deeply impresses the author, though Stanley Clisby Arthur's *Audubon: An Intimate Life of the American Woodsman,* New Orleans, 1937, runs it a close second. *Lafcadio Hearn's American Days,* by Edward Larocque Tinker, New York, 1924, is an indispensable book to any student of Hearn's ten years in New Orleans. In *The Incredible Yanqui,* New York, 1931, Hermann B. Deutsch covers the career of the filibusterer, Lee Christmas. *Huey Long: A Candid Biography,* by Forrest Davis, New York, 1935, was written on the eve of the dictator's assassination; it is useful, but not definitive.

Memoirists and travel writers have rejoiced for the past century and a quarter in the region's glamour, or sometimes have pulled long faces at its unregenerate Latin ways. First on the list comes Bernhard, Duke of Saxe-Weimar Eisenach, whose *Travels through North America* were published in Philadelphia in 1828. The Teutonic nobleman arrived by way of Lake Pontchartrain and found the charges for transportation to the city so exorbitant that he walked the whole way in from the mouth of the Bayou St. John. Yet he spent his money lavishly at balls and other entertainments, and filled his notebook with acute comments. Harriet Martineau is next with her *Retrospect of Western Travel,* London and New York, 1838. A. Oakey Hall's frothy volume of essays, *The Manhattaner in New Orleans,* New York, 1851, reflects the views of an observant wit determined not to acknowledge that Creole customs could ever be superior to those of New York.

In 1856 two books were issued under New York imprints: *Fifty Years in both Hemispheres, or Reminiscences of the Life of a Former Merchant,* by Vincent Nolte; and *A Journey in the Seaboard Slave States,* by Frederick Law Olmsted. Both contain long sections about New Orleans. Nolte had been in business there in the early days of the American regime and had thoroughly enjoyed the conditions which enabled him to prosper. Olmsted, coming half a century later to study those conditions and their upshot, found much to criticize, but on the whole was a just and tolerant spectator.

In 1857, Boston, appeared Theodore Clapp's *Autobiographical Sketches and Recollections*. Dr. Clapp was a minister whose long service in New Orleans coincided with the worst of the frightful epidemics—cholera as well as yellow fever—that scourged the city. His account of these visitations is a source from which every modern historian must draw, if he wishes to tell a rounded story—the gruesome along with the gay. Clapp is also informative about the beginnings of the Protestant churches in the *faubourg* built by Americans to balance the deeply Catholic Vieux Carré.

Published in 1912, New York, near the end of Eliza Moore Ripley's days, her *Social Life in Old New Orleans* is the best light commentary we have on the 1840's and 1850's. This record of customs, food, clothes, etc., provides excellent background material for the historical novelist. On the other hand, *New Orleans as It Was,* by Henry C. Castellanos, New Orleans, 1895, is a collection of strange true tales by a gay Bohemian, with accompanying characteristic remarks on the *mores* of his century. One is grateful that Castellanos was moved to write this book. He takes an interest in everything out of the ordinary, including voodoo, the African animist cult brought to Louisiana by the slaves of planters who had fled the Negro insurrection in Saint Domingue.

Other writers on voodoo are Lyle Saxon in *Fabulous New Orleans* (*op. cit.*), the anonymous contributors to *Gumbo Ya-Ya,* compiled by Lyle Saxon, Edward Dreyer and Robert Tallant, Boston and New York, 1945; and Lafcadio Hearn in fugitive pieces, some of which are to be found in the *Historical Sketch Book and Guide to New Orleans and Environs,* New York, 1885, as well as his *Creole Sketches,* Boston and New York, 1924. The subject is treated exhaustively in *Voodoo in New Orleans,* by Robert Tallant, New York, 1946.

Speaking of guidebooks, the city has been unusually well described in works of this sort. In addition to the *Historical Sketch Book and Guide,* credited to "Several Leading Writers of the New Orleans Press," and known to contain chapters by both Hearn and Cable, we have the following: *New Orleans Guide,* by James S. Zacherie, New Orleans, 1903; *The Picayune's Guide to New Orleans,* published by the *Times-Picayune,* New Orleans, fourteen editions, 1890 to 1928; the admirable *New*

Orleans City Guide, compiled as an activity of the Federal Writers' Project, Boston, 1938; and the equally good *Louisiana: A Guide to the State,* also a W.P.A. job, New York, 1945. Stanley Clisby Arthur's *Old New Orleans,* New Orleans, 1936, is a careful survey of the ancient and historical buildings of the Vieux Carré. Not a guidebook in the usual sense, Nathaniel Cortlandt Curtis' *New Orleans, Its Old Houses, Shops and Public Buildings,* Philadelphia, 1933, is a well-written appraisal from the viewpoint of the artist and architect.

Among recent historical works, Harnett T. Kane's *Louisiana Hayride,* New York, 1941, is a fine review of the Huey Long period. Hodding Carter's *Lower Mississippi,* New York, 1942, presents a multitude of facts and contains brilliant writing on the whole Delta region, including New Orleans. In *Storms, Floods and Sunshine,* New Orleans, 1945, Dr. Isaac Monroe Cline tells his personal story as an official of the United States Weather Bureau, stationed first at Galveston and then for many years at New Orleans.

Defying ordinary classifications, Herbert Asbury's *The French Quarter,* New York, 1936, concerns itself with the picaresque and the flamboyant. Asbury uses the subtitle, "An Informal History of the New Orleans Underworld." But though the appeal is frankly on the sensational side, the serious reader will find much of value in this book.

Perry Young's *The Mistick Krewe,* New Orleans, 1931, is an account of the part played by Carnival in the city's life, with emphasis on the society called the Mistick Krewe of Comus. The title of Percy Viosca, Jr.'s *Louisiana Out-of-Doors,* New Orleans, 1933, is self-explanatory.

The above does not pretend to be a complete bibliography on lower Louisiana. It comprises those books which were notably helpful to the writer in his approach to the New Orleans region through the back door of Lake Pontchartrain. Uncollected material in public and private libraries also was drawn upon. There are fewer learned societies here than one finds in the great northern cities. The Louisiana Historical Society and L'Athénée Louisianais are outstanding. The former has accumulated an immense amount of data which it willingly places at the disposal of scholars. Its *Publications* and *Quarterly* contain many valuable items.

The Howard-Tilton Memorial Library, New Orleans, is one of the South's great reference libraries. The person in quest of information on all periods of Louisiana history should go there first.

The Louisiana State Museum Library, Pontalba Building, maintained in connection with the museum in the Cabildo, New Orleans, is well stocked with colonial annals in manuscript form, the files of early newspapers, and rare books up to the end of the nineteenth century. It is weak on purchases of recent published material.

On the top floor of the New Orleans City Hall is a room where the back numbers of virtually all the newspapers ever published in the city may be consulted. The *Times-Picayune* courteously extends facilities to those who wish to work from the files of the different journals it issues or has absorbed: the existing *Times-Picayune* and *States,* and the former *Picayune, Times* and *Times-Democrat.*

INDEX

INDEX

OKLAHOMA

ARKANSAS

TEXAS

LOUISIANA

Mississippi River

MISSISS

LAKE PONTCHA

NEW ORLEANS

Gulf of Mexico

N

ce

and

Bienville founding New Orleans